W9-BZA-420

Praise from Canadian investors for
*Real Estate Investing in Canada:*
*How to Create Wealth with the ACRE System*
By Don R. Campbell

"This is a great book. The information in just one of the chapters alone saved me over $28,000."

~ *Michael Millenaar*

"Full of practical Canadian content and presented in an organized and respectful system. It directly addresses how you get the money and financing you need to purchase enough real estate to achieve your goals."

~ *Tamara MacLaren*

"The power of *Real Estate Investing in Canada* lies in the super simple, street-proven systems that it offers you. It makes real estate dreams possible and reachable for any Canadian. If you are serious about learning the truth, cutting through all the hype and being successful, this is your real estate bible!"

~ *Valden Palm, misterrrsp.com*

*Praise for the Authentic Canadian Real System from Canadian investors:*

"If you want a predictable real estate future, you must design it in advance. I know of no other real estate expert and educator who is as competent as Don Campbell. His research is unmatched and his results predictable."

~ *Gordon D. Wusyk, Founder and CEO of Predictable Futures Inc.*

"I learned more from the author in this time about character, business, investing, money flow and personal goal setting than I have in my entire career. Don R. Campbell is a mentor and an inspiration, who provides something unique and extremely helpful."

~ *Ernst Marsig, Investor and Business Owner, Y2 Marketing*

"I have thought about buying real estate for income for 30 years. The ACRE Quickstart program has changed my mindset from *thinking* about it to *doing it*—and believing that it is not just possible, but necessary."

~ *Joan Watson*

"Using the ACRE System, I bought 154 positive cash flow properties, all while working a full-time job. I now own over 350 properties."

~ *Arlen Dahlin*

"We've been implementing the various techniques in the system, with flawless results. Quite simply, this system is a must for all existing and prospective landlords. By implementing this system, you will increase your bottom line while significantly reducing your time commitment and headaches."

~ *Brent Beagle*

"I joined REIN and, using their ACRE Quickstart techniques and doing due diligence on my part, I was able to buy five investment properties in one month. Their extensive support, helpful forms, *Insider Reports*, and networking opportunities have given me the confidence and momentum to start my future full-steam ahead."

~ *Brian Simpson*

"It has allowed me to increase my net worth exponentially. The very valuable information helps me to manage my properties with ease and fosters a great business relationship with my tenants."

~ *Audrey Sloan*

"After joining the Real Estate Investment Network, our lives have completely changed and we are on the path to success. With the guidance of several members, we sold the house we were currently living in and turned it into four properties. One of these properties is the beautiful house we now live in and thoroughly love. The REIN system is so simple and easy to follow. All you have to do is take action and amazing things happen."

~ *Jeff Dick & Debbie Jeannotte*

"An absolute must for anyone interested in real estate investing. Don Campbell's concepts are simple, concise, ethical and best of all, relevant!"

~ *Darryl Cheung*

# 97 TIPS FOR CANADIAN REAL ESTATE INVESTORS

## DON R. CAMPBELL

PETER KINCH | BARRY MCGUIRE | RUSSELL WESTCOTT

WILEY

John Wiley & Sons Canada, Ltd.

**Copyright © 2006 by Don R. Campbell**

All rights reserved. No part of this work covered by the copyright herein may be reproduced or used in any form or by any means—graphic, electronic or mechanical without the prior written permission of the publisher. Any request for photocopying, recording, taping or information storage and retrieval systems of any part of this book shall be directed in writing to The Canadian Copyright Licensing Agency (Access Copyright). For an Access Copyright license, visit www.accesscopyright.ca or call toll free 1-800-893-5777.

Care has been taken to trace ownership of copyright material contained in this book. The publisher will gladly receive any information that will enable them to rectify any reference or credit line in subsequent editions.

*Library and Archives Canada Cataloguing in Publication Data*

Campbell, Don R.
    97 tips for Canadian real estate investors / Don R. Campbell.

ISBN-13 978-0-470-83808-2
ISBN-10 0-470-83808-6

    1. Real estate investment—Canada. I. Title. II. Title: Ninety-seven tips for Canadian real estate investors

HD316.C3175 2006          332.63'24'0971          C2005-907605-4

**Production Credits:**
Cover design: Ian Koo
Interior text design: Adrian So

Printer: Tri-Graphic Printing Ltd.

John Wiley & Sons Canada, Ltd.
6045 Freemont Blvd.
Mississauga, Ontario
L5R 4J3

Printed in Canada
6 7 8 9 TRI 10 09 08

# CONTENTS

The authors wish to acknowledge the creative effort of Joy Gregory in the preparation of the manuscript.

# INTRODUCTION

## WARNING: NEVER INVEST BASED ON TIPS!

This statement may seem to be a rather odd way to begin a book titled *97 Tips for Canadian Real Estate Investors*. However, if you have read *Real Estate Investing in Canada*, by Don R. Campbell, you know that real estate investing is all about following a proven system that dramatically reduces risk and helps you cut through all the hype and misinformation that characterizes the industry.

## NOW: THE GOOD NEWS ABOUT TIPS.

There are really two types of tips in the investment world. The first ones are the "Hot Tips" you hear from your neighbour, co-worker or family member. They're not really tips but rumours inspired by the hope of getting rich quickly. For instance, "This stock is going to go through the roof, and my friend knows someone who has insider information. You better buy now!" We've all heard dozens of these kinds of tips—and we're sure you know where most of these lead. *Nowhere.* I promise you that you won't find any of these dead-end tips in this book.

The second types of tips that exist are the insights and observations from veterans who have detailed experience in what they're talking about. No hype, no baloney. These tips are designed to give you advantages and strategies that make your current investments perform even better. Some tips will provide action steps that will provide results in the near-term term, and others focus on long-term wealth creation.

## WHAT'S IN THIS BOOK?

What you're going to discover in *97 Tips* is the wisdom and experience of four Canadian real estate experts, each with their own area of expertise: Barry McGuire, a legal expert; Peter Kinch, a mortgage and financing expert; Russell Westcott, one of Canada's leading real estate researchers and educators; and Don R. Campbell, an active investor with a portfolio of 250-plus properties, who is also President of the Real Estate Investment Network and a best-selling author.

We have dug deep into our decades of experience to uncover tips and secrets with the sole purpose of giving you an advantage in the real estate market. You'll read about mortgage secrets your banker may not even know. You'll discover legal land-mines you can avoid, even if your lawyer doesn't know they exist. How about closing and buying tips that can each save you thousands of dollars on *every* property you purchase!

In addition to these *97 Tips*, you will also hear from additional experts in their field who will talk about on-line advertising secrets for real estate investors; little-known GST rebate opportunities for investors; and powerful negotiations secrets. Plus, you'll discover the Critical Success Event in real estate—and how this knowledge will change your investment focus.

Each and every one of the 97 tips you'll find in this book has the potential to make your real estate investments run more easily and become more profitable. Veteran real estate investors understand how one simple tip can quickly save them thousands of dollars on their next transaction or refinance, and there are 97 of these key money- and time-saving tips at your fingertips in this easy-to-read guide.

Veteran and beginning real estate investors alike can instantly access these informative ideas and strategies any time, any place—expert insights that can make or break your next deal. In other words, this book will become your real estate reference guide you'll refer to over and over again. We highly recommend you read it with a highlighter and pen as it will spark many ideas and change how you invest, lowering risk and increasing results. It is a perfect companion to the Authentic Canadian Real Estate investment system found in the book *Real Estate Investing in Canada*.

Remember, successful real estate investing is all about focusing on the fundamentals and following a system that forces you to ask the tough questions. Use these 97 tips to help make your investment system even more fun and profitable.

# PART 1

## STOP THINKING! START KNOWING! THE FOUNDATION ON WHICH ALL IS BUILT

# TIP #1: GO ON FACTS—NOT ON HYPE.

*Forget guessing or hoping. Ask the tough questions of everyone involved— vendor, realtor and banker. If you are informed, you're investing. If you are uninformed (or guessing), you are speculating.*

Right up front in this book, we must be frank. We've all heard the stories about instant real estate riches, and there's a certain thrill in thinking the deal-of-a-lifetime is just around the corner. But in order to be a long term, wealth-creating investor (instead of a speculator), you need to be realistic. Real estate, like any investment vehicle, needs to have a system; a system that forces you to ask the tough questions ... and removes any guesswork.

To be successful in real estate investing is to build long-term wealth. The quest for the "right" property, the thrill of the negotiation and the adrenaline rush of the offer are all kind of exciting. They also complicate the process, and firmly underline the need to develop an *emotion-free* approach to decision making.

When experienced real estate investors talk about removing the emotion from their investment decisions, they're not talking about conducting business from behind an emotional wall. They're talking about making business decisions based on solid business information and what sophisticated investors call "market fundamentals."

## What do you need to do?

**COMMIT TO THE FACTS**

To make a decision based on fundamentals, always do your homework—all of it. Your homework will be complete once you can substitute the word "know" in the following sentences (where you may now be using the word "think"). For example:

> "I know (not think) these renters will stay after the property changes hands."
> "I know (not think) the economics of the region and the neighbour- hood are primed for long-term growth."
> "I know (not think) this property can be re-zoned to accommodate my plans."

"I know (not think) the income this investment generates will cover *all* of the expenses of the property."

### ADOPT A PROVEN INVESTMENT SYSTEM

You'll learn more about what it means to "know, not think" as you move through this book. For now, it's important to get a good handle on the idea that a real estate investment system means operating on *fact-based* decision making.

To be successful, a system must:

1. Be proven to work in your country, town and neighbourhood, thus not leading you down the wrong path.
2. Force you to ask the tough questions and not allow you to buy until *all* the homework is done (thus removing emotion).
3. Leave *very* little to chance, thus giving you a distinct advantage buying in any market that meets the criteria.

### 🅢 SOPHISTICATED INVESTOR TIP

Remember: "Fundamentals, not emotions!" Make this your business mantra. Never lose sight of the fact that when it comes to investing money, you need cold hard facts, not just hopes and dreams.

### ❶ KEY INSIGHT

In the beginning, investing with a system may proceed at a slower pace than you expect. However, with time and experience, you will learn to interpret critical information more quickly. A system-based approach means you'll never miss a critical piece of information and never get caught in a bad deal. That makes the extra effort worthwhile!

## TIP #2: FEAR: THE GREATEST MOTIVATOR AND THE GREATEST DE-MOTIVATOR. DEAL WITH IT.

*Analysis paralysis is an investment killer. You get over it if you have a proven system you can trust.*

There are a lot of good reasons never to invest in real estate.

That's right. Too much of the wrong kind of information can hold you back from making investment decisions. Even though you may feel like you are moving forward by collecting lots of information (some of which is useful and some of which is not), you will find that in the real world you will not make any money until you actually take the step and purchase a property.

We've all heard the "if only" stories of would-be investors. They're the offspring of those who never took any action because fear held them back. As with all things in life, action fuels success.

Novice investors need to face the fact that when it comes to the business of learning to be a successful investor, there comes a time when just listening will hold you back. Indeed, the ability to take action is the number-one difference between successful real investors and wannabes.

## What do you need to do?

**USE FEAR AS A TOOL — MAKE IT WORK IN YOUR FAVOUR**

Fear is an instinct designed to keep us alive, not control us. Use it as a motivator by turning the fear of action into the fear of missing out and you'll never have to tell those future grandkids about the time fear kept you from missing a real estate investment opportunity!

This step demands honesty. Ask yourself how often you've allowed fear to hold you back from making important decisions. Now ask yourself if that choice served you well financially. Recognize how the fear of stepping into real estate investment can keep us from earning long-term wealth.

**MIND YOUR W, S & Qs**

Use the Write–Scratch–Question approach to fear management and you will find yourself answering your toughest questions.

**Write:** Don't let yourself stew over a new excuse. Stop what you're doing and write the excuse down on a piece of paper.
**Scratch:** Now cross it out with your pen.
**Question:** Turn that excuse into a "positive-spin question." Even if X is true, what can I do about it? Get the answers you need to eliminate the fear.

Here's what that looks like in action:

**Write** the excuse: **"I heard that as a landlord you can get stuck with a bad tenant."**

Now, **Scratch** the excuse out.

Formulate the positive-spin **Question**: What system can I follow to ensure I provide great tenants with a great place to live?

**Answer:** Check credit and references. Set the standards by which you'll accept a tenant, and set them high. Remember, you're looking for an equity-building tenant—someone who wants to treat your property as if it were his own.

Use a lease agreement that covers all the details. (Include late penalties, non-sufficient funds (NSF) cheques, move-out notices, pets, noise, etc.)

Know your local tenancy laws and do a move-in inspection *before* the tenant moves in. Get post-dated cheques where allowed.

**Write** the excuse: **"I don't have time to invest."**

Now, **Scratch** out the excuse.

Formulate the positive-spin **Question**: What can I do to prioritize my time to find a couple of hours a week to focus on my real estate investment business?

**Answer**: Talk to your spouse/family. Look at the demands of your family life; where is extra time available?

Seek out joint-venture partners to share the time and capital investment. Explore creative but less time-intensive investment opportunities using joint ventures or registered retirement savings funds. Surround yourself with like-minded people who understand long-term investing; they will gladly teach you their tricks.

**Write** the excuse: **"I missed the market boom."**

Now, **Scratch** out the excuse.

Formulate the positive-spin **Question**: If real estate investment is about long-term wealth development, it must be about more than the "boom." Where can I find a trusted system to help me see the advantages of the current market?

**Answer**: You're in the real estate business to make money. Build a team of professionals that is designed to give you a market edge, not hold you back. Refer to the next tip for more on how to choose your team.

## $\circledS$ SOPHISTICATED INVESTOR TIP

Practice the win-win approach to team building. Don't waste your team's time and they'll learn to not waste yours.

Never (ever!) build your team based on a discount price for services rendered.

Discount Team Members = Potential For Disaster!

## $\circledbullet$ KEY INSIGHT

Learn to channel healthy fear into positive investment decisions. If the answers to your due-diligence questions aren't leading you toward actual investment action, keep following the proven system until they do! Fear keeps you sharp—just don't let it hold you back. If anyone gives you advice or an opinion, always look at the source to see if they really and truly know what they're talking about. There are a lot of instant real estate "experts" popping up across the country; don't let these fly-by-nighters steal your dreams.

# TIP #3: YOU'RE THE CAPTAIN, SO LEAD LIKE ONE!

*You can invest in an island ... you can't be the island.*

You now know that sophisticated real estate investors surround themselves with experienced professionals they come to view as part of their team. *If you focus on relationships instead of money, you will optimize your business results and avoid chasing deals that prove to be time-wasters.*

To surround yourself with experience that benefits your business, you want to make sure you are getting advice based on real-life expertise and knowledge. *You want advice based on business experience, not theory. You want action takers, not action talkers!*

## What do you need to do?

GO "PRO" (OR GO HOME)

Surround yourself with the best of the best experts and learn to use their talent and experience as much as possible. If you surround yourself with pretenders, you may become one!

**FOCUS ON YOUR SYSTEM**

Find a *real estate agent* for your system. When choosing your realtor, don't select the one you know from down the street or one you picked out of the Yellow Pages. Finding investment real estate for clients is a unique talent, so you want a realtor who has a few years of experience and who knows how to choose investment properties that fit your investment system. (See the book *Real Estate Investing in Canada* by Don R. Campbell for such a system.) These agents work for you. When you give them the parameters you're looking for and ask them not to waste your time with properties that don't even come close to fitting your system, they become valuable members of your team.

Be prepared to work with several before you find the right match, and then be prepared to listen to their advice. They may have inside information about what kind of renovations best increase value in a particular neighbourhood. They may know about problems that landlords are experiencing in the area, or the reasons particular vendors are "highly motivated" to sell a particular property.

*Find a mortgage broker.* Once again, you're probably not going to go with the guy down the street or your local banker. Because you are now in the business of investment real estate, you need a broker whose experience lies in getting mortgages for investment properties. There are bankers and brokers out there who do not fully understand the nuances of investment real estate. Don't use them. Remember, specific experience for what you need is critical. Instead, find one with extensive knowledge about mortgages for investments. Find out why they will get you the absolute best rates and the absolute best terms. The good news is, your mortgage broker gets paid by the banks—not you.

Your *accountant* must, and we mean *must*, have a complete grasp of all the tax laws and strategies that surround real estate investing. Many accountants specialize in working with real estate investors. They have studied this aspect of Canadian tax law and know the best structures and best systems to use. An accountant with this specialized knowledge is worth his or her weight in gold. A good accountant will save you a lot of money over the years, and help you to structure your real estate, so as to minimize taxes upon sale.

Work with a *lawyer* who has at least 10 years of real estate investment experience. A real estate legal specialist is critical to building wealth. A general-purpose lawyer can easily close the deal on your first home and will probably do an okay job on all your real estate purchases, but a real estate specialist lawyer can deliver you even more. They have the knowledge and strategies to save you a ton of money, protect you from liability and help you gain the confidence to keep moving your business forward.

### 🔘 KEY INSIGHT

Make sure each of the professionals on your team has experience specific to the investment real estate market. You also want them to have extensive experience in working with investors. A case in point: A real estate agent who knows you want undervalued homes to renovate and re-sell won't waste your time with homes already fetching market value.

### INTERVIEW POTENTIAL TEAM MEMBERS

Look for a real estate agent, banker, brokers, lawyer and accountant who own or have owned residential investment real estate. Experienced investors will understand why you're asking questions about their own portfolio.

### BUILD YOUR CIRCLE OF SUPPORT

Find appraisers, home inspectors and property managers that other investors know and respect.

Develop a win-win approach to business opportunities. If one lender gets all of your business, your relationship will mean more to him than if he recognizes you as a "constant shopper." If one lawyer or home inspector gets all your business, he may be more willing to help out with a tight deadline.

### 🚩 RED FLAG

Never choose a lawyer, accountant or any other professional based on price! This may well be the ultimate false economy as a deal could cost you thousands of dollars if things go awry. Real estate deals are complicated. Experienced lawyers look for the critical pieces hidden within a real estate deal and they protect you from the pitfalls.

## TIP #4: CHOOSE YOUR JOINT VENTURE PARTNERS CAREFULLY.

*You are the captain of your own investments. Joint-venture relationships, however, can make your money go further, faster.*

We've all heard the old maxim that it's not what you know, but who you know. In real estate it is very similar: It's who you know—and who knows what.

The opportunity to be part of joint-venture (JV) partnerships is a side benefit to building a strong real estate investment team. These partnerships help you and your like-minded partners pool money and expertise to buy more properties.

In parts 2 and 9 of this book, we will cover a number of tips about what you need to do to make these partnerships work. Here, we want to focus on the most basic elements of the successful joint-venture relationship.

*Choose your partners wisely.* A JV is most effective when two or more parties join together and each party brings something different to the relationship. It is quite easy to "partner" with someone in the same situation as yourself, but that will get you nowhere. For instance, if you have money but need expertise, don't partner with someone with money and no expertise. If you are well-versed in real estate and require investment funds, don't partner with someone who has the same strengths and weaknesses as yourself.

Build a partnership that is stronger than the two parties on their own. You may have time and expertise; your partners may have investment capital and relationships with key professionals. Together, you have the potential makings of a huge winner!

## What do you need to do?

### TAKE CONTROL

Even if it's not your deal, it is your money. There is never a valid excuse for not doing your full due diligence. Do rely upon your JV partner's expertise, but always take responsibility for the end result. Make sure your relationship is detailed in a written agreement that has been reviewed by all partners' lawyers. Design the divorce in advance!

Get a criminal and credit background check. (It's best to know in advance.) Have a written agreement and contract.

### ASK THE TOUGH QUESTIONS

If your partner will find and manage the property in return for your investing cash or credit, make sure she has the experience and expertise to fulfil that role. Check her references, learn what other joint-venture partners have experienced when working with her. Ask about her management experience with the specific kind of property you're about to invest in and visit some of the properties she is managing. Find out if her experience includes managing property through times of high and low vacancy rates.

Make sure you ask yourself the tough questions as well. Am I doing this joint venture because I have been "sold" on it? Is it the exact relationship I need to get my investments moving ahead? After doing a background check, what is my instinct telling me about this person? Can I trust her to be a partner who lives up to her obligations? And bottom line: does what I know about the partner fit my investment system?

## CHECK OUT THE DEAL YOURSELF

Take a close look at the basic details. Even if your partner is the one who finds the deals, it is still your responsibility to make sure all the due diligence is completed so you are happy with the deal.

JV deals are often bigger than those financed individually and that *will* be reflected in your financial responsibility. Sometimes a deal sounds too good to be true—because it is. Be realistic about rates of return and payback periods. Never assume your partners have done as much due diligence as you demand from yourself as a sophisticated investor. Tour every part of the property yourself some time before closing.

Never accept the basic facts at face value. Ask real estate agents familiar with the neighbourhood about current market prices. Better yet, have an accredited appraiser review the property. If renovations are required, are the cost estimates accurate and is there a 20% overrun factor built in?

If the JV involves a condominium unit purchase, get a copy of the deferred reserve plan study. Look at how maintenance issues are dealt with.

 **RED FLAG**

Don't be a silent partner unless the deal is going well. If something seems to be going off the rails, take immediate action. Make sure you request regular updates on how the property is performing, so there are no surprises.

 **KEY INSIGHT**

If the property is a distance from your market, it is even more important that you do your homework. This *must* include price comparisons and neighborhood analysis. And you must visit the property yourself! No exception!

# TIP #5: THE CRITICAL SUCCESS EVENT (CSE) IN REAL ESTATE: ASK FOR WHAT YOU WANT.

*Written by Alan Jacques, founder of REIN and author of upcoming book titled* The Q Solution *about producing breakthrough results in your business and personal life.*

A few years ago, I was interviewed for a program on success. A couple of days before the interview, the interviewer was kind enough to give me a list of all the questions he was going to ask, so I had time to prepare my answers. The interview went really well until we came to the last question—it wasn't on the list.

"Before we close," he said, "I have one last question for you, Alan. With all your success in developing and identifying systems in real estate, stocks, marketing and business, what is the single most important, multi-million dollar idea you've learned that, if you could only keep one, if you could only teach one, if you could only use one, this would be the one?"

There was a slight pause while I recovered from the surprise of getting a question that wasn't on the list. Then, without thinking, I said, "The critical success event."

There was another pause before the interviewer asked me to explain what the critical success event was. As I thought of ways to explore the critical success event concept, there was something in the way the interviewer asked me his question that caused me to reflect on my answer and deal with the concept at a much deeper level. As you will see, it has an immediate and very important application to real estate, but it applies to any area of your life.

If we stand back and observe human behaviour, we notice that most people spend most of their time working towards something. It could be completing a task at work, reading a book or making dinner. Most human activity has some sort of desired result attached to it—there is something we want to achieve. And generally humans are pretty good at doing this, especially with day-to-day tasks.

If we look more closely, we see most things that we accomplish are the result of completing a series of steps in a particular order. When this series of steps can be repeated over and over again, by different people, and still produce the same result, we call this a system.

Thus, if we want to grow a vegetable garden or buy an investment property or coach a team to victory, there are a series of steps we must take to complete the task. That's all rather obvious.

What's not so obvious is that in most processes or systems there is one critical step that, if done, virtually guarantees a result. If that same step is left undone, nothing happens. The key to being a success at anything, the key to producing the results you want, is *identifying this single "pivotal" event that leads to success.* This is the "critical success event" or "CSE." Once you identify this critical event, *all you have to do is keep doing it*! Sounds simple, doesn't it?

Let's look at a few examples. If you want to grow vegetables, the "critical success event" is planting the seeds. If you want to get in shape, the CSE is doing a physical activity, even just walking. Pretty obvious stuff.

To win a football game, the CSE is getting touchdowns. In hockey, it's shots on goal that beat the goaltender.

In business, many people get trapped by all distractions that go along with starting and running a business. Financial statements, business plans, financing, hiring staff, inventory control—the list goes on and on. But none of these is the CSE. How about making a profit? No, that's a goal, not an action step. The "critical success event" in business is selling something! In business, until something is sold, nothing happens.

Now, to real estate. The "critical success event" in real estate investing is *not* looking at properties, talking to realtors, doing renovations or finding investors. It's *not* getting good tenants, going through the MLS book, getting financing or even closing on a property.

No, it's none of these things. While many of these things may be important, they are really just the "extra stuff" that you may have to do. None of them are critical to your success as a real estate investor.

You see, many investors get caught up in this "extra stuff" and forget about their *real job*.

Your real job as a real estate investor, the key to wealth in real estate, the "critical success event," is ... **submitting offers**!

If you don't submit offers, you'll never own any real estate. If you don't submit offers, all you'll have is a bunch of ideas and dreams. They're a dime a dozen. Everybody has "great ideas" (and notice how many of these people are broke!). Until you actually submit an offer, you've done nothing!

How you structure your offer and how you make the deal will affect every aspect of owning that property—what resources you need now, how much cash flow will be generated while you own the property and ultimately how much money you'll make when you sell the property.

There's an old adage about real estate that is so true: "You make your money when you buy, not when you sell." If you buy it right, your profit will be built in from day one. Donald Trump's first book wasn't called *The Art of Property Analysis*. It was called *Trump: The Art of the Deal*. I'm not saying property analysis isn't important—it is. But until you make an offer in writing, you'll never own any real estate.

"But I'm broke, I have no cash!" If this is the case, then make offers that require no cash.

"But I can't qualify for any financing!" Then make offers that do not require you to qualify for financing.

"But I'm really broke, I need cash flow!" Then make offers that produce a positive cash flow.

Whatever your barrier is, submit an offer that deals with that barrier. The worst that can happen is the vendor says no. If a vendor declines your offer, so what? Move on to the next motivated vendor.

Look at this from the vendor's side for a moment. Once a property is listed for sale, what is the one thing the vendor, and indeed the vendor's realtor, is waiting for? Written offers. Believe me, they understand that no offer means no sale!

There's an extra bonus here that may not be immediately apparent. You will learn as much from offers that are *not* accepted as from the ones that are! You'll learn how to negotiate. You'll learn about the things that motivate vendors. You'll learn about realtors. You'll learn how to analyze a property. You'll learn about yourself. You'll learn "the art of the deal."

Remember the most important rule of negotiating: Ask for what you want.

## TIP #6: PATIENCE IS AN INVESTMENT VIRTUE. "GET RICH QUICK = GET POOR QUICK."

*If you focus on what you think will be "fast money," you'll waste time and resources chasing the next deal.*

Real estate markets are in constant flux, moving up and down as the months and years progress. You've probably met some real estate investors who chase the "fast money." As a matter of fact, we guarantee you have. They talk about each deal as if it's the *only* deal, that it is the one that will make them fabulously rich. When you see them a year later, they're often no better off financially, and still talking about the next deal that will make them fabulously rich. You'll notice they often appear anxious and exhausted. They're really up—or really down.

Worse yet, they often burn the relationship bridges that are meant to sustain their investment systems; they use people until they are done with them and then move on. Recreating their investment systems and relationships as they go along, they never ride the momentum of market fundamentals. Instead, these get-rich-quick artists become very good salespeople, with great stories about how you can join them and become fabulously wealthy. Their stories can be very compelling, even hard to resist. But resist you must if you truly want to make a long-term financial difference in your life and your family's. These short-term investors give real estate a bad name.

At the other end of the spectrum are investors who learn to practise the art of patience. Focusing on fundamentals, not emotions, will soon lead to a much more enjoyable and profitable way of investing. *Veteran real estate investors will tell you that it will take at least three years of real estate investing before you start to see the real fruits of your labour. Make sure you are emotionally prepared for this investment timeline.* Also, make sure your other partners, including your spouse, share your commitment to long-term wealth.

In an average market, it takes three years for a property to really start outperforming the market. In a hot market, your results will come more quickly. But the bottom line is simple: Don't quit your day job thinking you'll be eating your real estate profits in the first few years.

During these first three years of owning a property, you are building a foundation for your investment business. As you build that foundation, based on systems, relationships and follow-through, you will learn what it really means to make real estate investment decisions based on emotion-free market *fundamentals*.

 **SOPHISTICATED INVESTOR TIP**

Real estate investing should not be exciting; it should be boring. Indeed, a lack of excitement is one way to know your system is working well. Feel free to look for excitement elsewhere in your life, but not in your investments!

# What do you need to do?

**DEVELOP YOUR RESEARCH STRATEGY**

Sophisticated investors must be committed to uncovering the latest market information. Use that information to look at your target market and identify the direction the long-term real estate market is poised to move. In an average Canadian real estate market, properties will go up in some regions and down in others. Not every region is a good investment all the time. Follow the proven system outlined in the book *Real Estate Investing in Canada* and you will be sure to look at the long-term fundamentals of your market. Don't get caught by a slick salesperson—do your own research.

**USE ACCURATE AND TRUSTWORTHY INFORMATION**

Visit www.reincanada.com and sign up for the free *Canadian Real Estate Insider* newsletter. It discusses the latest trends and economic shifts and will help you keep apprised of where the markets are moving. Remember, once you start investing in real estate, you become a business owner. That means it's your job to stay informed about market trends, market shifts and opportunities. Read the business pages, look for opportunities, speak to experts in your target market, find out the inside information.

Learn your way around web sites with good economic statistics. Use the Internet to look for Canadian-specific economic analysis. Find local data and local contacts you can call to ask for more information.

Read economic analysis reports released by credible sources like the economics department of the major banks and Statistics Canada. Make sure the source is unbiased.

 **RED FLAG**

Avoid taking direction from a company with something to sell you. If a company delivers information about why a certain town is a great place to invest, look behind the curtain. Does that company have properties to sell in that region?

## TIP #7: BE PREPARED FOR THE UPS AND DOWNS: KNOW WHEN TO HANG ON AND WHEN TO CUT YOUR LOSSES.

*All investment systems require some financial commitment. You also need to be committed emotionally.*

Sophisticated investors learn to focus on economic fundamentals instead of the emotional aspects of investment deals. Still, there are times when emotions will creep into your investment decisions. In many cases, those emotions will be positive ones, like the good feeling that comes when you've completed a deal with lots of upside. Negative emotions can also impact decision making, although such emotions should be kept in check because you are following a system. An example may be the worry and exasperation you feel when a property is vacant and you have to carry it without rental income.

Negative emotions can lead to poor decision making. In the example above, for instance, among the worst things you could do are the following:

1. *Sell the property out of frustration, leaving profits on the table*. A sophisticated investor will gladly scoop the property from you—and will know your decision is based on emotions.
2. *Accept any tenant you can find*. This always backfires and ends up costing you more in the long run. Sophisticated investors follow a clear and un-wavering system to choose their tenants because they know a good tenant is worth waiting for—and that compromises are detrimental.

SUCCESS IS NOT A STRAIGHT LINE

Investors who take the time to develop a good investment system know they will need to be prepared for financial contingencies. That is why it is critical that you have a Staying Power Fund for all your properties. This should equal a minimum of two months' worth of mortgage, condo and tax payments. Think of these funds as being on stand-by. They're ready when you need them!

Once you own several properties, the fund could hold a lot of money. An emotional investor may want to use that money elsewhere. A wise, system-savvy investor will know that money needs to stay put in case it's ever needed to cover a contingency. These reserves level out the emotional highs and lows. It is much easier to sleep at night if these funds are sitting there.

The emotional impact of financial decisions can be tricky to handle. A healthy Staying Power Fund lets you manage the highs and lows without emotion impacting decisions.

## What do you need to do?

### DEVELOP A GAME PLAN FOR BEFORE AND AFTER YOU PURCHASE THE PROPERTY

Before you buy, follow your system and take an informed look at the deal, including the creation of your Staying Power Fund. Remove the emotions—*never* fall in love with an investment property!

After you own it, run it like a business. Use tested marketing strategies to make sure it is performing at or above your projections. If the property begins to underperform, do not panic or become an emotionally motivated vendor. If the property truly fit the system when you bought it, it probably still does. But do take immediate action to solve the problem. Address why the property is vacant. Look at why it's not generating positive cash flow. Talk to your network of real estate investors and get their advice. Use sound information to avoid making decisions based on desperation.

### BE HONEST WITH YOURSELF

Remember that your system is designed to help you understand how the numbers really work. If you make the emotional decision to sell too early, you will miss the eventual payoff. As long as you bought the property without emotion and the numbers worked, all you need to do is understand that this is a business and it is your job to make it work.

Some investments simply do take much longer to pay off. Do you have what it takes emotionally to stick with an investment for five to eight years or more?

Need to know if it is time to sell? Check out the following tip.

## TIP #8: KNOW WHEN TO SELL: THERE COMES A TIME WHEN CASHING IN IS THE BEST DECISION.

*There are two costs to every investment: a financial cost and an emotional cost. Learn to balance the two to make it easier on yourself.*

Most real estate investors will eventually find themselves holding a property that hasn't performed the way they wanted it to. In fact, if you haven't yet experienced this, you haven't owned enough properties. This is not like school where you get a big red "X" and are kept after school to write an essay about your mistakes. No, this is real life, where everyone makes mistakes. You need to deal with the mistake head-on, then learn from the experience and move forward.

This is true in all investments, from stocks to mutual funds to real estate. Not all investments will turn out exactly as planned. The difference between a successful investor and an unsuccessful investor lies in how they deal with these underperforming assets. Sadly, the majority of below-average real estate investors use one bad deal as an excuse to never invest in real estate again, thus killing their opportunity to create long-term wealth. Legendary investor Sir John Templeton was happy and wealthy when he was right 60% of the time.

But be prepared. Every once in a while, a poor performer will sneak into your portfolio. Let's deal with what to do if that happens. As soon as you find yourself *worrying* about whether you should sell a property, take a step back and recognize the obvious: *You are letting emotions cloud an investment decision. It is time to eliminate the emotions and look at just the facts*.

## What do you need to do?

**ASK THE OBVIOUS QUESTION**

Ask yourself, "Would I buy this investment right now?"

**If the answer is yes,** then your job as a sophisticated investor is to look for unique ways in which to make the property work again. You may need a creative marketing strategy to attract the right type of tenant, or a few small renovations to change the income level of the property. It may even be time to fire your property management company and get one that performs to the level you need, with no excuses.

Is the bad tenant experience making it seem like the property's not worth owning? If so, find a way to get rid of that tenant and find a new one. Each province has clear rules and regulations regarding eviction. Is vacancy an issue? Maybe you need to change your marketing strategy to attract a good tenant. Frustration over tenants—or a lack of tenants—can turn investors into the kind of emotionally-motivated vendor that sophisticated investors look for! Recognize the financial danger of selling too early, then focus on fixing the frustration.

Be honest with yourself. Were your revenue projections based in reality, or did you push the numbers to make them fit? Honest investors often find that underperforming properties didn't really fit the system and were bought based on assumptions that lacked hard and true facts. Learn from this for next time. Don't force a property to fit. It either fits the system, or it doesn't.

**If the answer is no**, then you need to analyze whether selling it would be the best choice. You need to look at the numbers, without emotion and, at the same time, identify any emotional attachment you may have to that property. Maybe property values haven't increased as you expected them to. Maybe they've actually dropped, or the property's cash-flow is negative, or development plans fell through that would have made the investment boom. Regardless of the specifics, it is sometimes best to take your losses, sell the property and move on to getting a positive cash flow property in your portfolio.

### ⑤ SOPHISTICATED INVESTOR TIP

Look for solutions, not problems.

### DO NOT WAIT. ONCE THE DECISION IS MADE, DO IT

Talk to your accountant about the best tax strategies for taking a loss. Then sell the property, take your cash and immediately get back on the horse and buy a property that fits a proven investment system. Do learn from the previous deal and tighten up your investment system. Also remember to stay focused: you need to cut your losses and look for a property that will outperform your projections.

### ⑩ KEY INSIGHT

The payoff associated with selling an underperforming property is not always easy to see. Once it's gone, however, you will experience a major decrease in your stress level. That alone will help you make better decisions and find a property you'll be proud to own.

## TIP #9: LEARN FROM YOUR MISTAKES—AND THE MISTAKES OF OTHERS.

*Everyone makes mistakes; the key is to make these lessons count.*

You must take full responsibility for your mistakes before you can take full responsibility for your wins. If you blame everything and everyone but yourself, you must then share the spotlight every time you do well.

Taking responsibility for investments that go well is easy. Sophisticated investors know they also have to take responsibility for the investments that don't meet performance expectations. More importantly, they know that every investment-gone-bad offers a valuable lesson about what they need to do better!

These mistakes make you aware that you are moving forward, not just sitting still. If you are not making mistakes, you are not being aggressive enough. Of course, don't go out with a plan to make a mistake just so you feel you're moving forward—that would be ridiculous. Just make sure that when you make mistakes (large and small), you learn from them.

Talk with like-minded real estate investors and learn from *their* mistakes as well as your own. Members of the Real Estate Investment Network (www. reincanada.com) share their mistakes and successes so that everyone can learn from the ups and downs. Find a place where you can do the same, so you are continually learning.

What's the biggest mistake you can make? Keep repeating the same mistake over and over. According to Albert Einstein, the definition of insanity is doing the same thing over and over—and expecting different results!

## What do you need to do?

**BASE EACH HOLD/SELL DECISION ON THE FACTS**

If you buy a property that initially "fit your system" and it isn't working out, decide if it is worth selling or fixing. Creating wealth takes some courage—courage to act and courage to wait. Follow a system so you know when to move and when to sit still.

Never let a mistake hold you back from taking future action. That's what unsuccessful investors do. And never let anyone in your life ridicule you for making a mistake; in most cases they are just jealous that you are moving forward and they don't understand that all *great* investors make mistakes.

### TAKE RESPONSIBILITY

Learn to acknowledge that you made a mistake, then learn from it. The insights you gain from experience will far outweigh what anyone else can ever teach you. What you know now probably would have influenced your decision to buy. That moves your personal knowledge of due diligence up a notch!

Keep your system intact; just tighten it up so you don't repeat your mistake, then move on to the next deal.

### DUPLICATE SUCCESS

The power of a proven investment system rests in its ability to consistently create results that can be duplicated. This is how you achieve what you really want—having financially consistent results over time. Practice your system and your tough decisions become simple.

### 🕐 KEY INSIGHT

Recognize the three components of a successful system based on duplication:

1. If it works, keep doing it.
2. If it doesn't work, stop doing it.
3. If it works, but you can't do it again, it doesn't work and it's not really a system!

(Suppose, for example, that you get lucky and the city buys a property from you because it needs to build a new highway. Or maybe you get a hot tip on a golf-course development coming to town and buy a key part of land they'll need to make the course happen. These aren't duplicatable investments. If it can't be duplicated, it's not part of a system.)

## TIP #10: BEWARE THE REAL ESTATE PRETENDER: THEY COME OUT OF THE WOODWORK WHENEVER THE REAL ESTATE MARKET GETS HOT.

*Hype sells. Your job as a sophisticated real estate investor is to pull back the curtain to see what's behind the hype.*

Sadly, the real estate market is often manipulated by two key emotions: hype and fear. These two emotions are commonly used to get investors to take action. Free seminars, late-night TV infomercials and syndicated shows that try to convince you a certain city or development is *the* place to buy into are all good examples of bad real estate hype. The seminars are free only until the pitch is made to you to buy their products. The infomercials you see on television are typically based on the market realities in the United States.

In fairness, some of the pitches might be good investments. But you'll only know if you do your *complete* due diligence. Similarly, some of the packages sold at so-called free seminars may be helpful. Just don't get caught up in the "there are only nine packages available" baloney. There are always more where they came from, but the promoters are capitalizing on the fear of missing out.

These are just a few of the many, many ways hucksters take advantage of your emotions in the real estate market. Your job is to cut through the hype and see what's real.

Just do your homework and make sure that the product you are about to buy is fact-based and proven for at least 10 years of market ups and downs—and actually works in your target geographic area! Real estate investing is not about getting rich quick, so don't buy into anyone who tells you it is.

Research can show you why the $5,000 investment in a seminar might be better spent investing in the actual real estate market. It will also help you understand that because the real estate market is constantly changing, the strategies that worked a few years ago might not work today. Similarly, the people you meet may have investment systems that truly do work for them, but won't work for you.

That's why it is so important to approach this business with a healthy perspective on what it is you plan to accomplish, served up alongside an equally healthy dose of skepticism.

## What do you need to do?

**YOU NEED TO BUY REAL ESTATE**

Always remember that your goal is to take action and buy real estate that fits *your* system. In real estate investment, submitting an offer that leads to closing a deal represents your Critical Success Event.

**KEEP IT REAL**

The tips outlined in this book and in the book *Real Estate Investing in Canada* will help you practice the real-world application of the old adage that information is power.

Never forget that you're responsible for the decisions you make based on the information you've gathered. Make sure the information you use is dependable and comes from dependable sources. You don't want to spend money needlessly and you certainly do not want to lose money. Avoid those who decide to call themselves real estate experts because they've done well in a hot market. Look for a long-term track record.

**KEEP IT RELEVANT**

You need to learn to make business decisions based on data that's relevant to your specific market. You'll discover that a national average price means *nothing* to you, although it is discussed frequently in the media and on the Internet.

 **RED FLAG**

A positive national real estate number does not directly affect your local region. Likewise, the positive investment economics of one city won't apply to every neighbourhood in that city, and not every property in the neighbourhood will perform the same as the neighbourhood as a whole. Do your homework: Use the Property Goldmine Score Card in the Appendix to ensure you are asking the key questions.

**ASK "WHAT'S BEHIND THE CURTAIN?"**

Apply the same "what's behind the curtain?" rationale to every deal you encounter. This is also true of every joint-venture partner, every mortgage broker, every "real estate guru" and every advisor you listen to. Find out what the truth is and uncover their *real* motivation. You may be disappointed.

 **RED FLAG**

As a novice investor, you're an obvious target for "experts" who want your money! They will try to sell you systems. They will try to talk you into deals. They will want cash up front—reducing their risk, but increasing yours.

**Learn the "What's Behind the Curtain?" Questions!**
Ask yourself:

1. What's in it for them?
2. Do they have a financial incentive to get me to take a particular action based on the information they're giving me?
3. Do they have experience in the market or are they part of the cult of opinion? (These guys know someone who knows someone who did something somewhere. That's not good enough for you!)
4. Are they currently investing in real estate and using the strategies they're teaching?
5. **Do they have a bare minimum of 20 real estate transactions** to their name, thereby giving them the experience of dealing with different buying and selling situations?
6. **Have they been investing for at least five years**, preferably 10 years, giving them experience in different market conditions? It's even better if they've been through a full up and down real estate cycle, which often takes a decade or more.

"General rules of thumb" are for those who don't really want to create long-term success. Be aware, don't get caught up in the hype of the market and, most importantly, do your own homework. It is easier to sit back and listen to someone tell you what to do, but that puts your future in someone else's hands—someone who may not have your best interests at heart. Ask yourself, "Are you truly ready to do that? Are you ready to take control?"

 **KEY INSIGHT**

Coulda. Woulda. Shoulda. These are the real estate investment world's three most depressing words! They also imply a lack of due diligence. If it's information that could make a difference tomorrow, you need to know it today.

**KEY INSIGHT**

This book will help you investigate every deal and every person that comes your way. Don't invest on basic rules of thumb. And definitely don't invest based on a list of 97 Tips! Use the tips to enhance an investment system like the REIN Quickstart system, a proven success with over $1.1 billion of real estate purchases.

## ⬭ FURTHER ACTION

Join the local chapter of the Real Estate Investment Network (see www.reincanada.com). There, you'll build a network of experienced, knowledgeable team members and access unbiased research to help you reduce the fear factor.

PART 2

MONEY MATTERS:
MORTGAGE AND
FINANCING TIPS

# TIP #11: CREDIT COUNTS.

*Boost your investment options with a good credit rating.*

Having a good credit rating is one of the most important factors in qualifying for a mortgage. But did you know your credit rating is based on a "scoring" system that can make—or break—your investment opportunities?

Before you even visit a lender, you can (make that *should!*) use the contact information at the end of this tip to get your credit score via the country's two major credit bureaus, Equifax and TransUnion. These bureaus use scoring systems called the Beacon and Emperica. The systems generate a score derived from data based on the five categories listed below. Study them. Then look for ways to use the information to improve or strengthen your credit rating. The percentages listed with each section outline the weight they are given when determining your overall score.

## Past payment performance - 35%
This is as straightforward as it gets. The fewer late payments, judgments, liens or collections against you, the better. More weight is given to recent history versus payment issues two years or older.

## Credit utilization - 30%
Low balances on a few cards are better than high balances on just one or two! So review your credit-card needs. Be aware that access to too many cards however (and frequent use) can be deemed detrimental.

## Credit history - 15%
Your record speaks for itself; the longer accounts have been open and are in good standing, the better.

## Types of credit in use - 10%
Finance company accounts score lower than traditional banking or retail accounts. In other words, too many buy-now-pay-later accounts may be interpreted as a potential for future risk.

**Inquiries - 10%**
Promotional or administrative inquiries (including credit grantor updates) will show on your report, but won't affect your score. Shopping for credit, however, can indicate a higher risk.

## What do you need to do?

**BE HONEST**

Problems happen. Be ready to explain any past issues. Hide nothing.

If you do have a problem with your credit history, make sure you include a detailed reason to your mortgage broker. The more information you provide, the better they will be able to sell your deal.

**WATCH YOUR CREDIT-CARD BALANCES**

Keep credit-card balances at or below 30% of the available credit. If you exceed 80% of the available credit on these cards, your score will dive.

**AVOID CREDIT SURFING**

Opening new accounts to pay down old accounts will earn you a red flag—fast.

When shopping for a mortgage, let your mortgage broker do the work. If you shop your deal from bank to bank, each bank will pull a credit report on you, thus lowering your credit score (see Inquiries, above). Brokers pull one credit history and use it for all the financial institutions.

**USE CREDIT WISELY**

Always remember: someone *is* watching. Every time you apply for a credit card or loan, your score is affected, so having too many credit cards in your name is *not* a great idea. If you need a credit card, get a couple at higher limits instead of a number of different ones.

Consolidate your consumer credit in a low-interest loan or line of credit. Keep your credit-card balances as low as possible. Using loans and mortgages wisely provides you with the leverage all investors need.

**KEEP THE BIG PICTURE IN MIND**

Sound credit choices generate a sound credit history. Poor choices may come back to haunt you.

**CHECK YOUR HISTORY EVERY SIX MONTHS!**

This step is really important. Contact the two main credit history providers at least twice a year to review your credit history. You may find inaccurate information on your file, which needs to be immediately removed. All it takes is one wrong keystroke to give you a bad credit rating based on someone else's record. Make sure your rating is based on accurate data.

## ⚑ RED FLAG

The frequency of fraud and identity theft is increasing, so it's even more important today to keep an eye on your credit file. Simple identity theft could leave you with a mortgage, loan or credit card that you never applied for. Imagine your shock when you get a call from a bank saying you've missed the last three payments on a mortgage you didn't even know you had! One key way to protect against this is to continually monitor your credit history. In fact, for a small fee, you can be advised electronically every time something changes on your credit file. It's a great investment and you can contact the credit bureaus to sign up!

## ❶ KEY INSIGHT

Mistakes happen. If your credit history has a few flaws, highlight them when talking to lenders. Provide them with the information they need to reconize that your borrowing strategies are back on track and what you're prepared to do to maintain a positive credit rating. Honesty is always the best policy.

To request a copy of your report and more information:

Equifax
T: 1-800-465-7166 or 514-493-2314
I: www.equifax.ca

TransUnion Canada:
T: 1-866-525-0262 or 905-525-0262
Quebec only: 1-877-713-3393 or 514-335-0374
I: www.tuc.ca

Get a copy of the report "Understanding Your Credit History and Credit Score" by registering as an owner of this book at www.realestateinvesting incanada.com. This 16-page guide, produced by the federal government and available at no charge, clearly outlines how to read and fix your credit history and credit score. Register your book today to receive it!

# TIP #12: THE TDSR: A RATIO TO REMEMBER.

*Get to know your Total Debt Service Ratio. It could make or break that mortgage application.*

You've got a new car, condo fees and a lifestyle that makes upscale dining a priority. That's great—as long as you understand that *all* of your expenses help generate a financial bottom line that could negatively impact your ability to get a mortgage when the bank calculates a formula called the Total Debt Service Ratio (TDSR).

The TDSR is the ratio of income to the amount of debt you must service in any given month. The maximum ratio for most front-line lenders is 40%. *In sum: The banks don't want you to spend more than 40% of your income on your monthly debt obligations, including all mortgage payments.*

To calculate your TDSR, begin with your Gross Debt Service Ratio (GDSR). This is the percentage of gross annual income required to cover payments associated with housing. Payments include mortgage principal, interest, and property taxes, and sometimes include secondary financing, heating, condo fees or pad rent. The GDS cannot exceed 32%.

$$\text{GDSR} = \frac{\text{Monthly mortgage payment (P+i) + monthly property taxes + heat + monthly condo/strata fee}}{\text{Verifiable monthly income} \times 12}$$

With GDSR, you can calculate you personal TDSR. Your TDSR will equal the percentage of gross annual income required to cover payments associated with housing and all other debts and obligations, such as car loans and credit cards.

$$\text{TDSR} = \frac{\text{Total monthly housing payment (from GDS calculation + monthly repayment on other debts)}}{\text{Verifiable monthly income} \times 12}$$

## What do you need to do?

**SHARPEN THAT PENCIL**

Multiply your *gross* monthly income by 40%. That figure represents the maximum amount most lenders will assume you can pay toward servicing all your debts. Now subtract your current monthly debt obligations—and don't leave anything out. Your property taxes and heating costs/condominium fees are part of the equation. Also include your minimum monthly payments for loans and credit cards and any secondary financing payments made on a monthly basis.

### 🄯 KEY INSIGHT

Lenders use your personal debt data to calculate mortgage eligibility and how much they're prepared to lend you. Lenders won't give you money based on fictitious numbers or a financial picture based on wishes. This is another important reason to keep track of your consumer (non-investment) debt and to check your credit history often.

## TIP #13: MAKE SURE IT'S *REALLY* PRE-APPROVED.

*Start your property hunting expedition with a visit to your banker or mortgage broker.*

Your relationship with your mortgage broker is going to be critical as you move forward as an investor. (Start building that relationship early; use the strategies outlined in *Real Estate Investing in Canada* to ensure you are maximizing the relationship.)

A good mortgage broker will do more than find you a mortgage. He or she will help you design a long-term plan so the types and terms of mortgages correlate with that plan. Any mortgage broker can get you a mortgage, but one with expertise and vision will make sure it fits into your plan. Be selective.

Have the initial discussion about the size of mortgage you can qualify for; you may even wish to get a mortgage pre-approved so you know which price range you will be investing in.

Novice real estate buyers beware. Being pre-approved is not a license to write an offer without a financing clause. A pre-approval is only an estimate of what could be approved when you finally bring the bank an offer to purchase.

An added bonus is that pre-approval locks in an interest rate. While the pre-approved mortgage estimates how large a mortgage you qualify for, it also secures a specific interest rate for up to 120 days.

## What do you need to do?

### UNDERSTAND WHAT A PRE-APPROVED MORTGAGE MEANS

A pre-approved mortgage is not a license to buy! The lender still needs to approve the property in terms of value, location, type and condition. Get the pre-approval in writing from your broker. (Verbal agreements *are* worth the paper they are printed on!)

### BEWARE WHAT ARE ESTIMATES ONLY

You cannot get a formal pre-approved mortgage over the Internet. Know that and act accordingly. Internet mortgage calculators do not give you permission to borrow funds from a specific lender, nor do they provide any kind of "guarantee" regarding how much money a certain lender will be prepared to let you borrow. **They are just estimates**.

Mortgage calculator tools available on various web sites, however, will help you determine how much you *may* be able to borrow. This can provide a useful starting point to help you apply for a pre-approved mortgage. These tools can also help you forecast what your monthly mortgage and interest costs will be.

### 🕐 KEY INSIGHT

When using on-line calculators and mortgage loan analysis tools, make sure you use Canadian sites. Mortgages are calculated differently in Canada than in the United States and you'll want to do your analysis based on Canadian calculations!

### SECURE A PRE-APPROVED MORTGAGE FROM A BONA FIDE LENDER

This gives financial clout to any offer you decide to make. Let your mortgage broker find the best deal for your long-term plan.

Even with a bona fide pre-approval, always include a clause on your offer to purchase that allows you to confirm that you can get financing that is acceptable to you; no exceptions!

### ASK FOR A "RATE HOLD"

If you're still not committed to a particular property, ask for a "rate hold," especially if interest rates are rising. This sets an interest rate for your future use, without committing you to that lender. If interest rates rise during the term of the "rate hold," you're protected. If rates go down or you find a better deal with another lender, you're under no obligation to use the rate-hold pre-approval.

Be aware that the size of the actual mortgage may change with the specific deal, including the precise amount of the down payment. Always confirm the numbers with your broker after you find a property.

### ⊘ RED FLAG

Never, ever remove your financing conditions on an offer to purchase based solely on a verbal mortgage approval. Just because your banker or broker says you are approved doesn't mean it is a done deal. Only after you receive an official written confirmation from the lending institution can you feel comfortable about removing financing conditions. *Don't get caught by acting too hastily!*

## TIP #14: OPTIMIZE YOUR DOWN PAYMENT OPTIONS.

*Learn to make a limited amount of investment capital cover a maximum number of investment properties.*

A pre-approved mortgage gives you some basic numbers to launch your search for investment property. But what happens when a traditional mortgage doesn't fit your investment plans? The standard down payment for most lenders, for example, is 25% and, in some cases, 35%. As an investor, you may plan to buy four, five or more properties over the next few years. Can you do that with a fixed or limited amount of money available for the down payment?

Absolutely. But it means knowing the kind of down payment options on the market. There are dozens of options available to a sophisticated real estate investor. Seven down-payment options are detailed on the following pages. Please note that some reference the programs offered by specific companies. These programs may have changed, so you'll need to do your own research.

*Heightened interest in real estate investing means new products are continually being released by lending institutions. Make sure you use a mortgage broker who is not stuck in the past. Remember to ask about any new down payment options their firms offer.*

For example, in Alberta, most mortgages are completely assumable, so that there is no requirement that the new buyer must qualify. This has obviously been an easy way for investors to buy properties. They pay the difference between the mortgage balance and the selling price, then start to make the mortgage payments.

## What do you need to do?

**EXPLORE ALL YOUR LEGITIMATE OPTIONS WITH A SOPHISTICATED BROKER. HERE ARE SEVEN OPTIONS TO GET YOU STARTED**

- **Use equity.**

  Use equity from an existing property to provide you with working investment capital. This is called an equity take-out strategy. It's the easiest option and it gets you the best rate available in the market with little or no fees.

  The equity you access can be a secured Line of Credit (LOC) set up against a property, such as your principal residence. It could also be from refinancing an existing revenue property with some built-up equity.

  Any interest paid on a LOC that is used for investment purposes is currently tax deductible. Check with your accountant for the best way to structure this.

- **CMHC-insured mortgages.**

  CMHC will insure a high-ratio mortgage on a rental property to a maximum of 85%. You can buy a rental with a lower down payment, if it's insured.

  The application fee for a CMHC-insured rental mortgage is between $600 and $900, depending on the number of units you're financing. The insurance premium can be as high as 4.5%. The insurance costs do change from time to time, so make sure you are working with the latest numbers. CMHC will often allow you to include this full fee onto the balance of the mortgage, so you are not directly out of pocket for it.

CMHC has strict criteria as to what types and conditions of properties they will insure, and in what areas. Not all properties fit what they are looking for. Make sure your broker has the latest information!

For buying your principal residence, CMHC will insure your mortgage to an even higher percentage, sometimes up to 100%.

 **RED FLAG**

CMHC will provide insured mortgages for larger multi-family buildings. Its criteria are very strict in these situations. However, a CMHC-insured mortgage will often get you a much lower mortgage interest rate, as it has reduced the risk to the lending institution. Just make sure your property analysis factors in the extra fees and the reduced interest rates.

- **15% down.**

  Some lending institutions, such as FirstLine Mortgages, offer innovative mortgage products that allow you to put just 15% down on a rental property. The rate is closer to posted levels and requires a small fee (around $300).

  This can be a good option for an investor whose analysis shows the property can carry itself even with the slightly higher monthly payments. It helps you preserve your capital so you can buy another property with the same amount of down payment. Just make sure the cash flow covers all the expenses.

- **10% down.**

  Another company, XCEED Mortgage, offers a product for investment properties that only requires 10% down. The maximum loan amount is $500,000. The mortgage interest rate is a little higher than posted bank rates and there is a small fee. Since the cost of borrowing will be higher than at conventional rates, this approach isn't for everyone, but it may be ideal for a property that's already creating substantial positive cash flow.

  Calculate the "opportunity cost" of putting 10% down instead of 25%. Balanced against the additional cost of borrowing, this could make the 10% down option viable. However, be wary that you do not put your property into a negative cash flow position that you can't handle every single month.

This product has no gross debt service (GDS) requirements. It also has a more flexible total debt service (TDS) limit and no minimum credit score requirement. XCEED Mortgage uses a standard sliding scale and offers rates based on A, B, C or C- credit. (The latter is a bankruptcy, one-year discharged, with established credit.) Yes, that means that even with a recent bankruptcy, they will look at financing your deal. This particular company also offers refinancing on rentals up to 85% and an aggressive rental offset policy that subtracts a percentage of the rent from the cost of borrowing.

This is complicated stuff, so do your homework and speak with your broker!

• **Subprime Lenders.**
A few American lenders are now making their way into the Canadian Market. Although they are primarily focused on the owner-occupied market and will lend up to 100% financing on a principle residence, they do have some products for the rental side of the business.

For instance, some of these companies will finance the purchase of a rental property with only 15% down, but the interest rates will be adjusted upwards, similar to XCEED Mortgages. These products are a strong option to consider if you have less than a stellar credit history.

• **Vendor Take-Back (VTB) mortgage.**
A vendor take-back mortgage is a mortgage (often in second position) that the vendor of the property provides to the purchaser. For instance, the vendor will "loan" the buyer $25,000 for a short period of time. This is in addition to the first mortgage you arrange at the bank.

This is a winner for the vendor, because they receive regular monthly income as if they were a bank and it is fully secured against a property they already know. It is a winner for the buyer because they don't need as much instant cash to purchase the property.

Over the last five years, we have seen this option become much more popular. A VTB is allowed by most banks up to a maximum of 15% of the purchase value. In almost all cases, the lending institution will want to see you put at least 10% of the value of the property into the deal.

In the past, getting a vendor take-back mortgage required a motivated vendor. With people exercising more care with their investments today, many vendors are now very open to providing them. The key is educating them and making them aware that it is an option. Your job is to clearly state how it works and how it benefits them.

• **Joint-Venture (JV) Partnerships.**

Joint ventures, when properly established, provide both partners with what they are looking for. (Review the joint-venture tip in Part 1.)

Finding a JV partner is how a high percentage of sophisticated investors build their portfolios. They help people who have capital, but not time or knowledge. The down payment is provided by the joint-venture partner and the sophisticated investor provides the partner with the opportunity. It is probably the best—and least used—down payment option of all.

So that each partner is protected, they will typically go on title and will need to do a combined application with the bank. Even if this is the first property for one of the partners, the other can use his properties to help the partnership qualify for the Critical 1.1 Rule as outlined below in Tip #16, Avoid the Debt-Service Wall.

### 🕐 KEY INSIGHT

"It's not illegal unless you get caught!" These are killer words from very poor advisors. No matter how desperate you are to get a property or a mortgage, *never ever* sign a document that outlines something you are not going to do. Some questionable mortgage brokers will ask investors to sign a document that states they are moving into the property, even though it is obvious they are not. This is not only lazy, it is bank fraud! Remember, brokers, real estate agents, accountants and lawyers work for you, not the other way around. Don't put yourself in a fraudulent situation just because you're told others are doing it. Remember, it will fall back into your lap when it gets discovered, and your advisors can claim innocence, leaving you to suffer the consequences of committing a fraudulent act.

# TIP #15: LET YOUR LONG-TERM PLAN SET YOUR RATE OPTION.

*To float or not to float? It's not as black and white as sink or swim!*

As an investor, you understand the importance of a good credit rating. You've explored your down-payment options and you've taken the first steps toward a pre-approved mortgage. Everything's going well—but you can't sleep because you're fretting over the float or not-to-float decision.

Many real estate investors spend more than a few hours debating the benefits of a variable (or floating) mortgage rate versus one that is locked in (or fixed) at a specific rate. Investors need to learn this is not a question that should keep you up at night. *More importantly, it's probably not even the right question to ask!*

First, some basics. A variable mortgage rate lets you float with prime. As the prime rate increases, so does your mortgage rate. In real-world terms, it's quite likely the low introductory rate you're floating at now may hit 7% by the time your five-year term is up. But that doesn't mean a variable rate is a bad choice. Paying more money for a guaranteed rate over the next 5 or 10 years is like paying an insurance premium to protect you against rising rates in the future. As a matter of fact, what you need to look at is the difference between the rates you can get on a floating versus a fixed mortgage. Only then can you tell what option might be best for you.

For a fixed-rate mortgage, the bank guarantees the mortgage interest rate for the entire term of the mortgage (1, 3, 5, 10 years, your choice). These are mortgages of certainty. Often the rates are substantially higher than with a variable-rate mortgage, yet some investors like the certainty of consistency.

## What do you need to do?

**UNDERSTAND YOUR OPTIONS**

As with most real estate questions there isn't a clear black and white answer. You must analyze how much you are willing to pay for certainty. Run the numbers, check to see how much more your mortgage payment will be with a fixed rather than a variable. Only by analyzing the true numbers will you know in which direction to go. Then make a decision that you—and your business plan—can live with.

## TAKE THE BLENDED OPTION AND SIT COMFORTABLY ON THE FENCE

Some lending institutions now offer a fence-sitting option. Here, you lock in a portion of your interest payment at a fixed rate. The rest fluctuates with the market. This gives you some protection against rate increases and lets you take advantage of the savings offered by low rates. This can be a good option when interest rates are low, but you're worried about what will happen when the rate rises.

## CHANGE YOUR MIND LATER

Canadian mortgages are much more flexible than they ever have been. This means that in many cases, depending on the strength of your banking relationships, you can change your mind on your mortgage, mid-term.

Most variable-rate mortgages have a lock-in option that allows you to convert your floating rate to a fixed rate. It is very helpful if interest rates begin a quick increase.

Even locked-in mortgages can be converted to new mortgages. A good mortgage broker will find a product for you that has a cash-back component that will help pay for any penalties you may incur when converting your locked-in mortgage.

Once you know how your mortgage works, calculate what it would cost you to move from one option to another. That cost will be clearly defined. Base your decision on what that research says—and move on!

Don't spend countless nights trying to decide which is the best option. Choose the one that balances your peace of mind with your economic analysis, then move on to the next property.

### 🕐 KEY INSIGHT

Keep the real facts in mind and don't get caught up in the hype. What is the real effect of a mortgage rate increase? A 1/4-point rate increase adds $7 a month for every $50,000 of mortgage. It's obvious there's no need to make a panic decision when rates move. Stay real. Avoid the hype!

### 🚩 RED FLAG

Some banks offer below prime variable-rate mortgages as enticements to get you to sign onto their mortgages. Make sure you read the fine print. The low rates are often only offered for the first few months of the mortgage, after which they jump. With these incentive mortgages, make sure you clearly

Red Flag continues

> understand your lock-in options. While some are better than others, you don't want to sign on the dotted line without knowing all the facts.

## TIP #16: AVOID THE DEBT-SERVICE WALL: USE THE 1.1 RULE.

*Apply the 1.1 rule to buy more properties.*

All real estate investors hit the debt-service wall at some time in their investment career. For some it happens early, for others it happens much later. Regardless, your banker or broker will eventually look at you and say, "Sorry we can't provide you any more mortgages, you've hit your limit." At this point you either panic, or you become proactive. I recommend the proactive option.

Investors who try to accumulate multiple properties may be stymied by their Total Debt Service Ratio (TDSR). As discussed in Tip #12, the TDSR formula calculates the ratio of your debt against your income and the banks don't like it to exceed 40%. *That is, you can't spend more than 40% of your verifiable income on your mortgage, loans, credit card debts, etc.*

The 40% margin may vary with some lenders, but it's darn tough to find a lender that will let you use the full 100% of the rental income from your properties to help you in your TDSR. In most cases, you will find they will take only 50% to 75% of your rental income, add this to your employment income and use that to calculate your TDSR. These rules quickly push your key ratio completely out of whack.

 **RED FLAG**

Many investors, depending on their employment income, find that once they own more than three properties, their TDSR is often well above the required 40%—a fact that limits the portfolios of modest investors unless they clearly understand the 1.1 Rule.

- **The 1.1 Rule—Live by it and you will never be limited!**
  The 1.1 Rule typically comes into play once you have three or more properties. A very select group of lending institutions will then start to analyze your rental properties as a portfolio. Once

that happens, the rules change. The lender will look for the magic number of 1.1 or more.

Your total portfolio (that is, three or more rental properties) will be assessed to determine that income (rents, etc.) amount to at least 110% of debt expenses (mortgage payments + property taxes + condo fees). If it does, you have just opened your portfolio to a whole new world of the bank saying YES! *In short, these properties generate $1.10 of income for every $1 of expense. This allows you to add more properties without needing a massive income to service the debt.*

### Rental Cash Flow Analysis Formula

$$\frac{\text{Rental income (less 5\% for vacancy hedge)}}{\text{Mortgage payment + taxes + condo fee (or housing costs)}} = \text{Debt Coverage Ratio}$$

If it is true that your portfolio meets or beats this criteria, the great news is that the banker ignores these properties when analyzing your TDSR. That's right, they ignore the mortgage debts you already have and, in essence, start from scratch. This rule is not discussed much in the mainstream, but investors who understand it will link up with a lender who uses it. Once that relationship is secured, the investor is pretty much handed the keys to the mortgage vault.

The only way the lender will decline a mortgage is if your next property doesn't fit the 1.1 Rule or your credit rating is poor. As long as you invest using the system outlined in *Real Estate Investing in Canada*, your properties will fit this magic 1.1 Rule, so the bank will just keep saying yes to you and your deals.

**Example:** You own three properties with a total rent of $3,300. As long as your mortgage payments + taxes + condo fees don't add up to more than $3,000, you have a winner in your banker's eyes.

## What do you need to do?

**FIND THE RIGHT LENDER FOR YOU**

If you're already working with a specific lender, talk to him or her about using Rental Cash Flow Analysis to treat revenue properties as a "portfolio" once you have three or more properties. If they allow the application of the 1.1 Rule, then keep using them and make sure you only bring them properties that will fit this critical rule.

If that's not possible with that lender, start looking for a knowledgeable broker or banker who will implement the 1.1 Rule to help you buy more investment properties.

### FIND THE RIGHT PROPERTIES

Once you own three properties, focus on new properties that meet the 1.1 Rule. That way you won't have to work so hard to get the banks to say yes. You'll also know that your real estate portfolio will perform well in the market. Once you put this rule in place stick with the system!

### 🟢 KEY INSIGHT

If you plan to have three or more properties in your portfolio, you need to know how the lending business works. With the 1.1 Rule, you can get approvals much more easily even if you have a modest income (or one that can't be verified). The key is making sure your properties meet the 1.1 requirement.

## TIP #17: SHAVE MONEY OFF THAT MORTGAGE.

*Keep your eye on the prize: Learn how prepayment options let you pay off your mortgage or accumulate equity sooner.*

The property is yours. Now what?

Real estate investors buy and sell property to generate long-term wealth. Sophisticated investors never lose sight of the fact they're working with borrowed money to create this wealth, and that by maximizing this financial leverage they will create wealth more quickly.

### 🅢 SOPHISTICATED INVESTOR TIP

Good debt vs. bad debt: Is there really a difference? The mainstream discussion regarding debt is that it is bad, so the more debt you have, the worse it is. That is true, but only in one sense. Debt is bad only if it is consumer debt or non-deductible debt. If the debt is used to create wealth through investing, then the debt is what we call good debt and it provides investors with the leverage

Sophisticated Investor Tip continues

they need. Make sure you analyze your debts, get rid of non-deductible and consumer debt and put deductible investment debt to good use.

So what's the bottom line? Mortgage prepayment options let you have a direct impact on your principal balance. Pre-payment options let you pay off your mortgage sooner and can reduce your interest costs by thousands of dollars while at the same time creating equity with no additional effort on your part. *That means more money in the bank—or more money to invest in future projects.*

Not all investors focus on paying down their investment mortgages, and some consider it a waste of good capital. However, if you can pay it down with no additional impact on your cash, then why not!

## What do you need to do?

### REVIEW YOUR PRE-PAYMENT OPTIONS

Learn how your mortgage pre-payment options work, then use any opportunity you can to pay off that principal.

### MAKE BI-WEEKLY PAYMENTS

The simple switch from monthly to bi-weekly payments lets you make 26 payments a year. That equals two extra payments every year. The extra cash is taken straight off the principal balance and you really haven't dramatically increased the amount you've paid every year.

### ROUND UP THAT NUMBER

A penny saved is a penny earned and that same principle applies when you round up your mortgage payments. Every additional dollar you pay is taken directly off the principal. If rounding up your payment won't dramatically affect your cash flow, or put you into a negative situation, then speak with your bank. The math can really pay off.

This is what it looks like when you round up a bi-weekly payment of $1,150:
Round up from $1,150 to $1,200
$50 x 26 payments = $1,300

That's $1,300 a year that goes straight off your principal.

## 🌕 KEY INSIGHT

Wise investing demands keen attention to what sophisticated investors might call "sweating the details." Never treat this as a sideline hobby, even if it is something you are doing very part time. Take this business seriously; explore all the options that can reduce your expenses. Ask yourself, "If I saw a $100 bill lying on the sidewalk, would I pick it up?" If the answer is yes, think the same about every $100 you can save in expenses. It is all the same $100!

**A Contrarian View:** Many banks will allow you to take a one- or two-month "payment holiday" on your mortgage every year. They just add back the missing interest onto the mortgage balance. This can have a huge positive effect on your annual cash flow. Imagine: you still receive 12 months of rental revenue, but only need to make 10 or 11 mortgage payments. If your goal is not to pay down your mortgage, but to maximize leverage, then this is an option you may wish to discuss with your bank.

## TIP #18: CHECK THE PAYOUT STATEMENT.

*Whether replacing the current mortgage with a new one, or paying it out completely, you are responsible for what you don't know.*

If additional payments on a mortgage are good, an outright payout must be better. Right? Maybe. It comes down to the math once again.

All mortgages have a payout penalty and one will be applied if you want to pay out a mortgage before its term ends. A typical penalty is three months' interest, which can be negotiable with some banks if you are refinancing with them. But three months of interest can quickly add up.

If you are going to pay out a mortgage for whatever reason, there is one strategy that will save you money. Most mortgages contain a provision that says you can pay out part of your mortgage without penalty. A 10% paydown used to be pretty standard, but some agreements go as high as 20 percent.

Here's how you take advantage of this clause to save you money. Before you pay out the whole mortgage, you should make the maximum no-penalty principal paydown, thus reducing the remaining balance. When the lender calculates the interest penalty on the mortgage you want to pay out, the penalty will be calculated on this reduced balance only.

# What do you need to do?

**GET YOUR PAYOUT STATEMENT**

Get a copy of the payout statement from the bank. If the rules regarding payout aren't clear, ask for clarification.

Make sure you know how your "penalty-free paydown" works. If you don't follow the right process, you may have to pay interest on the whole amount. You will likely need to provide *separate cheques*: One cheque is for the "free paydown." The second is for the rest of the mortgage, including the three months' interest on the portion left after the free paydown.

## TIP #19: BEWARE THE CASH-BACK MORTGAGE AND THE SIGNING BONUS CHEQUE.

*An early payout of a cash-back mortgage means you pay the normal payout penalty—and a cash-back penalty.*

Not all mortgages are created equal, and the cash-back mortgage is a great example of a mortgage that is a double-edged sword. One edge hands you money at closing. The other edge can take a big bite out of your bottom line!

A cash-back mortgage is defined as a mortgage a lender gives you, wherein they give you a cash incentive to sign on the dotted line. In other words, after you purchase your property, the bank gives you a signing-bonus cheque that you can use however you like. Investors often use this money for renovations on the property or toward the purchase of another property.

These cash-back mortgages don't have the best market interest rates (if they did they wouldn't have to give you a cash incentive to sign on). This interest rate can be as much as one full percentage point above the best non-cash-back rates. Before you take one of these mortgages, make sure you figure out what that money really costs you over the term of the mortgage!

The hitches continue. If, in the future, you are renegotiating the mortgage, paying it out or refinancing, you must be prepared to return a portion of that cash-back cheque to the bank. Remember, the lender provided funds for the full term of the mortgage, so if you're not going to full term, it will demand part of your signing bonus back.

## 🛈 KEY INSIGHT

If you are assuming an existing mortgage and have plans of not running it to the full term, make sure you know whether it was a cash-back mortgage. Even though you didn't receive the initial cash-back from the bank, you will be the one responsible to pay it back. OUCH!

Due diligence should identify the cash-back provisions. But it's better to be safe than sorry, and that means you *absolutely have to ask* if it's a cash-back mortgage. Believe it or not, many investors forget to cover this critical detail when assuming a mortgage, with or without qualification.

## What do you need to do?

### GET GOOD ADVICE

Get a real estate-savvy lawyer on your team. There are a lot of deals out there, and while the documents may weigh about the same amount, they don't necessarily read the same way! Ask your lawyer to look for a cash-back provision.

## 🚩 RED FLAG

Not knowing whether the mortgage you're assuming or arranging has a cash-back provision, and the penalties that may be involved, can make the difference between profit and loss.

### ASK NOW, SAVE LATER

Always ask the lender if the mortgage is a cash-back mortgage, regardless of whether it's a new or assumed mortgage. Also, when assuming financing with or without pre-qualifications, insist that your realtor obtain a "Mortgage Verification" form, completed by the lender, from the listing realtor.

## 🛈 KEY INSIGHT

Nothing in life is free. You shouldn't assume anyone is out to cheat you, or to conceal information that could cost you later on. But you *must* make sure you are doing all that you can to be fully informed. Due diligence means asking the right questions — *all* the right questions, *all* the time.

# TIP #20: GET THE GOODS ON MORTGAGE ASSUMPTION.

*The mortgage assumption picture is changing. Don't presume to assume.*

Alberta is currently the only province that allows buyers to assume a previous mortgage without qualification. Lenders in that province are, however, tightening up on mortgage assumptions. The end result is that many lenders are turning down attempts to assume a mortgage at the last minute—and catching investors by surprise and without adequate financing!

Other provinces and territories allow assumption of mortgages in certain cases, as long as the new buyer qualifies under their guidelines. This is often done to help the seller avoid massive interest payout penalties.

Lenders across the county, including those in Alberta, have dramatically tightened mortgage assumptions by requiring specific documentation and loan agreements. This is in response to mortgage fraud that has been perpetrated on them by unscrupulous brokers and borrowers. Any previously-held beliefs you may have had about assuming an existing mortgage may no longer hold true. In the very near future, no one will assume a mortgage until he's gone through the full mortgage qualification process.

Savvy investors know the one way around these changing rules is to maintain a good working relationship with your lender. Understand that policies are policies. Creative financing really comes down to the relationship you have with your banker.

## What do you need to do?

### GET YOUR LENDER ON-SIDE

A lender will be more interested in your deal, including a mortgage assumption, if she trusts your strategy and knows your business history. Use a Sophisticated Investment Binder (see Tip #25) to ensure full disclosure of information to your lender. Make it easy for them to say yes!

 **KEY INSIGHT**

Sophisticated investors know they can make money with legitimate transactions. They also know there is no long-term advantage to having a dishonest relationship with a lender. These are the people who loan you money, or

Key Insight continues

call those loans in. There is never any harm in asking a lender for what you want. But the relationship must have mutual benefits. You get a good deal. Your lender gets a reliable client. Remember, it is all about long-term trusting relationships with everyone on your team.

## TIP #21: DON'T RE-FINANCE YOUR HOUSE: USE A PERSONAL LINE OF CREDIT WHEN APPROPRIATE.

*Not all line of credit arrangements are created equal. Secure a line of credit that takes your investments where you want them to go.*

It's good to know lenders are offering more creative options for real estate investment financing. As you move through the investment process, however, you also need to understand how a personal line of credit (PLC) works and why it can be a very powerful financing tool for real estate investors. It is often a much less expensive and more flexible way to access the equity from your current residence to use for investing.

A PLC is like a bank loan, but it operates like a reverse bank account. You get approved to borrow a certain amount of money (the PLC limit), against which you can write cheques for any purpose you wish. You pay interest (and in some cases a small portion of the principal) only on the outstanding balance each month. If you are approved for $100,000, and you only use $15,000, you only make payments on the $15,000. This is much more effective way to take out equity from a property. In the re-mortgage scenario, you start paying interest and principal payments on the full $100,000, even if you aren't using it. With the PLC strategy, you only pay for money you actually use! PLCs are very flexible. You can pay them off anytime you wish without penalty.

There are two kinds of PLCs, secured and unsecured. An **unsecured PLC** is more difficult to get and has no specific collateral to back up the loan. As with any loan, you must meet the lender's income and credit-rating criteria. For an unsecured PLC, you typically have to pay interest and principal payments every month. The unsecured PLC has a higher interest rate than a secured line, typically prime plus 1% to 4%.

A **secured line of credit** is backed by some type of secure collateral, like the equity in your home or rental property, cash on deposit at the bank, or government bonds. The minimum monthly payment is often the monthly interest due that month (no principal payment required). The interest rate floats and is calculated every month. These lines are usually offered at around the prime lending rate.

With a secured Home Equity Line of Credit, you use your home as security and the bank effectively registers a second mortgage against your home. You will have to pay the appropriate legal fees (about $500 to $600) and you can usually get an interest rate equal to the bank's prime lending rate, or up to 1% above.

## What do you need to do?

**LEARN HOW PLCs WORK**

Not all PLCs are created equal. If you can only access the PLC by signing up for the lender's "deluxe" monthly package for a fee, calculate the hidden costs. PLCs often have an annual maintenance fee.

Some banks make you re-apply for the PLC or package service every year. This can be as much hassle as applying for the PLC in the first place!

 **RED FLAG**

The bank bases its PLC rate on their "personal loan base rate." This will be ½% or more above prime. You may think you're getting a prime plus 2% rate, when in fact you're being charged prime plus 2½% or more.

**BE READY TO CONVERT**

Watch the interest rate! Convert the PLC to a fixed-rate loan if you believe interest rates are about to skyrocket. You may have to pay a higher rate for a fixed-rate loan, but leaving it to float could equal cash flow trouble.

**WATCH THE CALL-IN**

With most PLCs, the bank maintains the right to "call in" the loan on very short notice. This would likely happen at the worst possible time, during an economic downturn, when your PLC is maxed, when you have a cash-flow problem or when you've just lost your job.

**INVESTIGATE YOUR OPTIONS**

Some lenders allow you to mix all your products under one umbrella. This gives you the flexibility to take your mortgage and split it into two, three or even four parts. Other lenders allow you to set up a matrix, which gives you a mortgage and a line of credit.

With the matrix-style mortgage, every time you reduce the principal on your mortgage, the available line of credit is increased. This is perfect for investors and business owners, and a wonderful way to turn your personal residence mortgage from a non-deductible debt to a deductible debt.

## 🌓 KEY INSIGHT

Never assume a lender has drafted the documents it wants you to sign for your benefit. These papers protect the lender's interest. Always review the complete agreement to ensure it meets your needs as well.

## TIP #22: KEEP FINANCING UPFRONT.

*Keep your lender in the loop and make disclosure of secondary financing a priority.*

Secondary financing is a blanket term that covers any additional funds (over and above the first mortgage) that are borrowed to make the deal work. This can include vendor take-back mortgages (as discussed in Tip #14), lines of credit, joint-venture or silent-partner funds, second and third mortgages and the like.

The bank will want to know where the funds are coming from to close the deal. In other words, it will be looking for a confirmation of funds that make up the difference between the purchase price and the first mortgage amount.

But secondary financing isn't as straightforward as it sounds. For one thing, some mortgage agreements disallow the practice. Where secondary financing is allowed, the total amount will be limited.

### What do you need to do?

**MAKE SURE SECONDARY FINANCING IS ALLOWED**

Contact your lender and confirm the mortgage instructions allow for second mortgage financing and to what level they allow it. Get this in writing.

When you put secondary financing in place, the banks will automatically be informed through the land registry of your province, so don't even think that you are sneaking it in after the fact. They are watching for this exact transaction.

If necessary, let the person who negotiated the mortgage (your broker) sort out any difficulties with second mortgage financing.

 **KEY INSIGHT**

Secondary financing is used all the time in real estate investing. As a matter of fact, the majority of sophisticated investors master secondary financing as part of their strategy. The best banks and brokers will work along with you to make it work. If you are ever told not to disclose secondary financing, run from that advisor as fast as you can. Surround yourself with professionals who conduct business legitimately!

## TIP #23: EVERY JOINT VENTURE IS UNIQUE. BE FAIR WITH YOUR PARTNER

*Let the situation dictate the type of deal you make.*

Joint ventures (JV) are business relationships that are especially effective in real estate investments. JVs are designed to put partners together to build on each other's strengths. A strong joint-venture partnership must be structured to be stronger than the sum of its parts. In other words, two weaknesses don't add up to one strength. Make sure you only enter a JV relationship with someone you can trust and someone who bolsters one of your weaknesses.

JV deals can be profitable, and if fairness rules partners' actions, a solid partnership can result.

There are countless ways in which to set up the financials for a joint-venture relationship. The key is to ensure that it is fair for both parties. Here are four examples of joint ventures the authors of this book have been involved with. Use them only as idea generators! There is no right or wrong way to structure the deal. What's important is that you structure the deal so all parties agree—and you make sure it enables each party to bring individual strengths to the table.

**🌓 KEY INSIGHT**

Make sure *all* aspects of the joint-venture relationship are detailed in a joint-venture agreement. This agreement must be written by an experienced lawyer and be confirmed by each party's lawyers. It must cover all the contingencies that can be thought of in advance, including the goal of the JV, the financial arrangements, the performance requirements of all partners, what happens if a partner doesn't perform his or her duties and the steps to dissolving the partnership. Make sure you talk about all the potential negative situations in advance, so there is less emotion should the situation ever arise!

## What do you need to do?

### THE CLASSIC 50/50 DEAL

This is the most traditional real estate deal. Here, both parties are registered as owners and have combined to arrange the mortgage financing. The deal is 50/50 with Investor A finding the property and Investor B putting up the cash down payment.

Positive cash flow is either split 50/50 or is put back into the Staying Power Fund. Upon sale of the property, Investor B gets her cash first. The remaining balance is then split 50/50.

### THE GUARANTEED MORTGAGE DEAL

In this case, Investor A (30%) guarantees the mortgage, put up 30% of the cash down payment, has good credit but not a lot of real estate expertise or additional time. Investor B finds the property and makes the rest of the cash down payment.

Upon sale of the property, Investor A and Investor B receive their initial cash investments back, and the remaining profit balance is split 30% to A and 70% to B.

### THE RENOVATION DEAL

The reno deal is a 50/50 arrangement, although each partner may contribute a different amount of cash. One may make the cash down payment, the other cover renovation costs.

Upon sale of the property, Investors A and B receive all their cash outlay. The balance is then split 50/50.

**COVERING NEGATIVE CASH FLOW**

In this deal, the partners share cash investment according to their own expertise, and investment goals, with Investor A covering negative cash flow and co-signing the mortgage with his partner.

Upon sale of the property, Investors A and B receive their initial cash investment. Investor A receives a cheque to cover all of the negative cash flow he covered and the balance is then split 30% to A and 70% to B.

## TIP #24: MULTI-FAMILY AND COMMERCIAL LENDERS USE DIFFERENT RULES.

*The rules change when you move from a typical house or condo to a multi-family building. It may even get easier for you!*

When you enter into the world of six-plexes and above, right through to massive apartment blocks, you are working with what are called "commercial lenders and brokers." This is a completely different world from single-family home mortgage lenders. It is a different world, with different rules.

Real estate investors soon learn the value in trading up. They move from buying a single-family home with a single tenant to buying a suited residence or a multi-family unit. The commercial mortgage market is one more step up the investment ladder.

Management complexities aside, real estate investors who are looking at small multi-unit apartments, mixed-use commercial, or the retail or light-industrial segments of the market are going to like what they see in terms of the growing number of commercial mortgage options. Like the single residential mortgage market, there are a growing number of very effective options.

The good news is, you and your credit rating become substantially less important in these larger transactions. It is more the building that the lender is concerned about. The big banks typically do not have much of an appetite for this type of real estate, until you get into the massive apartment blocks. This means you will mostly work with a quality commercial mortgage broker, or work directly with one of the second- and third-tier lenders.

When lenders do look at these deals, three areas get most of their attention:

1. The income the property creates.

2. The operating expense of the property.
3. The quality of the structure and the environmental liabilities around it.

If you take care of these three key concerns you will hear yes very often! Let's take a closer look at what's happening.

• **Proving income**: The lenders don't pay a whole lot of attention to your personal income (although it does play a small part). Instead, they want proof of the income the building produces, including rental income and any secondary income. They also want to know that, in the worst case, the property will carry itself even if you are not a part of the equation. The higher the income the property generates, the higher the mortgage amount you can receive. It's just that simple. The banker will still want to see your complete Sophisticated Investor Binder (see Tip #25) to check up on you and your partners. But it won't hold as much weight as the building itself. This is the exact opposite of the typical residential mortgage.

• **Operating Expenses**: The lender will want to do a detailed analysis of the operating expenses on the building. Don't be surprised if they don't believe the numbers you give them (even if they are accurate). Each lender has its own ratios for determining expenses versus income. These operating expenses will have to fit their criteria in order to be approved.

• **Structural and Environmental Reports**: The lender wants to confirm the property is going to take care of itself financially and will stay standing and not become a liability in the near future. They will demand a detailed structural review, including roof and mechanical. This must be completed by a professional.

They also want to know they are not lending against a property that could be considered an environmental hazard. You will be required to provide a Phase 1 Environmental Study report that says, at a minimum, "mostly clean." When a Phase 2 report is ordered, "just to be sure," the cost involved can push a real estate deal past the point of economic return. These reports must be planned for in advance as they do take some time and are an added expense.

The first piece of good news is that you, too, will also know that the building is in good shape and will be a strong performer.

The second piece of good news is that investors now have access to loans from $150,000 to $1.2 million. These loans don't carry the "income proof" and "heavy documentation" requirements a conventional loan demands. In addition, these loan programs provide financing for up to 80% of the value for multi-family buildings with five or more units. Only a few provinces currently allow this, but others are being brought on board. Talk with your mortgage broker to see if you can tap into these funds. Read all the fine print, but they just might provide you with the financing option you're looking for.

The loan-to-value ratio on each of these property types may vary and will be evaluated on a case-by-case basis, as will the interest rates. But it certainly ushers in a new era of opportunity for business owners who want to own the land on which they operate their business—and for investors who want to build a diverse portfolio but are concerned about qualifying under typical bank guidelines, or arranging private financing.

## What do you need to do?

**TALK TO LENDERS**

Talk to lenders about financing programs based on the appraised value of the real estate, versus the financial net worth of the borrower.

The best rates for commercial properties will come through conventional sources. Pursue those first. If you encounter roadblocks, look beyond conventional lenders to put the deal together. Then look for vendor take-back or joint-venture opportunities to finance the down payment. Vendor take-backs are much more common in these larger deals than in smaller single-family homes. Don't be afraid to ask. Sell your deal!

### 🅠 KEY INSIGHT

Commercial real estate investment deals are not the same as residential investment deals. The one thing both demand is a positive working relationship with a lender. If you take one point from this chapter, make it a new understanding of the investor/lender relationship. Your investment success depends on it. Get a strong referral from a successful investor or from your local Real Estate Investment Network chapter.

## TIP #25: COMPILE A SOPHISTICATED INVESTOR BINDER.

*When it comes to securing a mortgage, presentation matters.*

This section of the book has taken you through some key tips on mortgages and financing. You're now ready to look at the number one reason sophisticated investors get their deals done—and get their deals done faster.

Sophisticated investors know lenders need high-quality information to make decisions about mortgage financing. They know bankers and mortgage brokers must look at everything, from a potential client's credit history to the financial background of joint-venture partners.

They also know lenders are busy people who must prioritize their workloads. Therefore, anything you do to make their jobs easier will make your deal more palatable. The Sophisticated Investor Binder is the best way to make it easy for them to say yes. *That's right. Anything you can do to make their jobs easier will make your deal go faster.*

The Sophisticated Investment Binder will make that happen!

### 🌑 KEY INSIGHT

The Golden Rule of Real Estate: He who has the gold makes all the rules. In this case, the banks have the gold, so learn to play within their rules!

## What to you need to do?

**BUY A ONE-INCH BINDER**

Get a one-inch white binder with a clear overlay that lets you slide in a title page.

**CREATE A COVER LETTER**

This is a business letter personally addressed to your lender. That letter must include:

1. Contents of the binder: All the information the reader needs to know about you showing that you are a sophisticated investor waiting for a positive response to this particular application.

2. A reference to working with this lender in the future.
3. The date you expect to hear back from him. (And do make it reasonable. A too-short deadline is another reason to reject your request!)
4. An invitation for the reader to call you immediately regarding any questions.

### SHOW PROOF OF INCOME

You need to establish that you can repay a mortgage.

If you are an employee, get a letter of employment on company letterhead. It should state your employer and salary. If possible, have your employer personalize it with comments about your character and, if relevant, how long you've been at the company and where you're likely to go. Make sure the letter includes a reference who is happy to speak with the lender. This letter can be up to 90 days old but the more recent, the better.

If you are self-employed, you must provide documentation of your income. The Canada Revenue Agency provides a Notice of Assessment after you file your taxes. Include copies for the last two or three years. If your taxable income is low, include a financial statement.

In addition, ask your chartered accountant for a formal letter to your banker that clearly defines your business's actual income. This will include your salary, money received from shareholder loan repayments, expenses like rent from a home-based business, dividends, retained earnings, depreciation and other items you may find on an income tax statement.

 **RED FLAG**

Your accountant may not understand the importance of this letter. If that's an issue, draft the accountant's letter yourself, then ask him to modify it and sign it. Make sure your accountant is willing to be contacted for more information. This letter helps demonstrate your willingness to cooperate with a lender's needs.

### BE THOROUGH

Sophisticated investors speed up the mortgage application process (and build goodwill!) by giving a lender what he needs, when and where he needs it. That's why a sophisticated investor never waits for a lender to ask for information needed on the mortgage application.

Complete a generic mortgage application form. Provide your lender with the information you know he's going to need, long before he asks for it (SIN, postal code, employer's address, etc.) Make it look like you've done all this a hundred times before. Remember, this is a business decision and the banker is basing his decision on the numbers and on his perception of you. Be prepared!

If you use the bank's own form, you save your banker from having to re-input the data!

Do not write "see attached information" when completing the application. If it's information they need, make it handy!

 ## RED FLAG

If a banker transfers the information to his own form, read all of the fine print before you sign it. Once you sign an application, you authorize a credit search. Other applications may include hidden clauses with other implications. In Part 1 you learned to ask for what you want. In Part 2 you're learning how to make sure you get it!

### INCLUDE A CASH-FLOW SUMMARY

A detailed cash-flow summary includes all sources of income and helps show the lender you can make monthly payments. Summarize income from other revenue properties as "net real estate income." Make sure these numbers support information from employers or Canada Revenue Agency.

### GET A CREDIT BUREAU REPORT

Every time you sign a mortgage application, you authorize the bank to check your credit bureau report. But that report may contain inaccurate information!

By securing one for the bank, you get to check its accuracy before your banker sees it. To review the basics of a credit report, re-read Tip #11. In most cases, the bank will pull its own credit bureau record on you. By providing one in advance, you show them you are looking after the key details.

### INCLUDE A NET-WORTH STATEMENT

A net-worth statement takes time to compile, but it's critical. The statement must be current and list all your assets (including RRSPs) and liabilities (all loans and credit-card balances). To simplify future updates, use a basic Excel spreadsheet or a financial management program like Quicken to write the statement. You can see an example of a net-worth statement in *Real Estate Investing in Canada*.

**RED FLAG**

Make sure the money you're using as a down payment is listed on the net-worth statement and always sign and date your net worth statement. If someone is gifting you money to buy property, make sure your binder includes a letter signed and dated by the giver. It needs to state the amount, the date you received the money, and the fact the gift is completely non-repayable.

 **ADD A REAL ESTATE ASSESSMENT STATEMENT**

This statement shows all the details of the property you own, including mortgages held by you or others. It is especially critical when you own multiple properties and want the banker to apply the 110% Rule (Tip #16), versus a Total Debt Service Ratio. This statement should clearly outline the equity that is in each property along with the cash flow they create.

Make sure the totals match those in your net-worth statement. Include maturity dates of each mortgage. This shows your lender you may be a source of future business.

Create a computer version of this statement for easy updates.

 **RED FLAG**

This statement may be more difficult to explain to a lender who's not familiar with real estate investment (which is another argument to keep shopping until you find a sophisticated mortgage broker for your team!).

**MAKE THREE COPIES**

When the first Sophisticated Investment Binder is complete, make two more copies—immediately! This gives you one for your banker and two as backups. One of the backups is ready in case another deal comes along. The other is a master copy you'll update as needed.

 **KEY INSIGHT**

The Sophisticated Investment Binder takes time to put together. But all of the information it carries is relevant to *every* deal you make with a lender. In other words, you can present the information at the beginning of the mortgage application process, or scramble to find specific pieces under the tight time constraints of a pending deal. More importantly, a Sophisticated Investment Binder gives novice and experienced investors a distinct

Key Insight continues

advantage. It shows a level of professionalism not always evident in the investment business. The first tip of the next part of the book puts that into sharper perspective. You can do the work in advance, or scramble later and risk looking like every other investor.

## TIP #26: GO THE EXTRA 10% AS A SOPHISTICATED INVESTOR.

*Now take that binder—and make it shine!*

Your Sophisticated Investor Binder will take many lenders by surprise. Even if they are used to working with knowledgeable real estate investors, they probably won't be used to working with investors who are so organized!

The lasting beauty of the Sophisticated Investment Binder, however, goes well beyond the financial data you've included so far. Successful investors are those who "put in the extra 10%." A few more additions to your binder will make sure it packs a powerful communications punch.

## What do you need to do?

### PUT A FACE TO YOUR INVESTMENT PLANS

The first section of your binder should include a 5- x 7-inch colour photo of your family. Make it a formal shot, or something fun. Any copy shop can produce the print you want. Just make sure it's a top-quality print. This changes the transaction from bare numbers to a more personal decision.

### ADD A BIOGRAPHY

Now add a one-page bio of you (and your family). Tell your lender who you are, what you're interested in and what your background is. Make sure you include a sentence (or five!) about where you're heading with real estate.

### INCLUDE YOUR PROPERTY ANALYSIS

The next two parts take you through a tip-by-tip look at what it takes to know whether a specific property is worth your time and money. These tips form the basis of your property analysis and due diligence checklist (see the Appendix).

Put a copy of a completed checklist in your binder. This shows your lender you did your due diligence *before* asking to borrow money.

 **KEY INSIGHT**

> Rookie investors who compile a Sophisticated Investment Binder gain a definitive edge when meeting with lenders. Why? Because strict attention to quality due diligence shows that you understand what it really means to make the details of due diligence part of your investment system! As your investment experience grows, updated versions of the binder will demonstrate your ongoing commitment to making business decisions based on due diligence. Lenders will appreciate your commitment to clarity—and you'll appreciate how the binder keeps your business firmly focused on success. Better yet, your homework reduces your lender's risk and you may be compensated with a lower interest rate or better terms on the mortgage. Build a strong relationship by using the Sophisticated Investor Binder for *every* property, even if your banker has one from the last transaction.

## TIP #27: LINE UP THAT LENDER.

*Put that binder to work.*

Your Sophisticated Investment Binder is a great way to open communications about a specific property with a potential lender. But what happens if you've used the Property Goldmine Score Card to target a community worthy of more research, but you haven't yet lined up a property? *Use your binder to line up a lender.*

The Sophisticated Investment Binder carries all the information you need to get pre-approved for your first investment mortgage.

### What do you need to do?

**CALL LENDERS OR MORTGAGE BROKERS**

Contact two bankers or mortgage brokers recommended to you by other investors. Make an appointment to meet them. Look for a good personality fit and learn about their experience with creative real estate investors.

Ask the tough questions regarding "grey area transactions." Can they get quality financing without forcing you into a situation that may be considered close to fraudulent?

Tell them outright that you won't play any grey-area games.

 **Red Flag**

Remember who's in charge of the interview process. They're looking for a new client. You're looking for someone you can add to your support team. This should be a win-win relationship, but you need to make sure it will work for *you*.

### TAKE THE LENDER FOR LUNCH

Once you've chosen the banker or broker to work with, sit down with the lender in a more casual setting (like a lunch café or coffee shop). Don't talk business. Instead, focus on finding out his plans and aspirations. Find out if working with you will take him closer to his corporate or personal goals. Build a relationship based on each of you supporting each other's goals.

### MAKE THE PITCH

After the casual meeting, return to his office and give him a copy of your Sophisticated Investment Binder. If you have a property in mind, make sure the details (including the completed Property Analyzer form) are included in the binder contents. Give a date by which you'd like approval.

If you're looking for someone to add to your team, but don't yet have a property lined up, talk specifically about that.

 **Key Insight**

Your lender will always be one of the most significant members of your investment team. Cultivate that relationship. It will matter.

# PART 3

# HOW TO MAKE YOUR INVESTMENT SYSTEM WORK

# TIP #28: RELATIONSHIPS, RELATIONSHIPS, RELATIONSHIPS ... NOT LOCATION, LOCATION, LOCATION.

*Beginner or veteran, it's critical to surround yourself with a great team.*

Successful real estate investment is about *what* you know (and in Part 4 we'll discuss the fundamentals that drive the real estate market) and *who* you know. This may well be the most important tip of this book. If you only remember one thing, make it this tip: *For true, long-term success, surround yourself with experts and fellow investors who have the same vision. If you surround yourself with short-term, get-rich-quick thinkers, you will be so distracted by their vision that you'll never achieve your own!*

For this reason, it pays to be selfish when it comes to your time and your vision. Protect them as if you were guarding your last dollar. Time is a non-renewable resource that should not be wasted.

Building the right relationships takes the extra 10% effort we constantly talk about. It means doing the extra 10% other investors just aren't willing to do. Applied to the relationships you need for investment success, the extra 10% effort discussed in Tip #26 means acknowledging the need for a strong team—and then doing something about it!

It is, in essence, a choice. You can take the easier and more successful route to your goal, or choose the more difficult and more stressful. I highly recommend the former.

## What do you need to do?

### BUILD KEY RELATIONSHIPS

Build solid, mutually beneficial relationships with people who can nurture your success in real estate investment. (Review Tip #3 on how to choose a real estate agent, broker, accountant and lawyer.) There are enough dream-stealers out there, so make sure you avoid them whenever possible.

Learn as much as you can about the business goals of potential team members and see if they mesh with yours. If they plan to take six months off every year, or they only want to work two days a week, their plans won't fit yours if you are in the prime acquisition period of your plan; such a relationship won't benefit either of you. At least one of you will find it frustrating and stressful.

Every one of the experts you choose should be a member of a governing body. Check with the appropriate body to ensure they have clean records and are in good standing (e.g., call the local real estate associations, CGA Canada, CIMBL, provincial law associations, etc.).

Find a group of like-minded investors. Their positive support will go a long way to keeping your vision clear and keeping you on track to achieve it. Make sure the investment group you choose is a legitimate group with views that match your own. Even here, you still need to keep your eyes open. If you are going to do a deal with a fellow investor, for instance, make sure you do your own due diligence on the deal. Don't let yourself be blinded by another investor's reputation as an investment star or award winner.

### EMPOWER YOUR TEAM

Once you have a strong team in place, get out of its way and let the individuals do what they do best, which is pay attention to the details. This frees you to do what you do best—find properties. Don't try to outguess your lawyers, real estate agents, property inspectors or other investors.

### PRACTISE EXCELLENCE IN ALL THAT YOU DO

Do everything in real estate at a level of excellence, and demand the same of your team. If they are not willing to play at your level, you may wish to trade them for another expert and a first-round draft choice.

Practise your due diligence system so it becomes second nature. Find out how to mesh your system with that of your team, and chaos will start to disappear from your life!

### BE ACCOUNTABLE

No matter who's on your team, you are still the CEO and President of your real estate investment business and you are accountable for all the results. You did the extra 10% when it came to choosing your team; now apply it to the details. Read every document you sign, have them explained to you if you don't understand them, and never be embarrassed to ask questions.

### 🅢 SOPHISTICATED INVESTOR TIP

Many studies over the years have proven that your net worth and income end up being roughly the average of those you hang out with. If you want to increase your net worth and income, spend your time with people who earn more and have a higher net worth than you.

# TIP #29: GET YOUR SEASONS STRAIGHT.

Submitted by Tim Johnson, veteran investor and educator.

*There is a time to buy, a time to sell. A time to sow and a time to reap.*

One of the things a real system will help you do is identify if it is a good time to buy, a good time to hold, or a good time to sell. You'll see many "systems" out there that will teach you how to buy. But what good is that if you don't know where you are in the current real estate cycle? Buying can be exciting, but selling is where you actually reap the profits.

Experienced investors know there are four seasons in a real estate cycle. Because your system will be based on market fundamentals, you will discover how each season presents a different opportunity to strengthen your business. Veteran real estate investor and educator Tim Johnson descibes the market in the four different seasons—each characterized by its own specific actions to take.

## What do you need to do?

### STUDY THE REAL ESTATE SEASONS

To describe investment cycles as "seasons" has been a useful tool for experts from around the world who hold portfolios in all types of investments. In the real estate business, these are the four seasons, each of which requires certain actions from savvy investors.

Please note that an "investment season" does not correspond with the weather. Real estate seasons run for years at a time (not months) and the temperature doesn't change just because the real estate season changes!

The Four Seasons of Real Estate

**Autumn**
Harvest Profits

**Winter**
Plan, Study & Research

**Summer**
Manage

**Spring**
Buy

**Real Estate Winter: It's time to study the markets, do your research and wait for the buy signals.**

A real estate winter occurs when property values are in decline or returning to historic lows, and the economic fundamentals from the Property Goldmine Score Card show little or no strength. (The next tip provides a detailed approach to the score card.) Real estate winter is not a good time to buy real estate because the fundamentals will reveal no signs of life. If the fundamentals say NO, don't force it and buy anyway. This flies in the face of your system's focus on due diligence and is a recipe for disaster.

Sophisticated investors know that it's not winter everywhere. While the local market may be in real estate winter, other regions will be in real estate spring or summer. Use your system to find the regions that are in a different part of the cycle, and invest there.

Real estate winter is also a good time to learn more about how real estate investment works. Take courses, fine-tune your team, and build relationships with key people.

**Real Estate Spring: This is when the fundamentals start to look strong and prices are poised to increase.**

Real estate spring is the time to buy your investment real estate. The values fit your system, as shown by your analysis, and the market fundamentals show the prospects for good price increases ahead. Plant your "profit seeds" (buy real estate) in the spring so you can harvest them (sell) come real estate autumn. The more you plant, the better the harvest.

Buy quality investments that fit your system because they're supported by market fundamentals and take you closer to your personal goals. Always practise due diligence.

**Real Estate Summer: The fundamentals start to show; the frenzy is slowing down. The fundamentals are still strong, but not as strong as in spring.**

This is the part of the real estate cycle where you tend your properties. You make sure they are performing as well as they can, and you get them ready for sale. Here, it's all about maximizing income and keeping up with the maintenance.

You will still find good deals to buy in real estate summer, but buying won't be your biggest focus. By the time a real estate summer hits, you're seeing paper profits from your springtime investments. As your equity rises, so does the net worth of your portfolio. You can manage properties for maximum cash flow, re-finance them to take some cash out, and get them ready for harvest. You may even buy some new properties, taking care to make sure they fit your system and won't compromise your portfolio's health.

**Real Estate Autumn: The fundamentals show the market is slowing down even further. This is the time to reap that harvest.**
This is definitely not a panic sell time. In fact, you'll find that in most markets (as long as you bought using fundamentals) you will have a few years to start disposing of your properties and cashing in on your profits.

The counsel of your accountant will be critical during this time, to help you take advantage of tax strategies that will minimize your tax hit.

Sophisticated investors never try to "time" the market peak. Those who do try to sell at the peak often miss, leaving a lot of their profits on the table. Manage your assets to leave some profits in the deal for the next purchaser and you will do amazingly well.

### 🚫 KEY INSIGHT

The four seasons of the real estate cycle are based on the market fundamentals outlined in the next part and in detail in *Real Estate Investing in Canada*. The more you study the fundamentals and let them guide your investment choices, the faster you'll recognize the individual seasons and be guided in your investment activity.

## TIP #30: ADOPT A PROVEN SYSTEM: IT'S THE DIFFERENCE BETWEEN LONG-TERM WEALTH AND LONG-TERM FRUSTRATION.

*A proven real estate investment system is the foundation on which you will build your wealth.*

Adopting a system that has been proven over and over again will make all the difference in the world. A system is a tool or way of investing that will help you remove the emotions from the investment decisions as much as possible. It forces you to ask the key questions so you can truly analyze a property and predict how it will perform.

## Ⓢ SOPHISTICATED INVESTOR TIP

It is not a system if you can't easily *repeat* the actions and create the same or better results. Be wary of "new" systems that claim to be the latest hot thing. Approach them like you do a car in its first production year. Let someone else figure out all the bugs!

Sophisticated investors adopt systems so they can quickly and easily make real estate investment decisions that fit their personal goals. A real estate system helps investors zero in on the type of property they need to buy to be successful. It helps them locate and purchase property in a particular geographic area—and it keeps them from buying property that's a bad fit with their long-term business plans.

*Sophisticated investors use their systems to stay on track.*

## What do you need to do?

### FIND A SYSTEM THAT WORKS

A system that works is one that has proven successful for at least a decade. It must also be proven to work in the types of properties you want to own. If you are into buy-and-hold properties, don't waste your time with a quick-flip system.

The Authentic Canadian Real Estate (ACRE) system detailed in the book *Real Estate Investing in Canada* is a Canadian-specific system, and long-term investors have used it to purchase over $1.1 billion of Canadian investment real estate across the country. There are other systems with long track records. Just make sure they work in your area—and are truly designed to help you achieve the personal goals you have set for yourself.

If you are considering buying a system from an expert, make sure you check it out first. Never get caught up in the "There are only nine packages available tonight" hype. Make sure local investors have tested the system and proven it works.

### AIM FOR QUALITY

A quality investment system will include the following:

• A way to analyze the boom or bust cycle.
• A foolproof way to assess property.

- A specific plan-of-action regarding the kind of property you want to buy, buy-and-hold, or buy-and-sell.
- A detailed guide to financing, including strategies that help you get the financing you need to make your system work.
- Specific, proven strategies for placing offers and closing deals.

###  KEY INSIGHT

There's no need to reinvent the wheel. You can learn a lot from proven investment systems and experienced investors. Just remember that you need to make the system your own. That means you're in charge of the kind of properties you buy and you're in charge of how they're bought and managed.

## TIP #31: GET TO KNOW THE 10% RULE.

*Rules like this will save you time—and money.*

Flip open one of your local real estate newspapers or magazines and you come face-to-face with the number-one reason real estate investors discard the majority of properties they encounter—volume!

The simple truth about this business is that there is a lot of product on the market. Some have great potential to generate investment revenue, a lot more do not! And that's why you need a filter.

Some investors use a complex formula based on the interest rate, expense ratio, property price, down payment and market demand. You can learn to do that, or you can apply the 10% Rule. A property is worth more investigation and a more detailed analysis if *the gross annual rent is at least 10% of the purchase price.*

Monthly Rent x 12 = Gross Annual Rent*
Purchase Price x 10% must equal Gross Annual Rent* or less

## What do you need to do?

**USE THE 10% FILTER**

Apply the 10% Rule to decide if a property is worth further analysis. Remember that your goal is positive cash flow. Use market-based information to focus your time only on properties that are worth your investment.

### SOPHISTICATED INVESTOR TIP

Get over the idea that any deal is the "only" deal. Time is a non-renewable resource. You may miss out on a deal if the 10% filter discounts a property that could have generated positive cash flow. That's a cheap price to pay for the vast amount of time you'll save by not looking at properties that aren't worth your time.

## TIP #32: USE THE PROPERTY GOLDMINE SCORE CARD. IT'S YOUR REAL ESTATE TREASURE MAP.

*Believe it or not, this one piece of the system will tell you whether a city or town is poised to go up in value, or poised to drop. Use it no matter what investment system you follow.*

A copy of the Property Goldmine Score Card can be found in the Appendix. Developed from over 14 years of investing experience by the Real Estate Investment Network, the score card will guide experienced and novice investors through a series of questions about a specific property. Even if you don't have a full grasp of the economics that drive the real estate market, this one tool will force you to see behind the curtain so you understand exactly which way the market is headed.

*By the time you're finished reading this part of the book, you will see how this one tool lays the foundation for an investment system that bases business decisions on solid, market-based information ... not hype or emotions.*

## What do you need to do?

**STUDY THE SCORE CARD. UNDERSTAND THE QUESTIONS**

If you're intimidated by the concept of a real estate investment "system," turn to Appendix 2 and study the Property Goldmine Score Card to see just how simple the steps can be. Next, use the score card to analyze a particular piece of property that's caught your eye. If that property earns six checkmarks or more, it may be worth a closer look. If it fails to meet at least six checkmarks, you know your system just saved you some hard-earned cash!

Contact the local politician or economic development officer for the area you are investigating. If they can't answer your questions as per the score card, keep digging. The Internet is another great source of answers to score card questions. The score card is critical. Completing it is where you start to reap the rewards of putting in that extra 10% effort!

### 🔑 KEY INSIGHT

Many of the questions on the Property Goldmine Score Card require you to compare a local area or neighbourhood's statistics to those of a larger municipality or province. Your goal? Find the areas that outperform the averages.

### MAKE COPIES OF THE CARD

Keep a copy of the Property Goldmine Score Card in the glove compartment of your vehicle and in your briefcase. Practice using it to "test" areas. The questions will soon become second nature and you will start to see opportunities where others don't.

You will find yourself studying the media for opportunities others don't see. The announcement of a new highway or commuter train is big news. By using the Property Goldmine Score Card, you'll know these announcements signal important investment opportunities. While others yawn in indifference, you will jump all over the announcement and find the hidden real estate opportunities around it.

The great thing about a checklist is that it hones your insight. The more you use the list, the more you understand how the various criteria can positively or negatively impact each other.

### 🔑 KEY INSIGHT

Sophisticated investors know their systems depend on checklists like the Property Goldmine Score Card. This tool is critical to investment success. They take time to complete. They also save you time and money—which means they *make* you time and money!

## TIP #33: LET QUALITY RESEARCH DRIVE THE SYSTEM. NEVER AGAIN GET CAUGHT BY A SLICK SALES JOB!

*Some of the best sources of information are free!*

Novice investors find the questions on the Property Goldmine Score Card to be a breath of fresh air. Instead of fuelling an investment system with the excitement of nervous tension, the score card gives them a series of specific questions carefully designed to take them calmly and rationally to where they want to go. All they need now are the answers to those questions.

Veteran investors use the score card to ramp up their "buying machine" and target only areas with huge upside potential. These include towns or neighbourhoods that earn 10 or more checkmarks, meaning they have a distinct advantage in the marketplace. Quality market research is a prerequisite of quality real estate investments, so don't ever skimp on your fundamental research. If you do, you dramatically increase the risk and will likely be caught in deals based on emotions. Worst of all, you could be the last to know the property is a loser—and your own laziness will be your only excuse!

Quality answers to score card questions are not difficult to find and, better yet, are often free! There are people out there who are paid to give you this information. These include economic development officers, statisticians and politicians. All you have to do is ask!

### 🕐 KEY INSIGHT

Never buy a property blind! It doesn't matter who is selling you the property and what story they have told you, it is imperative that you, or a *very* trusted partner, go to the area you're thinking about investing in and spend time investigating the economics. If you've already got a property in mind, make sure you or that trusted partner do a detailed inspection before you buy.

## What do you need to do?

PICK UP A NEWSPAPER (OR THREE)

Economic articles and announcements should be the first thing you read every morning. Is the government trumpeting huge job increases (or losses) in your target investment area? Is a new company moving in and bringing employees, or is a well-established one moving out? Have officials just confirmed a new local transit system improvement, or identified where new stations will go? How about a new overpass or a major new residential development? These are examples of the kind of announcements that sophisticated real estate investors recognize as yielding significant investment opportunities. Most people ignore these signs, then call others "lucky" because they take advantage of the investment potential others missed!

Don't pay too much attention to the "national average" numbers that are often quoted in the media because they don't help you to see what's happening in your local area. Relying on these national averages is like saying your head is in a hot oven and your feet are in the freezer, so on average you're doing fine. Your investment system depends on quality information. Dig deep!

Continually review the display and classified advertisements published in your target area. They will tell you a story you can't find anywhere else. This includes current market data on the *true* vacancy story, which holds that a higher-than-usual number of rent ads equals a higher vacancy rate and vice versa. Current ads also give you a realistic look at rents in your target market. That information will help you make market-savvy adjustments.

### DROP BY THE PUBLIC LIBRARY

Check out local directories and newspapers. They will tell you lots of "street" news the major media won't cover because the stories are too small. Crime rates and the location of grow-ops that were busted are front-page news. So are new schools and hospital expansions.

### PAY ATTENTION TO BUSINESS MOVES

Take a look at who's moving in and out of a community. If a Wal-Mart or Costco or Canadian Tire is moving in, someone else has done a lot of research for you.

The key is to look for employment level trends, both good and bad. The economic development departments will have the most up-to-date stats for who's moving in and who's moving out.

Also, be aware of long-term trends. If it is a forestry town, look at demand for the products it produces. If long-term demand is good, find out if there is a large enough disease- and bug-free source of mature trees to feed the local mills. Ditto with mining towns and stable demand and supplies of ore.

This long-term approach avoids the hype and emotion of current headlines that could lead you to inaccurate conclusions.

### STUDY HOUSING PRICES

Royal LePage releases a quarterly survey of Canadian housing prices that's worth its weight in gold. It lists most major towns and cities and can be picked up at any Royal LePage office, or on the Internet. Combine these stats with stats from the local real estate boards to get a true picture of the market.

### LOOK AT VACANCIES

Call your local CMHC office to see if they have stats for a particular community. As these vacancy rates may be dated in smaller regions, make sure you check the date the survey was taken and *not* when it was published. The implications are enormous. For instance, if you investigate a college town and the survey shows high vacancy rates, there's a good chance the survey was done when school was out for the summer.

Use the local classified ads as the major indicator of your competition and the vacancy for the town. This data will give you rental market shifts from month to month and that's apt to be more up to date than formal surveys.

### VISIT THE LOCAL CHAMBER OF COMMERCE

Talk to staff about what's going on in the region and tell them you have suites for rent in the area. People from out of town often call the local Chamber of Commerce to get some direction about where to look.

Join the chamber and network. This helps keep your finger on the pulse of the local business community. Announcements of business expansions or contractions are often shared at meetings and you can use that information to fine-tune your investment strategy.

### VISIT LOCAL BUSINESS OWNERS

Strike up a friendly conversation with every business owner you can. In small communities, the owner is often behind the cash register and they will have an ear to the ground as to the health of the town's economy. Ask them questions such as: Are sales up or down? Are they re-developing any regions? Are the mayor and council business-friendly or not?

## COLLECT MUNICIPAL DATA

Visit the local municipal office and ask for a zoning map, a copy of the official community plan and a copy of the bylaws.

Speak with the local economic development departments; they are there to stimulate economic development, and that is what you are doing as a real estate investor—bringing money into their community. The savvy economic development people will welcome you with open arms. That's also a good sign they will do the same when major employers consider moving into town. The less-than-helpful ones will be difficult to deal with. They'll be "too busy" to help and act like they're doing you a favour. That same growth-impeding attitude will likely prevail when companies and employers come looking for their help. If this is what you experience, look into whether the economic development staff are sending economic opportunities off to more welcoming towns.

## MEET THE LOCALS

Cab drivers, bartenders, newspaper editors and local politicians can be a very good source of information and give you a good "sense" of the community.

## TALK TO REAL ESTATE AGENTS

Talk to a number of different agents. Ask to see reports such as the Royal LePage real estate quarterly report. Interview the agents you like; then select one and bring her aboard your team. Make sure you fact-check all the information on neighbourhoods, etc.

## PICK UP MLS BOOKS, HOT SHEETS AND OTHER LISTINGS

Pick these up at the local real estate office. The back of most Multiple Listing Service (MLS) books lists prices and properties sold for the last six to 12 months.

## VISIT REAL ESTATE BOARDS ON THE INTERNET

They often have great stats on current and historical real estate prices. Sometimes the data is free, while other times you'll pay. A good real estate agent on your team should be able to access any of the information you require.

### TALK TO PROPERTY MANAGERS

Talk to several property managers. They can be a good source of information on what's really going on in the rental market. Be aware that many are overworked and underpaid, factors that may cloud their comments, even in a booming market.

Sophisticated investors will tell you they won't buy until they've lined up a good manager for that property. So consider this part of your due diligence background work for the next phase: purchase and management.

### TAP INTO THE PROVINCIAL STATISTICS

Provincial departments often have specific information on particular cities and towns. Staff can also direct you to other departments (economic development, agriculture, industry) that may have other useful information on what's happening in a community.

Overall provincial stats are what you'll compare your local numbers against to see if your target area performs better or worse than the provincial average.

### ACCESS INFORMATION FROM STATISTICS CANADA

Statistics Canada has excellent economic and population data. It's often in "raw" form and you'll need to wade in to find what you need. (Remember: you're looking for information other investors don't have!)

Stats Can fees depend on the data you want. Sign up for their free advisory service, a daily e-mail announcing their latest findings and press releases.

### LOOK FOR RESEARCH REPORTS PUT OUT BY THE REAL ESTATE INVESTMENT NETWORK (REIN) AND OTHER CREDIBLE RESEARCH COMPANIES

The Real Estate Investment Network and other economic research firms across the country release investment information such as reports and press releases. Get on to *every* credible research report e-mail list you can find and use the data to stay on top of the latest trends. Here are a few organizations to check out:

Real Estate Investment Network : www.reincanada.com
Royal LePage: www.royallepage.ca
Statistics Canada: www.statcan.ca
Clayton Research: www.clayton-research.com

**BUY A STREET MAP OF THE AREA**

Last, but not least, a good street map will get you where you want to go, literally! It's especially helpful if you're buying in an area you don't frequent. Look for everything a tenant will want to have access to, including parks, schools, shopping, transit and transportation. This is easy to do with a map but is far more difficult if you're just driving around aimlessly!

Always locate your target property on the map and see if there is potential in the surrounding neighbourhoods.

# TIP #34: CONTROL THE PAPER TIGER WITH A PROVEN FILE SYSTEM.

*Win the paper war with a file system that buys your time back!*

One of the first things you learn about buying real estate is that it creates a storm of paper. You can let it overwhelm you or adopt a proven file system that lets you find specific documents in seconds.

The Power Paperwork System was developed by the Real Estate Investment Network (REIN). It is easy to use, compatible with Canada Revenue Agency rules regarding paper trails, provides the best results over time—and can be used when buying single or multi-family properties. *Put this in place now—or set it up before you buy your first property!*

## What do you need to do?

**BUY A FILING CABINET THAT WILL HOUSE LEGAL-SIZE DOCUMENTS**

This is essential. The legal documents and paperwork you need to file your taxes must be kept in an accessible place. This is the absolute best way to do that.

**BUY GOOD QUALITY FILE FOLDERS AND HANGERS**

You need four different colours of folders and hangers. Every time you buy a piece of real estate, add four new file folders to your cabinet.

*Red:* For all tenant information. This includes all rental information, move-in and move-out inspection reports, the completed tenant questionnaire, lease or rental agreements, a CD of property pictures and all correspondence with the tenant.

*Yellow:* For property miscellaneous. This is where you put general property information, warranties, your master key and all maintenance and inspection information.

*Blue:* For all legal documents. Because this file won't be accessed very much after closing, blue files go into the bottom file drawer. Documents will include a copy of the offer to purchase, all due diligence documents, the survey (or title insurance certificate), the appraisal and all closing documents.

*Green:* Ongoing monthly receipts. This is the file you will open most often. It holds all of the receipts for any expenses related to that property. At the end of each month, gather all of the receipts from a file and put them in a #10 envelope marked with the month and year. On the outside of the envelope, list the company name, the amount paid for each receipt and the classification (office expenses, marketing, maintenance). This greatly speeds up your computer accounting records and provides a replicable record if your computer crashes or you are audited.

### KEEP YOUR ACCOUNTING RECORDS UP-TO-DATE

All of the receipts in your green files must be entered into a QuickBooks-style accounting program at least once a month. Always write all of the key details of the receipt on the actual paper. Your accountant will love it—and it's a wonderful way to answer an auditor's questions!

 **RED FLAG**

Legitimate expenses will be denied if you don't keep receipts and make sure you know what they're for! Handwrite notes on every receipt!

### ESTABLISH A CLASSIFICATION CODING SYSTEM

Keep track of individual expenses with a proven classification system. According to information from the Canada Revenue Agency, a statement of expenses related to real estate rental investments can be classified according to the following:

- Advertising
- Caretaking
- Financing and borrowing costs
- First mortgage interest
- Second mortgage interest
- Condo fees
- General repairs & maintenance
- Insurance
- Legal and accounting
- Property management
- Property taxes
- Utilities
- Auto expenses

**USE YOUR SYSTEM TO SAVE MONEY!**

Get into the habit of tracking expenses as you go. By using the file folder and monthly envelope suggestions outlined above, you will make it very easy for your bookkeeper and accountant to advise you about how your portfolio is performing. These systems also save you accounting fees and allow you to make decisions based on facts, not emotions.

 **KEY INSIGHT**

Set up a simple spreadsheet program so you won't miss out on all the deductions for simple things like a $5 box of Tim Hortons doughnuts. With a program like QuickBooks, you can set it up to press Control D every time you enter a doughnut receipt.

## TIP #35: CELEBRATE YOUR SUCCESSES.

*Make investing fun ... and enjoy the journey, not just the destination.*

Real estate investment demands hard work and patience. Sophisticated investors use a system they can depend on and sometimes the system makes real estate so simple it is boring. Don't go looking for excitement in your investments. However, that is not to say that real estate investing should not be fun and enjoyable.

The key is to not wait until you've "made it" to celebrate. Celebrate each step along the way. When an offer is accepted, take your favourite person out to dinner. When you close on a property, go do something you love. When you have all your suites rented, find a way to celebrate your success. Make it fun—and make it something you wouldn't normally do.

What you are doing is rewarding action and the more you reward action, the more action you'll take toward achieving your goal.

Of course, when you sell a property for a good profit, treat yourself big—you earned it!

## What do you need to do?

**STAY FOCUSED, YET HAVE FUN**

Take real estate investing seriously—it is a long-term commitment to wealth creation. But don't get so caught up in the business end of your investment life that you forget about life and loved ones.

Continue to follow your system and build in celebration points along the way. Small rewards remind us that success is a cumulative process.

# PART 4

## FOCUS ON THE TWO TYPES OF ECONOMIC FUNDAMENTALS AND DRAMATICALLY INCREASE YOUR BOTTOM-LINE RESULTS

*Part 3 walked you through the importance of following a proven real estate investment system. Among other things, it introduced you to specific people to speak with to access the critical market information you need to become a successful real estate investor.*

*Now that you know where to look, this part of the book will walk you through a list of what sophisticated investors call "the market fundamentals" that will help you find towns and neighbourhoods that have the best opportunity to outperform the rest of the real estate market. Once you understand how the fundamentals impact property value, you will be able to look at the nitty-gritty of optimizing actual investments, which is the topic of Part 5.*

# TIP #36: DIG FOR SPECIFIC INFORMATION AND IGNORE GENERALITIES.

*Knowledge = Advantage = Long Term Results. Never buy into hype or emotions.*

Sure you can get lucky in the real estate market—many people have. But a lot more have been unlucky. The last thing you want to do as a real estate investor is rely on luck and chance. That's not investment. It's called "speculation"—and you might as well play the lottery to fund your retirement!

Successful wealth creation through real estate investment is all about uncovering the market fundamentals that can tell you whether a property is poised to increase in value or decrease. And the good news is the numbers are easy to get, but most investors don't know the right questions to ask.

We're looking for markets with a future not a past. A town or neighbourhood may show rising values today, but sophisticated investors look at how it will perform in the future. Please note that we are talking about specific town or neighbourhood research, not market generalities. General provincial or national real estate stats mean nothing to a sophisticated investor. Sure, they're interesting to read, but they are really useless to an investor because they don't drill down into a specific target area.

For example, you may hear the media report that the average Canadian or provincial real estate price increased 5%—a finding that is generally useless. It could mean that some markets are up 10%, while others are down 5%, thus averaging 5%. If you based your investment decisions on such a general number, you might say, "Great, real estate prices are up again, so let's buy some more." However, if you're not paying attention to local numbers, you could be the one buying in a region where prices are dropping.

## What do you need to do?

### UNDERSTAND THE TWO TYPES OF FUNDAMENTALS

Some market fundamentals are passive, meaning they're outside the investor's control. Although passive, they often have the largest impact on the long-term value of your properties.

Other fundamentals are within the control of the investor, such as "sweat equity." The key is to find properties where you have a combination of both.

You need to understand how both kinds of factors impact the investment environment.

 **REVIEW THE PROPERTY GOLDMINE SCORE CARD**

As you read this tip, refer to the Property Goldmine Score Card in the Appendix. You should develop a strong appreciation for how this checklist can support your investment system and power your decisions with real-world information.

## 🚩 RED FLAG

> The Property Goldmine Score Card will help you pinpoint the market fundamentals of a particular community, thus narrowing your search for a property to buy. You can also use it to "test" a particular property in a specific community. Either way, the power of the market fundamentals holds true: Find a town or neighbourhood that, according to the checklist, delivers the most potential.

**WARNING!** Don't just buy *any* property in a region that offers great fundamentals. The property must also fit detailed investment criteria. Not all properties will work, even if the fundamentals are there!

### The Market Fundamentals: The Foundation upon which Your Real Estate Portfolio Is Built

Build your portfolio on a strong foundation of fundamentals and it will create long-term wealth. Build it on hype and poor fundamentals, and it becomes higher risk and could bring potential financial disaster.

Here's a quick overview of the real estate investor's fundamentals discussed in detail in *Real Estate Investing in Canada*. The fundamentals discussed here will play a major role in your long-term success as an investor. Fundamental market research is provided to investors from groups as diverse as the economics departments of RBC (Wealth Effect & Affordability Index) and TD (Increased Job Growth & Gentrification), to regional bureaucracies (infrastructure expansion, zoning and renewal), to real estate sales firms (Boom Effect), to specific research firms such as the Real Estate Investment Network and Clayton Research. Make sure that you tap into as many un-biased resources as you can, study their reports and become a knowledgeable investor.

**1. Passive factors: Use them as indicators of future strength**
These factors wield a direct influence on market strength, but are outside an investor's control.

• Mortgage Interest Rates
• Wealth Effect
• Affordability Index
• Increased Job Growth
• The Boom Effect
• The Economic Development Office's Attitude
• Infrastructure Expansion
• Gentrification and Renewal

**2. Active factors: Where you can have a direct impact**
Market-savvy investors know these factors help them boost investment value.

• Maximizing Zoning and Value
• Direct Renovations
• Stand Out from the Crowd
• Divide and Profit
• Jumping the Gun

## TIP #37: LOW MORTGAGE RATES ARE A NEUTRAL FACTOR FOR INVESTORS.

> *Sophisticated investors know interest rate hype when they see it. Learn why low interest rates are a neutral factor for investors and often an increasing interest rate is a good thing!*

Mortgage rates, hockey and the weather are national obsessions. Most Canadians assume low mortgage rates drive values upward and high interest rates keep values down. If that's true, then a low-interest-rate environment should benefit real estate investors.

Sophisticated investors take a general statement like this and dig a little deeper. Interest rates play only one role with respect to value increases in real estate. They are talked about so much because the relationship between interest rates and value sounds logical. But to get the truth you must dig a little deeper.

# What do you need to do?

**ASK THE OBVIOUS. WHAT DOES A LOW MORTGAGE RATE REALLY MEAN?**

The answer depends on your investment system and your portfolio plan!

A low-interest rate for a mortgage keeps an investor's expenses down by allowing access to investment funds more cheaply, which is great in the short term. However, low mortgage interest rates also allow more renters to become homeowners, and while this increase in demand for real estate will drive the values upward, it will also expose the investor to higher vacancy rates. Investors will be competing for a shrinking cohort of renters. So, where an investor wins on the interest rate side, they lose on the vacancy side; that is, if they only use obtaining a low interest rate as the reason to invest.

Since values increase lock-step with vacancies, low interest rates are a neutral issue for investors.

**DON'T GENERALIZE ABOUT INTEREST RATES AND INVESTMENT**

If you're buying and flipping properties, low interest rates are good for business, providing you a larger market of buyers.

If you're buying and renting to generate a long-term source of passive income and long-term wealth, slight increases in interest rates can be a good thing over the term of your investment. If interest rates are in the historical low zone (but not at historic lows), then the investor has a much more balanced market.

Remember that mortgage rates and the Bank of Canada's prime interest rates are not always heading in the same direction. Always access information relevant to the current market.

- Which way are interest rates going today? Up? Down? Flat?
- How does that compare to historical numbers? Low? Average? High?

**🔑 KEY INSIGHT**

Keep your perspective when interest rates shift. If, for example, the interest rate on a $100,000 mortgage increases from 5.0% to 5.25%, it really is only a $17-per-month difference. If this $17 a month turns your investment deal into a money-losing deal, it was a bad deal to begin with!

# TIP #38: STUDY THE NET WEALTH EFFECT.

*There is a direct correlation between property values and how people feel about their wealth and disposable income. Use this data to predict future value.*

The key number here is *not* average income, but average "disposal" income. Disposable income as defined by sophisticated investors is *available income after taxes and regular household expenses* are deducted. In other words, money that is left over at the end of the month. The factor that has the most impact is, of course, the tax component (both on property and income). This number can differ dramatically from region to region.

Of course incomes could be increasing quickly in a given area; however, if tax pressures are increasing quickly as well, real estate values will not be positively affected. On the flip side, you may find a region where incomes aren't skyrocketing, but taxes and living expenses are decreasing, even dramatically, as we witnessed in Alberta between 2000 and 2004. This combination led to a spike in real estate values.

In real estate markets, perception is reality. If people can, or think they can, afford higher real estate prices because they feel wealthier, then prices move up. If they feel constrained by high expenses, high real estate values or high taxes, values will flatten. This ties directly into the Housing Affordability Index in the following tip: *As a region's populace feels increasingly "wealthy," real estate values will move upward due to the perceived rise in affordability.*

## What do you need to do?

### IDENTIFY WHERE AFFLUENCE LIVES

Identify a town where people tend to spend more money on retail items than is the average. This is a sure sign that the wealth effect is in place and you will see real estate values increasing more quickly than the average. Focus your investment strategy on towns where income and retail sales are increasing at a higher rate than the provincial and national averages.

### TRACK MEDIA STORIES

Follow Statistics Canada's income numbers, then drill down to the provincial and local numbers. Save articles from print and electronic media discussing increases in retail sales or disposable income measurements. Remember to compare the numbers to the provincial and national averages.

**WATCH FOR ANOMALIES!**

Beware—there are communities that break the rules.

In towns with a lot of retirees, for example, demand for quality housing may drive market values upwards. However, net disposable incomes will decline and the perceived Wealth Effect will be negative for long-term values in the region. These communities may have some good opportunities for short-term or specialized housing investments, but without a positive Wealth Effect, increases in real estate values will not be sustainable over the long term.

## 🔴 KEY INSIGHT

Sophisticated investors look for information others miss. You are looking for a town that outperforms the rest of the marketplace, in regions where the overall tax burden is decreasing. Even when the values across a whole province are on the rise, a town with a higher-than-average-gross wealth effect will often outperform its peers. Just look at what has occurred in Ft. McMurray, Alberta over the last five years!

# TIP #39: APPLY "AFFORDABILITY" DATA.

*Use the Housing Affordability Index to test a community's investment potential.*

Economists at the Royal Bank of Canada produce a quarterly report that analyzes the affordability of housing in specific markets across the country. This tool has proven to be a very accurate source of real estate market health across Canada.

In these reports, you will find the percentage of median income that is required for a median home in each province, as well as in select major cities; in a recent improvement, the report breaks out different housing types. This helps investors determine whether a market is overpriced or undervalued compared to the rest of the country.

As a rule of thumb, a well-balanced market for investors is a market that has a Housing Affordability Index of about 33%. That means that it takes

33% of pre-tax income to make the monthly payments for a median piece of property.

 **RED FLAG**

Cities and towns that are above this rate are often overpriced for investors. Even though prices may be skyrocketing, if the city's index is 5% or more above this mark, it indicates the market is turning speculative and the fundamentals are getting out of balance.

## What do you need to do?

**LOOK FOR 33 PERCENT**

Get the latest Housing Affordability Index Report by visiting www.rbc.com/economics. Focus your extended research on areas where the index shows 33% or less. If a community meets that test and the rest of your indicators are strong, you may have zeroed in on an area that will outperform the rest of the market—but only if other fundamentals are in place. A low affordability index doesn't necessarily mean it's destined to go up. Some regions just happen to always outperform in this fundamental.

Be wary of regions where the Housing Affordability Index is too low, as this is a sign that renters are able to become home-owners quite easily.

**DO YOUR OWN CALCULATIONS**

For most towns and cities, you will have to do your own math to determine where the town sits on the scale. Yes, it is worth the effort as the majority of investors aren't willing to do that extra step to uncover the real investment gems. This is one of the most important indicators of a community's investment potential.

## TIP #40: IDENTIFY WHERE INCREASED JOB GROWTH IS HAPPENING.

*Look for an area where people are moving to fill tremendous job opportunities.*

Savvy real estate investors know it pays to read the newspaper and Internet news sites, and watch the media. Always be on the lookout for major announcements of new jobs, major expansions or new employers moving into an area. This is a good sign of a future increase in residential housing demand. It's also a signal of an increasing Wealth Effect.

Here's how it works. When companies or governments make a major announcement of new jobs or new business relocations, the announcement will trigger a significant increase in housing demand. Naturally, the housing supply takes time to catch up to this demand, but often never does. From this increased demand and fixed supply, real estate prices are driven upwards in a given area more quickly than the regional average. You can see this occurring today in regions as diverse as Barrie, Ontario, Ft. McMurray, Alberta and Ft. St. John, B.C.

## What do you need to do?

### LOOK FOR JOBS, JOBS, JOBS

When analyzing a region, look for cities, towns and neighbourhoods in high demand because of what's happening in the local labour market in terms of an increase in jobs or easier access to jobs.

Your goal is to find areas where the population is growing faster than the provincial average due to an influx of jobs. In some towns, the population will be growing because the town has become a retirees' haven or is a cheap place to live, but this does not always lead to increased real estate values. You want to find cities, towns and neighbourhoods that are gaining a reputation as great places to live and have a growing economy.

Visit the Economic Development Office of towns you have picked for potential investment. (You'll discover more about the importance of this office in Tip #42.)

### STUDY BOTH COMPONENTS OF NEW RESIDENTS

People moving into a town to fill new jobs come from two main sources. *Immigration* occurs when people move from other countries into a new country; *intra-migration* occurs when people move from one part of the country to another. People generally speaking look for rental properties until they are settled (usually for two years). After two years, those with savings look to buy a home, so investors win in both cases. They have a market for their rentals and a stable market for the properties you wish to sell in the future.

These sources of in-migration can exist independent of each other, or combine to provide a very strong market. What you'll generally find is that if a region is creating a lot more jobs than the average, the immigration and in-migration numbers will be very strong. As people migrate to your target region, it will affect everything you have to offer to your marketing plan. Make sure you know which type of in-migration your business plan will focus on.

##  KEY INSIGHT

Work with the Human Resources Departments of the employers who are hiring. Become a solution to their new employees' housing concerns. Make it easy for them and they'll make it easy for you.

## 🚩 RED FLAG

If you discover or are investigating a region where there is a net *loss* of migration and immigration, seriously reconsider any long-term real estate investments in this region as your market will continue to shrink while available housing units will increase. Less demand + fixed supply = decreasing prices.

# TIP # 41: SURROUND THE BOOM FOR BEST RESULTS.

*It's not always a great idea to invest right in the boom, as the best deals may have disappeared. However, the Boom Effect will have a major impact on surrounding area's real estate.*

When a specific area experiences a boom in residential real estate prices, it impacts real estate markets in the surrounding areas in a delayed fashion. There are two reasons why this occurs: first, demand for the less expensive real estate surrounding a boom area increases rapidly, because those who can't afford the higher prices in the boom area move out into the surrounding regions.

Second, perception becomes reality. That's right, human nature once again kicks in, and those who live in the boom's surrounding areas begin to believe that their area is also going to boom and therefore drive prices up.

People will begin to ask more for their properties, right when the demand is increasing. A perfect economic storm occurs.

For a sophisticated investor, it is often easier to invest in areas that surround the initial boom, because the prices will be lower there but the rents will be very similar to the initial boom region. This lag can be from anywhere from six months to six years, depending on how far out from the initial boom the property is located and how many other of the Key Factors are in place driving the region's market.

On a macro scale, for example, Calgary, Alberta had a late 1990s boom and property values in areas surrounding the city were pushed up quickly along with it. The value of real estate in towns closest to the city increased first, and then in areas farther out. You can witness this effect in every area across the country where there has been a marked increase in value. In Toronto, in 2003, when prices began to outstrip what the average income earner could afford, property values in the surrounding cities and towns really started to take off as people chose to move farther out so they could still live the dream of home ownership.

The same effect occurs on a micro scale. When a neighbourhood is redeveloped or goes through a gentrification, the older, untouched neighbourhoods near it also increase in value.

Some investors develop their investment strategies around the Boom Effect. They identify the boom, then analyze areas outside the boom and use that information to buy properties at great prices before the positive boom affects the area.

## What do you need to do?

### FOCUS ON FACTS, NOT SPECULATION

Never be the first into an area you "think" will benefit from a close-by boom. Instead, make sure the value increases have already kicked in, thus reducing the risk of buying in a region the boom may silently pass by.

Since blind speculation is risky, always review the facts of the region and property. Zoning changes, for example, do not mean a development will proceed. Announcements of new condo developments don't mean that they will always be built. Let the speculators take the first dollars off the table as they are the riskiest profits. After the boom has truly taken a grip, that's when the risk is diminished and sophisticated long-term investors move in.

## 🛈 KEY INSIGHT

Look for new neighbourhoods being built in or near older neighbourhoods. The micro-ripple effect will dramatically increase the values of the neighbouring older homes. Another reason to buy resale instead of new as an investment is that over a five-year-plus time line, resale property values increase more quickly than new homes.

## TIP #42: BUSINESS FRIENDLY EQUALS REAL ESTATE FRIENDLY.

*Jobs and taxation directly affect real estate values. Look for regions where development is wanted, not shunned.*

Real estate investment is a complicated business impacted by the local Economic Development Office. In a perfect investment world, you want to invest in an area with the potential to attract and sustain a good supply of quality renters and eventual buyers. That means an area with strong economic growth potential in terms of new industries and new jobs. *It also means finding a business-friendly environment with minimal taxation (personal and property) and with a fair landlord and tenant law structure!*

If you find a region with dynamic and forward-looking Economic Development officers, you have just identified an area that has a great potential for attracting employers. Their job is to "sell" the region to major employers, and if they understand this role, you will know by your first conversation with them. Discuss potential deals they're working on, look at their overall plans, and make sure the region still has land to be developed to attract major employers.

If, on the other hand, while doing your due diligence and asking the key questions on your Property Goldmine Score Card you feel you are constantly being blocked or even directly put off by the local Office, be wary. This attitude will be a deterrent to investment by potential employers. You'd be surprised at the number of Economic Development Offices that act like Economic Deterrent Offices.

Remember, no matter what your political leaning, if you wish to be successful in the business of real estate investing, you want to have a business-friendly atmosphere which is designed to attract people. You want a town or city that promotes itself and actively attracts investment, as this will help your business succeed. Real estate investing is a business, so you want to look for business friendly atmospheres.

A macro-level analysis of a province's tax and tenant laws is just the beginning. You will find provinces and municipalities that offer a distinct advantage in both of these areas. You also must look at municipal tax structures for both business and property.

## What do you need to do?

**LEARN WHO'S WHO**

You do not need to contact local or provincial politicians on a regular basis, but it is a good idea to know who's who, and it makes sense to call or e-mail local and provincial politicians with your reaction when you hear about plans that positively or negatively impact your business.

Be politically active on subjects that will help your business succeed. It is easy to sit back and complain like the masses do, but as a real estate investor, you can make a real difference by making your voice heard on key subjects like income, business and property taxes, and zoning bylaws.

Look for regions where the government and bureaucracy support what you want to do—avoid regions where the support doesn't exist. There are enough areas of opportunity available to you, so why add the risk of a poor political climate into your portfolio?

**GET INVOLVED**

Join the local landlord association and/or a local Real Estate Investment Network. Through the association you will have access to the decision makers and be able to keep your finger on the pulse of your target investment region.

**DO YOUR HOMEWORK**

Find out why nearly identical properties in different communities are priced differently. Get your information from people who live and work in the community, including real estate agents.

Take a look at how local tenancy laws impact the region's real estate investment opportunities and learn how actual or proposed zoning bylaws can nourish or strangle local property values.

See the Appendix for a list of Support Tools and Key Contacts that can help you find out about landlord and tenant laws across Canada.

## TIP #43: TRAINS, PLANES, AUTOMOBILES (AND SEWERS): PAY ATTENTION TO REGIONAL INFRASTRUCTURE GROWTH.

*Access, access, access—that's all that matters.*

Paying attention will pay you dividends. When you read an announcement of a major infrastructure improvement in the works, get off your couch and check it out, using the "what's behind the curtain?" approach to analyze the potential benefits. These announcements could be the annexation of new land by a city, a new transportation development, a new sewer or water plant—all of which show signs of a region looking forward to growth potential.

There are many towns in the country that have the potential to grow, and have a number of economic fundamentals going for them, but they lack the capacity to add to the sewer system; are running out of industrial land that could bring in more jobs; or are very difficult to get to. All of these factors will negatively affect long-term values in the region.

### 🅚 KEY INSIGHT

Transportation Infrastructure: Picture in your mind an area near your region that currently has a highway servicing it. Now take away that highway and picture how that would affect the access to the region—and its desirability. In most if not all cases, you will see that the region could *never* have grown to its current status without transportation infrastructure.

Now, the reverse is also true. Once the transportation improvement is completed, the serviced region will grow at a much faster rate. Demand for real estate will increase, more jobs will move to the region and, best of all, people will follow. This is just one of many infrastructure improvements you can take advantage of.

When Calgary, Alberta started building its C-Train a couple of decades back, some local real estate investors thought C-Train proximity would hurt long-term property values. Sophisticated investors, backed by the experience of investing in major metropolitan markets like Toronto and Montreal, saw what others missed: proximity to light-rail transportation commuting routes pushes property values up by giving commuters better access to the downtown core.

It is not just new transportation that drives these values. Watch for widening of highways and the construction of highway extensions and over-passes. With reduced commuting times in these areas, property values and rents will increase.

## What do you need to do?

**KEEP INFORMED**

Read the major media; watch for any announcement of major infrastructure improvements being announced in your target investment region. These will signal a region that is set to grow more rapidly than average.

Read the local press of the region you are targeting for investment; this is where the real gems will be found. Befriend the local Economic Development department, as the staff will be able to keep you informed of major infrastructure proposals and projects being built.

**ALWAYS ANALYZE A NEIGHBOURHOOD AS IF IT WERE A TOWN ON ITS OWN**

Ask yourself:

"Where do the people who live here work?"

"Is the investment value of their homes recognized and respected by municipal leaders when they make decisions about area roads and land-use changes?"

"What will the demand be when the infrastructure improvement is completed?"

 **RED FLAG**

Governments like to announce, then re-announce, then re-annouce again infrastructure improvement projects, a great vote-buying scheme. Never invest based solely on announcements—many projects never come to frui-tion. Sophisticated investors wait until they "see the smoke"; in other words, they wait to see the project actually being worked on, making it less likely to be stopped.

## Tip #44: Look for Gentrification and Renewal. Renewal Will Renew Your Bank Account.

*Is it shabby or chic? Watch for clues that show a neighbourhood is moving from one economic class to the next.*

Often described as tough but funky, older neighbourhoods that turn into good investment opportunities typically got their start as working-class communities on the "outskirts" of a more centralized hub. Many feature once well-kept homes that slid into disrepair—and out of residential real estate favour—as suburban neighbourhoods sprouted up in the 1970s and 1980s.

These days, these regions are easy to recognize. These regions tend to have a few houses that show signs of recent renovation, located alongside a mix of older, unrenovated character homes. These regions often turn into great family neighbourhoods, as they have larger lots or older landscaping, and are close to transit or job locations.

Before you invest in these renewal areas, you *must* drive through them to look for signs of increasing pride of ownership. These include tended gardens, new paint or siding being added to properties, and newer cars in the driveways. These properties will be surrounded by others that have not yet begun this transition; these are your target properties. Look at what has occurred in the Junction area of Toronto, Inner City of Calgary and the Yaletown neighbourhood in Vancouver; then you'll see the real impact.

### 🏴 RED FLAG

Never buy the best property in the neighbourhood. Buy the worst and bring it up to the neighbourhood benchmark and you will get the biggest bang for you investment dollar. And never be the first to invest in a renewal area as sometimes the gentrification doesn't fully take hold and neglect still characterizes the neighbourhood. Reduce the risk; wait for the renewal to really take hold.

These transitional neighbourhoods aren't all located in neighbourhoods just outside of a community's "inner core." Some of these neighbourhoods are right downtown, where old, run-down warehouses are being refurbished as apartments or upscale luxury condominium lofts.

In other regions, look for dilapidated industrial buildings that are being torn down or renovated. These include in-fill developments, where developers knock down old buildings and construct narrow, zero-lot-line houses or townhouses.

 **KEY INSIGHT**

You can use these redevelopments as part of your Boom Effect fundamental strategy. As the region's older industrial buildings are redeveloped, the areas surrounding them will dramatically increase in demand.

## What do you need to do?

**LOOK FOR CLUES**

How do you know if you've caught the neighbourhood in the right time? Look for tell-tale signs of continued improvement. These include a mixture of older-model cars and new vehicles. The gentrification is more advanced if the number of new cars has outstripped older models.

Look for media stories about neighbourhoods whose long-time and new property owners talk about "taking back" their neighbourhood from prostitutes and drug dealers. Meet with the local Neighbourhood Watch or neighbourhood community group to see what's going on and where they want to take the community. Like people in the Economic Development departments, you will find groups that have a forward-looking vision and others that don't have this quality. Invest in regions where the leadership is strong and they want to renew their neighbourhood.

**EXERCISE PRUDENT PATIENCE**

Renewal areas have long-term profit potential. But you do *not* want to be the first investor into an area you believe is going to be in transition.

 **RED FLAG**

When you invest in a neighbourhood where renewal has begun, it often means you are buying into a neighbourhood with a tougher tenant profile and lower-than-average rents. The tenant situation will improve and the values increase as the renewal progresses, but it will take time. You will need patience to buy in transition areas.

**🟊 KEY INSIGHT**

Local investors are often the last to discover neighbourhoods going through the process of renewal. That's because they let their personal beliefs about where *they* would live obscure the fundamentals of their investment system. They let their emotions and past history affect their investments. This is an example of what goes wrong when you make decisions based on emotions versus facts—you miss the biggest opportunities.

## TIP #45: MAXIMIZE VALUE AND ZONING OPPORTUNITIES.

*Always look for ways to make a good deal better.*

The types of property available for investment are as varied as people's investment needs. Sophisticated investors learn to look at a property's physical attributes, where the property is located and what it's currently used for. The they examine how they may be able to change that property's use—called Divide and Profit—to optimize return, an investment strategy that goes way beyond renovating an existing property to add re-sale value.

For example, you could purchase a rundown hotel and convert it to condominiums or rental units. This takes the property from a below-average performer to its highest and best use, with positive cash flow. The same can be true if you are buying raw land and selling it off by the building lot, thus increasing the overall value of the property.

Another example—and a much simpler one—involves buying a property that is currently a single-family dwelling and converting it to a multi-family or student housing property. This is done by investors across the country, every day. You will need to know your local zoning and tenant regulations to make this transition successful; however, these changes will dramatically affect not only the value of the property but the income you generate from it.

Zoning will always be the key determinant; it is not just the simple act of making changes to the property. You have to do it so that it fits all of the local rules and regulations—and there are many.

# What do you need to do?

**EXPLORE THE ZONE**

When you're looking at an area, always check into the zoning and what it allows. Examine the city's redevelopment or long-term plans for the region. Do you have the opportunity to change the zoning to fit their plans? That strategy is easily applied to a plot of raw land on the edge of a growing city or a small town or an area that the city would like to see an increased housing density.

Ask yourself key questions like "Can warehouses or old office buildings be transformed into trendy loft-style apartments or condominiums? Can a single-family home near a university or college be turned into a home that's rented out by the room? In other words, suited?"

Simple math shows how a four-bedroom home that typically rents for $1,000 a month could generate $1,600 if each renter paid $400. You would need separate lease agreements with each tenant. Rooms left vacant over the four-month summer break could be rented to summer students via short-term agreements.

Be certain you understand exactly what needs to be done to ensure changes meet local zoning requirements and safety codes.

 **KEY INSIGHT**

It costs money to change the way a property is used, and profitability may depend on getting those changes in place. If you don't have the knowledge or funds to make the changes happen, partner with someone who does.

**RED FLAG**

Learn to think outside the box, but never "assume" a property-use change will be a) easy or b) possible! Avoid costly mistakes by getting the facts before you buy or by making it a condition of the purchase contract. Look for opportunities that others can't readily see and you will have no lack of properties to invest in.

**TAKE ANOTHER LOOK AT THAT GARAGE OR STORAGE SHED**

If the property has an unattached garage, think about renting it out separately if bylaws allow. Sophisticated investors rent unattached garages for anywhere from $50 to $300 per month. They rent the garages to the tenants renting the house, or to someone else who wants the space for storage or parking. The additional income vastly increases monthly positive cash flow.

This is also true of extra parking you may have on the property. Especially if it is near a major employment region with limited parking. The same thing goes for property with separate storage areas. Look at the local economy to determine possible renters. Would the site be attractive to people with large recreational vehicles?

## 🌀 SOPHISTICATED INVESTOR TIP

*If you do rent out that garage ... you need to know that, in most provinces, garage rental is not covered by the landlord and tenant laws. In all cases, use a separate and non-residential lease for the garage. This improves your ability to set garage rents. Market-savvy investors also arrange for their garage leases to end during the wintertime. They know it's much easier to renew the lease when the weather is colder!*

# Tip #46: Buy Below True Market Value.

*There is a huge difference between current market value and true market value. Discover the difference and see profits where others can't.*

There's an old stock market joke that says everyone can make money from stocks as long as they follow the cardinal rule: Buy low and sell high. Real estate investment has a similar axiom. Fortunately, at least for real estate investors, the buy-low-sell-high supposition actually works for those who understand hidden values in properties—and how to buy substantially below true market value.

*True market value* is defined as the final retail value that an investor can garner for a property after they have fixed a problem and maximized its use. Sometimes this entails a massive restructuring, as in turning raw land into a subdivision. At other times it is a much simpler process, such as buying an apartment building and selling the individual units as condominiums.

This is one of the real estate investment industry's least-well-understood markets, but there are a number of investors who focus their efforts on this smaller yet very profitable investment strategy and is something that all investors should keep their eyes open for. This happens in several ways.

## Foreclosures and Pre-foreclosures: Not as Simple as It Seems

In this instance, you buy properties from lenders who have foreclosed on unpaid debt, or from homeowners trying to avoid bankruptcy or increase their cash flow—fast. In Canada, unlike many other countries in the world, accessing these properties is not as simple as it may sound. Our privacy laws are very strict, making it much more difficult for investors to identify potential foreclosure properties and obtain owner contact information. In the U.S. the process is much easier.

The best market is the pre-foreclosure market, where by being proactive through advertising an investor can attract property owners who have too much property and too little income. This strategy helps you solve their problem by paying them a fair value for the property, which helps them to save their credit rating. A true win-win. *Never ever* be a vulture and try to steal their property from them for next to nothing just because they are desperate.

## Condominium Conversion

Investors may purchase a larger, multi-family property, such as an entire apartment building, then convert the property so each suite has an individual title. As individual units, the units are worth far more than they were valued as a single multi-family unit. The process is known as *condominiumization* or *stratification*.

In some regions, these individual units can be sold immediately. In other areas, you have to hold them in your portfolio for years before you can sell them at a worthwhile profit. During this holding period you can rent them out to create income until it becomes time to sell.

The development of raw land is also covered under this scenario. Here, you buy the land and convert it to individual lots to be sold at retail. Although not a strict condominiumization, you are still buying a large block and selling it in smaller pieces.

 **RED FLAG**

Condominiumization tends to increase demand and property values in neighbouring areas. Remember this fact when you are assessing a property's long-term prospects. Will your investment benefit your own long-term wealth creation? Will it improve other local property values faster?

# What do you need to do?

BUILD A NETWORK OF MOTIVATED VENDOR CONTACTS

Find out "who knows what" on the pre-foreclosure front in your target area. Foreclosure lawyers and trustees, for example, do look for buyers they can count on to make a deal go through. Their job is to get a fair market value for the property.

Advertise for motivated vendors who need your help with getting out of the property. Be creative!

At the same time you need to build your list of buyers who want to buy the properties from you now or in the future. Most investors forget about building their buyer's list when, in fact, this is the most important and often most difficult list to build. Build a portfolio of prospective buyers for the properties you buy and convert, and then you will be able to confidently purchase an ever-increasing number of under-true-valued properties.

Learn the art of the "simultaneous close." Here, you use your contacts to buy an under-true-value property. You then assist a new buyer in purchasing the property from you for a slight profit on the same day you take possession. Make sure that full disclosure is used to all parties and that you are only selling the property at true market value or below. The person buying from you often pays less than the appraised value (remember, always leave some profit on the table for the next owner), but probably has to do a certain amount of work to get the property ready for the traditional market. The initial vendor will be happy because you solved their financial situation, your new buyer will be happy because you were able to offer them a property below market value, and you will be happy because you will have made a small profit on the deal.

SCOUT CONDOMINIUMIZATION PROSPECTS

Identify multi-family properties where condominiumization is possible. Speak to a local expert who has worked on conversions and be aware that the local government will have a big say in whether they will allow it and what steps you must do to get it condominiumized. Issues will include fire code standards all the way to more political concerns, such as your activity will deplete the rental market stock. In all cases the local politicians and bureaucrats will have a lot to say about your conversion.

> ## ◗ RED FLAG
>
> Condominium conversion investments take deep pockets and expertise to get started. You must realize that all of your costs are up front and your return is derived only from the sale of the property. Your business plan must take this into consideration. If you need to hold individual units in your portfolio for several years, make sure your business plan reflects that reality!

# TIP #47: ADD VALUE WITH A MARKET NICHE.

*The more focused your real estate business, the more profitable it will be.*

Newcomers to the real estate investment market often follow a pretty linear train of thought. They see real estate investments as generating long-term wealth in one of two main ways. You buy and hold quality rental properties that appreciate over time, or you adopt a quicker-cash strategy via the reno-and-flip deal.

Reality paints a different picture and savvy investors will explore niche-market opportunities like those outlined below.

## Rent-to-Own

Find quality tenants for quality properties and set up a formal agreement whereby they can move from renters to owners. The renter gets a limited down payment rate in return for owner financing and proving they are a good credit risk. (This subject is covered extensively at Real Estate Investment Network Workshops and has proven to create tremendous relationships between landlords and tenants.) Tenant hassles disappear as tenants begin to treat the property as if it was their long-term home, and tenants save money every single month towards their purchase. A great way to give back to society by showing people who thought they would never be able to own a property how they can become home owners.

## Furnished Suites for Rent

A highly mobile workforce means large urban centres have a growing number of employees who only live in their cities on a part-time basis. When major construction or engineering projects are announced in a region an instant opportunity arises. These large projects attract experts from across the country for short stays, often in hotels. However, many would prefer to stay in a rental property as it is not only cheaper but much more comfortable (especially in smaller centres). You furnish your rental property with comfortable yet simple furnishings and then be creative with your marketing to attract these professionals. The rent is often 50% to 100% above market rents for an empty suite, and is still cheaper than a hotel.

There are literally dozens of these unique niche strategies you can use to increase your investment returns. Make sure that you are following one that has been proven to work in Canada over a long term.

## What do you need to do?

**EDUCATE YOURSELF**

Identify your target demographic and figure out who needs your "product." Learn what's important to them in terms of amenities (schools, work, recreational areas) and investigate market prices for a similar product.

If small families are your target for a building, look for unique ways in which to attract them. (Alert people to local schools and daycare facilities, extra large washers and dryers, etc.) Identify a niche and then put yourself in the tenant's shoes. Advertise where they read, talk directly to them in your ads. (Do not write generic ads—be creative. See Tip #50.)

Develop a quality marketing program that zeroes in on your target market.

**BE SERVICE-ORIENTED**

Tenants most interested in the rent-to-own category may have encountered bankruptcy, or be close to that position. They may not know they could qualify for a new mortgage a year after declaring bankruptcy. To improve the deal's rent-to-own success, include financial counselling in their rent-to-own agreement.

Find out what amenities (Internet, cable TV, on-site parking) your furnished-suite clients need most and then supply it. Also make sure your kitchens and bathrooms are well equipped. Do your suites offer a toaster, blender, microwave, good set of knives and a hair dryer?

## 🏴 RED FLAG

Make sure your niche actually exists and is reachable. For instance, don't try to force furnished suites in an area that already has too many hotel rooms. Check the student housing situation *before* considering them as a target. If the local schools are growing, then you have lots of potential; if the student population is declining, then the demand will already have been filled, so look for another niche.

## TIP #48: STAND OUT FROM THE CROWD: THE DIFFERENCE BETWEEN PROFIT AND LOSS.

*No matter what real estate strategy you are following, you will have competition. Learn how to get your message out so it's heard!*

Everything you do in your business must have a consistent and clear theme. From the first contact with a vendor, to attracting new renters, to working with your bankers, consistency in message is critical. Dan S. Kennedy states, "No matter what business you're in, you're always in the business of marketing." And that is especially true in real estate.

The important point to note here is that we're not talking about marketing or selling a property—we're talking about your whole message.

Small, focused marketing steps can make all of the difference in the world. Once again it is all about knowledge and learning what your target market is looking to hear. From classified ads to billboards and flyer drops, marketing is the engine that drives your real estate business. How you answer the phone is marketing; once you get the prospect to the door, curb appeal and inside suite condition become a part of your marketing. How the prospect is treated while viewing the suite is also part of the marketing strategy. Every step of the process must be thought of as a marketing opportunity.

## 💲 SOPHISTICATED INVESTOR TIP

Matching your message to your prospective target is critical. If you are trying to get a mortgage, target your message and presentation to a banker's point of view. If you are trying to attract motivated sellers for your property,

*Sophisticated Investor Tip continues*

make sure you are speaking their language. In other words, put yourself in their shoes, think about what they will be looking for—then give it to them wherever possible.

## What you need to do?

**GET EDUCATED**

Read all you can about marketing in the real estate industry. Then put the best nuggets into action.

**DEFINE YOUR MARKET**

Clearly define whom it is you are targeting and what you want your ads to achieve once people read them. Define your niche, get into prospective tenants' heads, and figure out exactly what they are looking for from you. Then make your message match their needs. This may sound obvious, but if you look at most ads today you will see that they target a general public—and ads like this will not produce results. The more you speak directly to your prospect, the better results you will have. (See Tip #50 on classified ad writing.)

Turn every conversation into a real estate discussion. Be proud of what you do and tell everyone. You never know where your next renter, property or investor may come from, and everyone you know is a potential deal-maker for you.

## Tip # 49: Never Advertise—Always Market!

*Hone your ad-writing skills and generate the data you need for other marketing materials.*

The great thing about a great classified advertisement is the process you use to write that ad will help you develop other marketing materials, including reports you plan to give to prospective investors.

The most important thing you need to remember about a quality marketing program is that it is designed to deliver business, pure and simple. *Research shows a quality marketing program yields higher-than-market rents and premium property values.*

# What do you need to do?

**BECOME A STUDENT OF MARKETING (NOT ADVERTISING)**

Read all that you can about street-smart direct response marketing. Direct response means that the ad is designed to have the reader take immediate action; it has nothing to do with creating a brand!

**IDENTIFY YOUR BUSINESS NEEDS**

Once you have identified your business needs (renters, sellers, etc.), you need to design your marketing program to fill these needs.

Once the need is identified, target media and on-line spots where your prospect will be reading or gathering. For instance, if you need renters and you are near a local hospital or school, why not use their bulletin boards for marketing?

 **KEY INSIGHT**

> *Lead-generating ads*: Use a lead-generating ad to fill longer-term or on-going needs. Are you building your list of prospective buyers for your properties? Do you want to line up future renters, rent-to-own clients or joint venture partners? Most of these are part of an ongoing business plan that requires consistent new leads.

**CREATE YOUR DATA SHEET**

List everything you can think of about your product and service. Include facts (spacious kitchen, new siding, rent price) and benefits (client can make money by buying and renovating your property, immediate access for a family looking to rent, etc.).

Be creative. Identify the details that caught your eye and made you think about the property as if you planned to rent or buy it. ("Recent renovations means your work is done." "Basement games room ready for action." "Private deck ideal for entertaining.")

Use the data sheet as part of the "Free Report" you give to prospective clients and investors.

**REVIEW THE POWERFUL WORDS LIST**

Review Tip #50's list of powerful words. Where appropriate, work them into your other marketing materials, including the data sheet.

# TIP #50: CLASSIFIED AD WRITING SECRETS.

*Never follow the crowd if you want real results!*

Classified ads, both on-line and off-line, are a crucial part of any real estate investor's plan, providing you with renters, buyers, sellers—and much more. Because of this, it is important to learn the secrets to writing classified ads that work. The good news is that since so many people do such a poor job of writing their classified ads, it is quite simple to write ads that stand out from the competition.

Newspapers and on-line rental sites provide you with targeted prospects. Since their readers are actively looking for what you have to offer, your job becomes to make them choose your product over the hundreds of other advertisers.

Most sites and newspapers filter your prospects for you by geographic region, so you are truly only talking to a very select group. For example, the *Ottawa Citizen* or the *Saskatoon Star Phoenix* service a particular geographic area. Because advertisements are grouped by product (for example, "Suites for Rent" or "Single Family Homes for Sale"), motivated readers save search time.

## What do you need to do?

**THINK ABOUT YOUR CLIENT**

Review your amenity list and rate each item on a scale of 1 to 5 in importance to the individual who will buy or rent your property. Put yourself in the shoes of your prospects: What are they *really* looking for in a property to buy or rent? How do you convey this to them in your ad?

**WRITE A CATCHY HEADLINE**

Choose the top two items you rated as being the most important features your client wants or needs. Now choose two items that make the home unique. Take one or two of these top four items and use them to write a creative classified ad headline that attracts immediate attention.

Examples:

"Get Naked with a Good Friend" (features a two-person tub)

"Free Utilities—Free View" (free utilities and a great view of the city)

"Warmth in the Winter" (fireplace on main floor and in lower-level recreation area)

Go bold with the headline, but don't use only capital letters (they make a headline hard to read!). Avoid abbreviations and do be creative! Use eye-catching phrases ("Must Rent—Off to Cuba) or name the benefit the buyer or renter will receive from your property. ("Finally—A Place To Call Home. Be Proud Every Time Your Friends Visit!")

### ADDRESS THE POTENTIAL RENTER'S NEEDS AND WANTS

Think like one of your prospects and make your classified ad stand out by using catchy sentences and adjectives to paint a "word picture" of what the owners/renters can expect. "Bright Kitchen" and "Private Deck" have lots of appeal. "Instant Access" and "5-minute Walk to Two Elementary Schools" offer peace of mind.

Write as if you're talking to one person not a group. The words "you" and "yours" are very powerful—use them often. ("Come home to your 3-bedroom bungalow located on a quiet cul-de-sac just minutes from schools and shopping.")

### MAKE THE AD ONLY AS LONG AS IT NEEDS TO BE

Keep your sentences "tight," but don't sell a property short by leaving important details out. You want to attract a long-term tenant who will pay you thousands and thousands of dollars over the time of their tenancy. Don't cut down on words to save a few dollars, thus missing out on attracting the right tenant. The people reading your ad are already looking for a specific product. Tell them what they need to know so they can make an informed decision!

Pique the prospect's interest with talk of benefits and when they call, make sure you (or your voice-mail) give them an even more visual picture of the property and the area. No more "You've reached Bob, leave a message after the beep." Be eloquent, spend a minute describing benefits that you couldn't fit in the ad.

### LEAVE READERS WITH A FEELING OR EMOTION

Use emotive words such as home, comfort, enjoy, private, bright, relax, easy, instant, and back them up with pertinent details about the area ("Walk to school parks and the river valley"). Tell readers about the lifestyle your property offers ("Enjoy the sunset in your fully-fenced backyard" or "Warm days on your private deck—warm nights by your fireplace").

Once you create desire for your property, add a call to action and ask for the sale or tenancy, such as: "This home can't last. Don't wimp out! Call today."

 **RED FLAG**

Writing a classified ad takes time and effort, but it is well worth it to learn what works and what doesn't. Watch for ads that you yourself respond to. Assess what elements really stood out. Keep ads you like and look for ways to use their ideas in your own.

### USE ADVERTISING'S MOST POWERFUL WORDS

Re-edit that classified ad. Where possible, use real estate advertising's most powerful words. They are:

Free (utilities)
Discover (quiet lifestyle)
Proven (Safe)
You, your
Save (on heating)
New (renovated)
Easy (access to transit)
Announcing (rental rebates)
Home
Warmth
Bright
Clean

**FREE REPORT FOR READERS**

Register your book and get the latest version of the *Classified Ad Secrets* report. By visiting www.realestateinvestingincanada.com and registering your book, you will receive an e-mail outlining exactly how to receive your *free* copy. Written by Don R. Campbell, it will clearly give you *all* the tips you need to write classified ads that jump off the page and have readers grabbing their telephones to call you.

# Tip #51: Renovation: A Dusty and Dirty Way to Wealth.

*Renovation shows proliferate on TV today (and it's not as easy as they make it seem). Don't buy into the dream without having very specific knowledge. See the direct warning in Tip #63!*

Renovating properties has been and always will be one of the most commonly discussed real estate subjects. There are dozens of books and at least that many TV shows, all devoted to the massive results you can create with a little paint and floor coverings. Sadly this has really muddied the waters for real estate investors.

Let us be clear—the renovations you complete on your personal home differ dramatically to the renovations you should be doing on your rental or re-sale suites if you are interested in making a profit.

All warnings about the downside of Do-It-Yourself (DIY) projects aside, many investors get into real estate to renovate and re-sell properties as a way to build their own pool of working capital. That approach can work, but only if you know what to renovate and what to leave alone. Not every fixer-upper is worth your personal sweat equity. Make sure you value your time and you learn the secrets to properly estimating and renovating a property.

> **CANADIAN RENOVATION SECRETS**
> You can get a Canadian-specific renovations system titled *Renovation Secrets: Renovating & Flipping Houses for Quick Cash*. Written by two Canadian experts who have transacted over 788 properties, it has been tested and proven for over a decade. The results that Canadians are achieving with it are quite amazing. It is available to readers of this book at a special discount by visiting www.realestateinvestingincanada.com and clicking on the Renovations Secrets menu item on the left side of the screen. This program will literally save you thousands on your renovation projects.

## What do you need to do?

### IDENTIFY THE RIGHT PROPERTY

Be picky. Increase the odds of success by adopting proven strategies for the renovate-and-resell market. Look for quality-built properties in areas that show an increase in pride of ownership and always use a qualified house inspector to make sure the property is structurally sound. Never compromise on this step. Major structural repairs are often not worth the dollars you might save on the purchase price.

Properties that are slightly neglected can be a goldmine, because repair and clean-up costs may be less than a major renovation. Similarly, "cosmetic" changes are the simplest and least costly, but these can include new flooring, drywall, paint and cabinets.

Assess those changes or upgrades that could prove expensive. Be honest with yourself. Your focus should always start and end with curb appeal; those upgrades that will make the property attractive to the renter or buyer.

 **RED FLAG**

Skip the property inspection at your own peril. Use an expert inspector to avoid major post-deal issues related to problems the untrained eye might not see, including mould due to water damage, roof repair problems or hazards linked to electrical wiring. A comprehensive inspection report also gives you a kind of quick list for repairs.

**KEY INSIGHT**

Many investors complete the renovations on the first one or two properties they buy to renovate and re-sell. Then they start to use trusted contractors to do the improvements. You will start to really make money when you focus on buying properties with potential and then let others do the physical work.

## TIP #52: JUMPING THE GUN: INVESTING ON A WISH AND A PRAYER.

*Speculation is not investment—it is fraught with risk. Know the difference between investing and speculation.*

Speculation in the real estate market can lead to significant financial gains. Speculators who jumped into the Sea-to-Sky corridor between Whistler Mountain and Vancouver, B.C., soon after Vancouver's Olympic bid was accepted, rapidly drove up property values. There, speculators made money because values rose and stayed high, giving initial speculators a chance to bail out, cash in hand. The fundamentals showed that prices were not sustainable and there wasn't much supporting them; however, values continued to sky-rocket. Why? All because of speculation.

As a speculator you can make massive amounts of profit in a fairly short time; however, this is not the same as investing. Investing is based on long-term fundamentals, whereas speculation is based on taking advantage of a unique and often short-term-demand increase. As an analogy, investors are to value-stock investors as speculators are to day-traders. Money can be made in each, but the risk levels are very different.

We don't discuss speculation in *Real Estate Investing in Canada* or any of our other books because it doesn't fit the ACRE system of investing, and speculation is not a "system" per se you can duplicate. You can't consistently read the markets when speculating; you're reacting to quick market shifts and acting on gut response. For a system to prove itself, there must be results that can be duplicated. With speculating there are too many variables that are out of your control and the risks are high—too high for investors who keep their eye on their own Personal Belize.

 **RED FLAG**

Get the facts. Speculation on a single deal can put your whole portfolio at risk. Sure, it's tempting to get rich quick; that's why you see so many late-night advertisements, but sophisticated investors are long-term value investors.

## What do you need to do?

**RECOGNIZE THE DANGER SIGNS**

When the excitement of the deal detracts from the fundamentals and emotions become more important than market facts, it's easy to be drawn into the hype. Remember, it is your job to ask the tough questions so you cut through the hype and get to the facts. To get your plan back on track, pull out that Property Goldmine Score Card.

**REFUSE TO PLAY THE GAME**

Speculative investments throw market fundamentals to the wind. When you run across a speculative deal, recognize the hype for what it is—and what it is not. If your goal is long-term wealth, then keep asking the questions until you get the answers you need. Speculation, and those who engage in it, often use the promise of quick cash to distract you from your fundamentals. Watch out for the "Gotta Act Now or You'll Miss Out!" sales pitch. It's a good sign the deal is speculative (and someone else is out to get rich quick).

## TIP #53: ANALYZE A PROPERTY RIGHT DOWN TO THE LAST NICKLE.

*It's time to crunch numbers—even "future" numbers.*

Many beginning investors only analyze the absolute basic expenses when deciding whether a property's income will cover the operating expenses. The most common cry of the soon-to-be-broke investors is, "I found a property and the rent will cover both my mortgage and my taxes!" Sadly this uninformed view of investing has led these neophytes into some very bad deals.

Once again the critical key is to be brutally honest about a property's potential. Assess the "true" income that it can deliver (rather than what you hope it will) along with all of the ongoing expenses you'll need to cover with this revenue (much more than just the mortgage and taxes).

This is also true of the costs of closing on a property. Many beginning investors fail to assess the true cost of buying a property, which adds up to much more than just the down payment and legal costs. Sophisticated investors know that there are many additional costs that need to be budgeted for well in advance.

## What do you need to do?

**CRUNCH THE NUMBERS**

Take a harsh look at all properties you will be investing in. Don't ever get caught wearing rose-coloured glasses when doing your analysis. Sophisticated real estate investment comes down to bare-bones number analysis. (At the end of this tip, we'll give you a checklist you can use to ensure you are analyzing in detail.)

**BE THOROUGH**

Remember all the talk about how successful investors go the extra 10%? This is where that 10% saves and makes you money. Leave no details out.

Sure it takes an extra few minutes, but this analysis will tell you the truth about the property and save you from getting caught in a bad deal.

**Cash-Flow Analysis Numbers**: Make sure you get accurate numbers for all of these and any others that are specific to your property:

*Income:*
    Rent
    Laundry
    Parking
    Other

*Expenses:*
    Heat
    Electricity
    Water/Sewer
    Property Taxes
    Condo Fees
    Insurance
    Property Management
    Vacancy Allowance
    Repairs & Maintenance
    Snow Clearing/Landscaping
    Mortgage Payments

*Closing Costs:*
    Legal Costs
    Legal Disbursements
    Professional Inspection
    Appraisal
    Title Insurance
    Property Survey
    Mortgage Fees
    CMHC Fees
    Land Transfer Tax
    Property Insurance
    Renovations
    Reserve Fund

## TIP #54: PERFORM SPECIAL DUE DILIGENCE ON VACATION PROPERTY.

*The fundamentals for vacation property are a little different.*

There are two kinds of recreational property: personal use and pure investment. Make sure you are honest with yourself as to what is driving your recreational property investment. If it has a personal-use component to it, feel free to let emotions come into the equation, however if it is truly an investment piece, then emotions *must* be taken out of the equation.

The wonderful thing about owning recreational property is that you may be able to use it for revenue and your own R&R. The drawback about buying recreational property as revenue property is that it could compromise your whole system, leading to less R&R—and way more stress.

The most important thing to understand here is that due diligence regarding vacation property involves more than the basic market fundamentals.

 **RED FLAG**

*It may not be a real estate investment, even if it looks like one!*

This is true in all types of real estate investment, but is most common in recreational or tropical property. It is only a real estate investment if you have full 100% control over the title of the property. You will get a full certificate that outlines your exact suite or property, and you have the regular real estate market to sell it into if you ever wish to.

Sadly, many people believe that buying a time-share or a percentage interest in a property is a real estate investment when it is really a security like a stock.

The key is full control of a specific property. If you don't have control so you can solve problems, increase value, increase rents, do renovations and all the things that sophisticated investors do to increase value—you aren't investing in real estate.

Another test as to whether it is a true real estate investment is available exit options. A true real estate investment will provide you many and varied exit options that are in your control. An investment that limits your market (i.e., there turns out to be no market for your time share or your percentage interest in a property, or puts limits on who you can sell to, is *not* a real estate investment.

Make sure you are taking the emotions out of these decisions. Base decisions on fact. If you are buying a security supported by a property, it is still a security. And *always* review your exit strategies; if they are limited, the value will be greatly diminished in your portfolio. If you can't cash in your profits, the profits are no good to you!

## What do you need to do?

**CHECK EMOTIONS AT THE INVESTMENT DOOR**

The recreational market is not like a traditional market for revenue property. For one thing, demand for recreational real estate usually spikes during its peak-use season, putting upward pressure on prices, too. If you are going to buy in the recreational market, buy in the off-season when there is less competition.

Let your strategy lead. If it's a summer property, return to the area in the winter when purchasers are few and far between and vendors are much more motivated. Also, it will help you identify the underlying strength of the region's economy. If the economy and therefore the strength of your investment is based on a short three-month season, you may wish to consider whether your investment money will perform better in a 12-month fundamentally strong region, and use a portion of those profits to rent the best place on the best beach for the whole high season in the recreational property area.

*Never ever* be influenced by a smooth sales pitch. Never be embarrassed to ask the tough questions! It's your hard earned money; don't let it be thrown away.

### EXERCISE A HIGHER LEVEL OF DUE DILIGENCE

The amount of due diligence you need to apply increases along with the distance you have to travel to see the property.

If it is being rented out on your behalf, make sure you are digging deeply into the management company and its track record. Sadly, you will find inexperienced managers running the show because they don't cost as much, but this will cost you more in problems and vacancies that will arise.

### ESTABLISH OWNERSHIP

Sounds too easy? This can be a bigger problem in some foreign countries. You need to know who owns the title to the property and precisely where the property's lot lines are. (Can renters using your ocean-front cabana actually access that ocean?)

It may sound exciting to own property in a tropical paradise. Just remember, however, "You're not in Canada anymore," so you can forget the rules and regulations we have all become used to.

In some regions squatters can move onto your property and in just 30 days become the rightful dwellers on your property. You can't kick them off, no matter what your ownership papers say.

### VISIT THE PROPERTY

Get past the marketing messages. You must see it before you believe it. Also be wary of promises like "a new development" or "future airport." You want to be sure everything's in place before you buy. You *must* differentiate what is real from what is marketing hype.

If you are going to buy in a foreign locale, especially in tropical countries, visit it in the high season as well as the low season. Try to live in similar conditions as the property you are buying. We've seen many people visit a region, stay in a five-star hotel and love the experience. Then, when they return at another time to try out their "investment property," real life hits home and paradise is not all that it seems.

Learn the language, speak with the locals, and ask about the property. The locals will know the current owners, how they treat people, what problems they have and much more. (This holds true for any locale you are investigating.)

### BEWARE THE MARK-UP

When you visit the property, find out how much similar properties cost on the local market. You may find comparable properties at dramatically lower prices.

You will find that many properties that are being sold at a distance are overpriced compared to the reality of the local market. This is because our *perception* of property value inflates prices.

If you seriously want to buy in a region (especially recreational or tropical), visit the place and start looking for yourself. Never use the excuse that it is too much time or hassle. While there you will discover just how much these distant marketed properties have been marked up. Not doing this type of homework is like buying in a small town in northern Canada because the prices are cheaper than where you live. That kind of unsophisticated investing leads to trouble.

### USE YOUR OWN LAWYER

Vet the deal through your own lawyer/solicitor, not one used by the seller. You need solid details on everything from your property lines (how close to the shoreline do you own?) to restricted uses, dispute procedures and how money will be transferred to you.

A different legal system and culture also puts different legal issues into play. What are the squatters' rights for the area, for example? What about the responsibilities and liabilities of the owners? Each country has different rules and, sadly, even the sales team or developers don't know all the rules.

**BE ACCOUNTABLE**

Ask yourself, "Who will be 100% responsible for your investment?" It won't be the "local representative" noted in the contract—so invest accordingly!

## 🌀 KEY INSIGHT

The property can be down the street, around the corner, or across the world. But if you're buying it as an investment, the fundamentals of your investment risk strategy always stay the same. Look at every property for what it is: an investment in your future. Don't get caught with the lure of "tropical or lake-side paradise." Make sure you have done *all* of your homework well in advance. Remove the emotion!

# PART 5

## DATA, BRICKS AND MORTAR: THE PRACTICAL SIDE OF WEALTH CREATION THROUGH REAL ESTATE INVESTMENT

# TIP #55: ASK THESE CRITICAL QUESTIONS BEFORE BUYING *ANY* PROPERTY.

*Uncover the hidden problems and opportunities. Never skip a question.*

Pilots never skip their pre-flight checklist—and neither do sophisticated real estate investors. No matter how thorough a sophisticated investor becomes in completing his or her due diligence, they know a checklist of questions will help them to avoid a property with problems. And when it comes to real estate investing, avoiding problem properties is just as important as finding solid investment properties!

Here are the questions you must have answered before you even consider buying a property.

## What do you need to do?

### ASK: IS THIS THE RIGHT AREA?

Step one is to determine that you are looking in the right area. You answer this question by working through the macro questions outlined on the Property Goldmine Score Card (see the Appendix).

### ASK: WHAT DOES YOUR DUE DILIGENCE TELL YOU?

Here, you dig into the micro questions of a particular property by getting answers to the questions in the Every Property Due Diligence Checklist (see the Appendix). These questions help you determine the facts on the specific property. They cut through any of the hype or emotion that surrounds purchasing the property.

The more often you ask these questions, the faster you'll get to the answers. To speed up the process, many sophisticated investors have their real estate agents get answers to these questions *before* they even present the property to the investor. This saves the agent and investor real time, since they both get to focus on properties that fit the investor's system. When you focus on the facts, you fine-tune your system and improve your portfolio!

## 🌓 KEY INSIGHT

If you have trouble getting answers to your questions from a vendor, that's a sign there could be some hidden problems they would rather not discuss with you. This is great news, as you now know you either need more clarity, or you need to walk away from a potential problem property.

## 🌀 SOPHISTICATED INVESTOR ACTION STEP

Due diligence accomplishes more than you might think! Once you are happy with the answers to the questions on your checklist, you can present your findings to your lender when applying for a mortgage. This extra due diligence gives your banker more good reasons to say yes to your loan. For a refresher on the value of quality information delivered in a quality presentation, review Tip #25.

# TIP #56: COVER YOUR ASSETS WELL.

*You've worked hard to build your portfolio. Make sure you spend time to ensure you're insured properly.*

Not all insurers are created equal, and not all properties can be insured equally. Insuring rental properties is much more difficult than insuring your home. There is a lot more to consider, especially since many insurance companies have dramatically reduced their coverage of rental or investment properties, further complicating the whole issue of asset insurance. The crux of the matter is that every insurance company has its own rules and guidelines, some good and some bad. That's why it is critical to have a veteran investment real estate insurance broker on your team.

The different insurance regulations on rental properties take beginner investors by surprise. You need to understand that insurance policies have *exclusion clauses*. In other words, insurance covers some things—and not others!

Insurers may, for example, require a change of electrical service before the company will insure a residential property, while others will accept it as is. You will want to have this discussion with your insurance agent *long* before you remove conditions on the property.

## KEY INSIGHT

Insurance companies are revising their policies all the time. As a purchaser, then, ensure that your purchase offer includes a clause that gives you time to have a property analyzed for insurability. Many unsophisticated investors don't consider the insurance needs of a property until after they have removed conditions. They then run into difficulty when they find out that they can't get insurance on the property without investing in extensive renovations. A finance company will not provide funds on an uninsured property. *Never* remove conditions of a purchase without first confirming insurability.

## RED FLAG

Many insurance companies won't insure a residential property with 60-amp service. They will stick to this guideline even if it costs them the rest of your business. Others might not insure a home with suites that share 100-amp service. They require a 100-amp panel per suite. Be clear with your insurance broker as to what is required, well in advance!

## What do you need to do?

### PUT AN INSURANCE AGENT ON YOUR TEAM

Find an insurance agent who has worked with owners of rental properties. Make sure he knows what you're doing and understands your real estate investment portfolio. There is a vast difference between an insurance broker with rental property experience and one who has only dabbled in it. Find a veteran and tap into their expertise. If your broker often turns down your insurance requests, you are probably working with the wrong broker.

Discuss discount opportunities for bulk purchases. Ask about their discount levels and how you can achieve them. Discounts are often based on the number of properties or the value of your complete portfolio.

### MAKE APPROPRIATE INSURANCE A CONDITION OF CLOSING

To avoid closing a deal on property that's difficult to insure, add the following to your offer: *"Subject to Vendor arranging appropriate insurance on property within 10 days of acceptance."*

Talk to your insurer before you remove the final conditions on the property and you won't get caught in a bind at the last minute.

## TALK INSURANCE SPECIFICS

Ask your broker about policy exclusions. Determine whether you need a basic policy, a mid-level policy or a premium policy. Learn about the differences in costs and coverage.

Be aware of hidden rules. Find out, for instance, what your liabilities are if the property becomes vacant. You may have to pay an increased premium. Be specific and ask whether the coverage is still in effect, since some policies become void if the property is vacant.

### RED FLAG

Your insurance will not cover tenants' personal property. Make sure they know that and encourage them to insure their belongings. Insurance companies offer tenant insurance. As many tenants aren't aware they're not covered, you can pass this information on to the tenant as a service.

## FIND OUT ABOUT REPLACEMENT-COST AND RENTAL-LOSS INSURANCE

Make sure your property is covered with replacement-cost insurance. This applies to condos, too. When buying a condominium, have your professional review the insurance policy the condominium corporation has on the building. Look for specific provisions such as the replacement cost if the property should happen to burn down.

Do your best to arrange rental loss insurance. This will cover you in case your property becomes uninhabitable due to an insurable event. It will pay you what your monthly rent would have been until the property is in condition to rent out again. This simple clause has saved investors hundreds of thousands of dollars over the years.

### KEY INSIGHT

The banks will want their mortgage payments even if a property has been burned and is uninhabitable. Rental loss insurance will provide you this critical source of revenue. Discuss this with your insurance agent up front.

## TIP #57: A MULTI-FAMILY PURCHASE GETS COMPLICATED—FAST. BE PREPARED.

*These deals promise easier management. But they're definitely more complicated.*

Multi-family purchases (MFP) are a great way to optimize your time and cash flow. Instead of six tenants living in six separate properties scattered across the region, you can have all six living in a six-unit dwelling at one address. This can result in far fewer hassles and often yields substantial monthly savings on your operating expenses.

Imagine only one roof, one heating system, one yard to maintain. That is a positive aspect of multi-family unit ownership. But the good news comes with a buyer beware. If single-family homes are at the first level of real estate investment complexity, then multi-family properties are a definite step up—way up. With multi-family purchases, the purchase and due diligence are more complex and you have additional issues with choosing tenants that will get along (or at least not bother each other).

## What do you need to do?

### APPLY THE MFP RULES OF DUE DILIGENCE

As discussed in Tip #24, the due diligence required of an MFP is more complex and more expensive as it takes you into the world of the "large commercial lender." With an MFP, you often deal with what the industry calls a commercial mortgage lender. And these lenders have a completely different set of rules.

In addition to all the regular analysis and due diligence, you will often be required to undertake an environmental study of the land and an engineering report on the infrastructure of the building. This will cost you substantially more than single-family-home due diligence.

### UNDERSTAND THE ENVIRONMENTAL STUDY

Almost all commercial lenders require a Phase 1 environmental study to help them determine if there are any current or future environmental issues that will devalue this property. If the Phase 1 study uncovers potential issues, you may be required to go to Phase 2, and that is where costs start to skyrocket.

### KNOW THE FIRE CODE

Your due diligence should also include reports from the local fire department to make sure the property meets the required fire code. Many jurisdictions now require multi-family owners to bring their properties up to current fire codes, even if the property was built decades ago, under a different code.

These repairs easily run into the tens of thousands of dollars, and if you are not aware of them, they can make a good deal go sour very quickly.

### GET THE BUILDING INSPECTED

Most lenders will be very specific on the building infrastructure inspection. They will require an engineering firm to sign off on the complete inspection. Obviously, this makes it much more expensive than a regular house inspector's report.

### 🕐 KEY INSIGHT

A detailed inspection gives you the approximate costs of any required repairs. This information gives you an opportunity to negotiate purchase conditions with the vendor. You can present the "third party" report from the engineer and require that the repairs be done before the purchase is finalized (closes), or negotiate a discount off your purchase price. The inspection will also help you decide on purchasing or not; if the building requires substantial repairs and you are not getting it at a substantial discount, it may be better to walk away.

### EXAMINE THE MFP RECORD

Many municipal jurisdictions keep records of complaints against residential properties. The emergency response department (ERD) may not go out and search properties for violations, but they may keep records of properties against which complaints have been filed. If those complaints led to a work order and that work order was not completed, you may be responsible. (Example: Basement windows that are smaller than current requirements for that property type. If you don't complete your due diligence by checking with the city bylaw enforcement team, you could be stuck with an order to immediately replace each and every basement window at your cost.) If, on the other hand, you find this out in advance of removing your conditions, you can go to the vendor and negotiate compensation.

### 🚩 RED FLAG

The MFP record and ERD file are especially important if the seller doesn't have, won't provide, or insists on an "as is" condition regarding a property you haven't been able to inspect. Any time your questions go unanswered, you need to see it as a sign of hidden trouble. Dig deeper!

### GET THE TENANT FILES

In Part 8, we will discuss the basics of tenancy. Here we will just say that regardless of whether you have one tenant, or many, the rules are the same: You need to confirm tenant information *before* you remove conditions or take possession of the property. Too many investors are left with a very bad deal simply because they did not confirm the tenant information in advance. For example, a vendor may embellish the rent rolls or promise certain rental incentives. If you don't get confirmation from the tenants in advance, you will be stuck fulfilling these promises even though you did not budget for it.

Ideally, you need to obtain tenant files to ensure there are written leases signed by both parties. Then review each tenant file with the lease, the move-in report and the tenant application. Record this information on a spreadsheet if you can't take copies with you.

### KNOW YOUR LENDER'S REQUIREMENTS

Most MFP vendors provide buyers with an opportunity to review the rent roll and see what vacancies are. If you're getting new financing, the new lender will likely demand a certified rent roll where the seller warrants that the vacancies are at a certain level. Your lender then approves the mortgage based on a certain vacancy level.

If at closing (perhaps two or three months later), the vacancy level is higher than the level at which your mortgage was approved, most lenders will hold back some of the funding until the approved vacancy level is achieved.

In extreme cases, the lender can refuse to fund at all and reverse their mortgage approval if the vacancies (and, therefore, the income) are not at the level agreed to in the mortgage confirmation letter.

### GET A POST-CLOSING ADJUSTMENT AGREEMENT

With your offer, include a post-closing adjustment agreement. Add this as a schedule to your contract and ask that it be signed and returned with the contract. A post-closing agreement allows your lawyer to hold back some funds to take care of anything the vendor promised to do but didn't complete. In most cases, these funds aren't required because the vendor fulfils his obligations. The funds are then immediately transferred to the vendor. The agreement protects you from cases where the required work is not complete. This hold-back for post-closing adjustments is there for you to complete the work without the money coming out of your pocket.

You'll also want to arrange tenant estoppel forms, sometimes known as rental confirmation forms. These forms, signed by the tenants, confirm their rent levels, the amount of their security deposit, and any side deals they may have with the vendor. Once you receive these forms, make sure you compare them to the information you have from their tenant file and the certified rent roll that was provided you. This is another use for the post-closing hold-back of funds.

### SPEND SOME TIME ON THAT VACANCY ISSUE

While the deal is conditional, get your lender to state clearly in writing what vacancy level they will accept. Compare the lender's vacancy requirement against the current building situation.

Make sure your seller knows what your lender wants and negotiate further how the lender's requirements will be achieved. After you have removed conditions, even though you haven't yet taken possession, you may wish to assume responsibility for choosing tenants. As the current owner will no longer be responsible for long-term tenant choices, this ensures you won't get stuck with less-than-desirable tenants.

### FACTOR IN "NORMALIZATION"

No matter how thick the contract and how diligent the research, you can expect some unforeseen time and expense associated with assuming an MFP.

There will always be a normalization period after you take over the property. During this period (often three to six months depending on the quality of the building) don't expect to be taking out much in the way of positive cash flow. There will always be surprises and these surprises inevitably cost you money. Make sure you are prepared for this and budget accordingly.

# TIP #58: PROPERTY TAXES ARE INEVITABLE—SPREAD THE PAIN!

*Make property taxes part of your monthly cash-flow calculation.*

Real estate investment is all about managing cash flow. Sophisticated investors know the mental pain involved with writing a large cheque for property taxes every year. They also know monthly tax payments will ease that pain—and help you stay on top of important information about how your property is performing every month. *This tip is especially critical if you have a number of properties with taxes all due on the same date!*

## What do you need to do?

**WORK WITH THE LOCAL TAX AUTHORITY**

Call the local tax authority and find out what you need to do to make regular monthly payments instead of a large lump-sum payment. Set it up so these payments come directly from your bank account. This makes them part of your monthly cash-flow calculation.

### 🅢 SOPHISTICATED INVESTOR TIP

If this monthly approach is one you would like to adopt, implement it in January. All of your quarterly, semi-annual and annual cash flow assessments will now include a critical piece of information.

## TIP #59: BE REALISTIC ABOUT SUBDIVISIONS.

*These developments look like a great way to "get rich quick." In reality, they are much more complicated and expensive than most think.*

We've all seen the advertisements. Ten acres of pristine land overlooking a beautiful natural area. Good access to a commuting highway and utilities that run right up to the property line. The land's currently zoned as agricultural. But hey! It's obvious the parcel is destined for residential subdivision success and all you need is the cash to start making it happen.

The dreamiest part? You'll recoup that initial cash payout and use the money to build your own dream home in a neighbourhood you put together. Pull in a few other investors and you even cut the cost of the initial risk. Sad to say, but this is often a pipe dream. If you don't have the experience and contacts to put together a subdivision deal, you will often bump up against some solid brick walls.

# What do you need to do?

**FIND OUT WHAT'S REALLY INVOLVED IN SUCH A DEVELOPMENT**

Sophisticated real estate investors know there's money to be made in land development. They also know these deals are much more complex than buying and owning residential rental properties. Before you ever try to bring a subdivision to birth on your own, consider the following facts:

• Development agreements require a good working relationship with the local municipality. If it's the business you want to be in, make sure you know who you'll need onside. With these deals, politics can be as important as subdivision experience.

• Never assume a zoning change will happen, or will happen in a particular time frame. Take the timeline you have planned and double it. Remember to factor these extra costs into your model.

• If the land includes lakefront property, expect other levels of government to be involved with issues concerning land use that impacts the shoreline and water quality.

• Utility providers: Get as many details as you can regarding their expected timelines for delivering their services into your potential subdivision—then double these timelines.

• Utility provision costs money. Find out exactly how much it will cost to service the lots you plan to sell.

• Hire a team of experts in the subdivision development business. If you jump in yourself, hoping that it will work, you will invariably be shocked at hidden costs you never even considered. These experts are worth their weight in gold.

## 🏴 RED FLAG

Lenders will not advance millions of dollars on a good idea, and sophisticated investors wouldn't dream of asking for it! With this kind of deep-pocket project, your due diligence package must be extremely detailed and include a full business plan, market research on target buyers, and a backup plan if the deal doesn't come to fruition. The lender will be looking at the property and at the experience of the people involved. And don't expect full 75%-plus financing—or to get all the money at once.

### BEWARE THE DEBENTURE

A debenture is an unsecured bond that is backed by the credit of the issuer but not by any specific collateral. There are two things you need to know about debentures:

1) They can be an efficient way to share the financial risk of an expensive project.
2) They can be an efficient way for many people to lose money on a single project.

Before you buy into a debentured real estate investment, do your own research. Run the project/site plan through the Property Goldmine Score Card (see Appendix). If you are thinking of being a financial partner in a subdivision, you are still obliged to do your own full due diligence. Consider the Property Goldmine Score Care as a bare minimum. If you blindly go in without doing your own homework, you compromise your portfolio with unnecessary risk.

### DEMAND DETAILS FROM THE DEVELOPER

Look at the developer's background and subdivision experience. Find out if the company has enough staff to complete the project and whether it has access to the cash the project needs for completion. Check to see what safeguards are in place to make sure money raised to support this project won't be used on another. Find out what the reporting structure will be like. When will you receive reports? When will you get paid-out—with the first dollars or the last? All of these are key considerations.

Also, remember that this is not a true real estate investment. Here, you are a financial partner. You are buying a type of security, not a piece of property. This greatly limits your exit strategies.

## TIP #60: GET UP CLOSE AND PERSONAL WITH THE RESIDENTIAL ZONING CODE.

*Is that suite legal, illegal, conforming, non-conforming or something else altogether?*

Sophisticated real estate investors learn to survey a property for innovative ways to optimize their cash flow. They see a detached garage and think, "I can rent that out." They see a separate entrance to the basement and think, "This single-family home can accommodate two renters."

So far, so good.

The problem with some of the "obvious" revenue-generators is they may not fall within a particular municipality's regulations regarding residential zoning laws. Many jurisdictions across the country do not license additional suites in property they designate as single family homes. This means the city or municipality may knock on your door (at any time!) and shut down your secondary suite, turning your great investment into a poor one in a single day.

Of course there are thousands of secondary suites across the country. Some areas have very clear guidelines that, if met, will allow you to license your basement suite and rent it out. Other municipalities appear to turn a blind eye, knowing that if they shut down all "non-conforming" suites there would be a housing crisis in the town.

If you are considering secondary suites in your property, make sure you know the regulations and the level of enforcement.

###  RED FLAG

Most regions will ignore your secondary suites until there is a complaint. This complaint can come from anyone: tenants, neighbours, friends or jealous family members. Make sure you do not rely on this added income to make your deal work.

## What do you need to do?

**GET THE FACTS**

Call the municipal government's development office to ascertain the latest rules and regulations. Find out how a particular municipality defines "self-contained dwellings located in a larger detached dwelling." If one is allowed, do you need to have separate cooking, sleeping and bathing facilities? Are legal parking spaces (usually, these are narrowly defined) required for each unit within a home?

Ask how you can determine if a particular suite (sometimes called a "secondary suite") is a "listed" use or a "discretionary" use. Speak with fellow investors in the region to discover what their experiences have been with the local authorities as they pertain to secondary suites.

**NOW DIG DEEPER**

Vendors who advertise a house with a "basement suite," "in-law suite" or "non-conforming suite" may know their suite doesn't meet the code, or meets only certain aspects of it. A non-conforming suite may be one grandfathered into that particular dwelling. It may also be "vendor-speak" for illegal! The vendor might know that, in some municipalities, development officers don't have time to investigate claims made in real estate advertisements. If the suite is non-conforming, then the value of the property is less to you as an investor. Factor that in when negotiations begin.

**BE SURE—BEFORE YOU BUY!**

Make sure your investment is based on fact, not conjecture. Secondary suites are not allowed in some zoning classifications. Some suites may have been "grandfathered" into new zoning regulations, while others may never have been legal. There is a definite risk in buying an investment property that does not meet local zoning requirements!

Take the address to the local planning department to see if the suite is actually conforming—*before* you remove your conditions.

 **KEY INSIGHT**

Real estate investment has developed a certain amount of its own "lingo." Make sure you base business decisions on what that lingo really means. A "suite-able" dwelling isn't so sweet if the building and zoning codes don't actually allow another tenant. Sure, you may be able to run the non-conforming suite for a while, but you will not be able to plan on that income over the long term since there is always the threat of this second income being taken away.

## TIP #61: OBTAIN A FULL SURVEY OF THE PROPERTY— OR USE TITLE INSURANCE TO COVER YOUR FUTURE.

*The survey will immediately advise you of non-compliance issues. These issues can become very costly if you haven't done your homework. Base your purchase decisions on the hard facts of a real property report.*

The survey certificate is called many different things across the country (including a Real Property Report and a Surveyor's Real Property Report).

Drawn up by surveyors, it is a two-dimensional picture of your property and locates the buildings, including garages, tool sheds and decks, on the land. It also outlines how far each building is from the property lines as well as any easements or rights-of-way on the property.

**Compliance** is the term that describes what happens when a municipality looks at that property report and decides it meets their bylaws. Compliance issues include the physical location of all buildings, which must be a certain distance from property lines. Compliance occurs when permits for these buildings are properly issued.

Compliance also covers land and property-use issues. You can't generally keep farm animals within an urban municipality. Without the right permissions, you also can't turn a single-family home into a rental property with self-contained living quarters on the upper and lower levels.

The reason you need a real property report and compliance is that the real property report tells the lender (and you) there are no compliance issues on the property. This means you won't have to take the garage down because it is too close to the property line, or change an overhang that passes over the property boundaries. Your lender uses the information to protect its investment and make sure you will not have to decrease the value of the property to make it comply.

 **RED FLAG**

Non-compliance issues cost real estate investors cold, hard cash. You may have to remove an illegal basement suite. A non-conforming deck that encroaches on a municipal right-of-way may have to be torn down at your expense. Be aware.

## What do you need to do?

**PERFORM YOUR DUE DILIGENCE**

Never, ever, take a vendor at his or her word. Real property reports and compliance are not hassles; they're documents that support your due diligence.

Write contracts that stipulate the seller will provide the real property report and evidence of compliance 10 days before closing the deal. Make it the seller's responsibility. Once you get the report, keep it in your files so you can provide it to the person who purchases the property from you in the future.

Be forewarned that decks, especially covered decks, often are non-compliant. The encroachment of decks on the utility right-of-way is a major (not a minor!) encroachment. In a worst-case scenario, the municipality can order non-compliance issues rectified immediately—even *before* it will allow the property to be transferred at the Land Titles office. The municipality can refuse the permits and order that the deck be torn down and removed. If a deck encroaches on the municipal right-of-way and it interferes with any work the municipality has to do in the future, you could be responsible for the cost of removing that deck.

A vendor's lawyer could claim you are being unreasonable in not wanting to close a deal despite issues related to permits and encroachments. This could lead to a demand that you pay late-closing interest costs. It can be a significant amount of money—and such an aggravation is avoidable if you've stipulated that being provided with real property reports and compliance are part of your closing terms.

If encroachment is the issue, have the vendor's lawyer obtain an encroachment agreement from the municipality. A standard agreement will state:

a) If the decks are ever removed they cannot be built in the same place; and
b) If the municipality ever has to work in the right-of-way, the property owner assumes the risk if anything happens to the deck, as well as the responsibility to repair it.

 **KEY INSIGHT**

A real-estate-savvy law firm may not start a title registration process unless it has seen a real property report or that title insurance is in place. Its goal is to make sure you understand the legal implications of a purchase and the risk of buying property that doesn't match a real property report or meet municipal compliance.

**SOPHISTICATED INVESTOR TIP**

Title insurance has become increasingly popular in Canada. It is used extensively in the east and is slowly being adopted out west. Title insurance is used in place of, or in addition to, a formal survey certificate/real property report. It provides you with select coverage in case the property is found not to conform

Sophisticated Investor Tip continues

in the future. In addition to many other benefits, some title insurance policies will even pay for the renovations required to make it conform—so make sure you shop around! Title insurance also helps you close on a property more quickly than if you were to arrange a new survey certificate.

## TIP #62: KNOW THE BASICS OF CONDO PROPERTY MANAGEMENT.

*Multi-unit rental projects owned by individual investors require three levels of management.*

The legal and practical aspects of property management are quite different when a strata-titled multi-unit rental property is owned by numerous individual investors. Investors should understand the basics of the three management levels, and know how one builds on the other.

Each province has its own set of rules that control the operations of a condominiumized property. Make sure you become well versed in your obligations as a condo owner and learn what the regulations state for rentals, reserve funds and special assessments.

## What do you need to do?

**UNDERSTAND THE THREE LEVELS**

Owner/occupiers and the occasional investor who do their own management would be at Level 1 Strata or Condo Management. Investors who do not want to be part of a management pool would be at Level 2 (Tenant acquisition and administration), and most other investors would be at Level 3 Rental Pool Management. In projects owned by one investor, the distinction between the three levels is much less important.

### 🚩 RED FLAG

Property management is not cheap and, as with most purchases, you get what you pay for. Find a property management company with extensive condominium experience. Its personnel will be much more aware of key and hidden regulations and, more importantly, know how to deal with issues that arise.

*Red Flag continues*

These condo experts are often *not* the same management companies that will be managing your single-family or smaller multi-family properties. Go with the experts; the extra costs will be well worth the hassle-free management they'll provide. That said, don't assume a company offers better management just because it charges more than the market average. Get *lots* of references.

## ❶ KEY INSIGHT

Get into the habit of reviewing all property-management costs on a project before you invest, then review the costs again after you've owned it for a while. Watch for "fee creep." This occurs when small, incremental fees are added by management over time. You'll find that most management companies are 100% above board. But it's your business and you want to ensure the people you have put in charge of your business are doing their job for a fair "wage."

## TIP #63: PUT YOUR RENOVATIONS TO WORK. (IT'S NOT AS EASY AS MOST THINK!)

*Factor renovations into your investment plan, and make sure you finance the work with profit in mind.*

We all know renovations can make you money. However, it can be fiscally dangerous to jump into a renovation project without following a system, especially since the rules about renovating a rental suite are substantially different from those involved with renovating your home. When it comes to your home, emotions are allowed to run wild. Unless you are thinking specifically of re-sale, you can choose colours, textures, fixtures and appliances based on your personal taste. In a rental property, that same approach drives the budget up beyond economic hope. It can also make your property difficult to rent.

Treat a rental suite reno like it's part of your business. You need to re-move your personal preferences, replace them with information about what your target renter wants—and still be cost effective. A whole book could be written on this subject! A proven Canadian-specific system is available for investors looking to know exactly what renovations to do and which ones to avoid at all costs. It is titled *Renovation Secrets* and is available at www.realestateinvestingincanada.com.

You need to make sure the renovation *financing* won't eat away the profit from that new kitchen—or flush the cost of a new bathroom down the drain! When estimating the cost of the renovations, make sure you add a 50% buffer to cover the issues that will inevitably arise. Remember to be honest with your banker. Presenting an honest reno budget is further evidence of your willingness to do the extra 10%!

## • The LOC option

A Line of Credit (LOC) may be the best way to finance a home renovation that costs less than 75% of the home's value. An LOC can be registered as a second mortgage, leaving the first mortgage in place.

Canada's chartered banks can't lend a homeowner more than 75% of the value of a home without having the loan insured. Those premiums can add a significant cost to a renovation project and must be factored into your business plan. (A 2% insurance premium on a loan of $90,000 would cost a borrower $1,800.)

## • The PPIL option

A Purchase Plus Improvements Loan (PPIL) is used when buying a home where improvements are necessary to add value to the house. PPILs are also good for renovations. The key? They must add value to the house. PPILs can save you money because lenders will let you borrow based on the post-renovated value. That negates the 75% rule—and saves the insurance premium.

## What do you need to do?

**CALCULATE THE REAL COSTS**

Determine the pre-renovation value of your house and the cost of the renovations.

**GET AN APPRAISAL**

Have the property appraised as-is and request the appraisal include an "After Renovated Value." Take both of these to your banker or mortgage broker. The bank will give you the mortgage based on the post-renovated value. The catch? The renovating cash (a cash holdback) will be held in trust or by the bank until the renovations are done. Once that happens, the holdback is released.

## 🕐 KEY INSIGHT

A failure to calculate accurate renovation costs is one of the main reasons greenhorn investors don't turn a profit when re-selling renovated properties. Fixing up a basement in a single-family home is a bad investment for most investment properties. You won't recoup this $25,000 in the increased value of the home. However, that money spent on the above-ground floors (especially on the kitchen, bathroom and light fixtures) will give you an immediate return on your investment. Remember to always follow a proven system, like the *Renovation Secrets* program mentioned previously. The small subtleties make all the difference. Never guess what the renter or next purchaser wants—go with the facts. You can and should learn from the mistakes of others. Make sure your plan for the property covers the added costs of the borrowed funds used to complete the renovations.

## TIP #64: DON'T CRY THOSE CONTRACTOR BLUES: PROTECT YOURSELF WITH CONTRACTS IN WRITING.

*Quality contractors can be tough to find. Use written contracts to protect both parties–and to build solid business relationships with contractors you can trust.*

You can build a home, renovate a personal residence or make-over an investment property, but the cardinal rules of contractor negotiations remain the same:

1. Get quotes and contracts in writing.
2. Decisions regarding quality and cost are not interchangeable.

### What do you need to do?

**MEET THE CONTRACTOR**

This is an obvious requirement for most projects you are about to begin. But many forget to do this when buying a property where a renovation has already begun and the contractor is already on-site. Here, your relationship with and trust of the contractor's ability to get the job done on time and on budget is very important. A dependable and knowledgeable

renovator is your best friend when working on fixer-upper properties.
Treat them like gold.

## PUT THE DEAL IN WRITING

Even though you have developed a relationship based on trust and professionalism, make sure you have a very clearly written contract in place
(hence the name contractor). The contract should outline all aspects of
the renovations, including plans, price and timing. It should also cover
payment schedules—what needs to be completed and at what stages of
completion you will make payments. It must have a clear definition of
what occurs if the work is not up to your stated standard, or your timeline.
Penalties and holdbacks are very commonly used to keep the project on
time and on budget.

Any changes to the timeline, plan or pricing *must* be given in writing
and agreed to by all involved so there are no disputes at the end.

---

### Contractor checklist: What your written deal should cover

- **The job**
  What's to be done? Make sure the contract describes the job completely
  and correctly. Go for detail.
- **The material**
  What materials and products will be used and who will make those
  decisions?
- **The permits**
  Who will obtain the appropriate zoning approval and building
  permits?
- **The business**
  How will you handle deficiencies and mistakes? How will payment be
  determined? (Pay-as-you-go? Instalments? Upon completion?) Who
  provides workers with the space, access and utilities they need to do
  their jobs?
- **Insurance requirements**
  Define what insurance the contractor must have in order to work on the
  property and to fulfil the requirements from your insurance company.

## MAKE QUALITY A BUSINESS PRIORITY

A quality renovation project needs to suit the requirements of your business plan. At the most basic level, contracted improvements need to:

a) look good
b) last a long time and
c) have a positive impact on your business plan's financial bottom line.

*In other words, the work has to make your property more valuable for the re-sale or tenant market.*

That might not mean granite countertops and hardwood floors, even if that is your taste. What you're looking for is a solid return on your renovation dollar with quality products and quality craftsmanship.

---

**To protect your investment, expect the following:**
Your contractor should:

1. Be licensed.
2. Perform the work as contracted and then take responsibility for making sure changes are authorized in writing.
3. Hire skilled trades to your level of expectation.
4. Oversee the work.
5. Maintain liability and property damage insurance.
6. Maintain workers' compensation insurance.
7. Have extensive experience in your type of renovations. Don't hire a high-end craftsman to do a quick reno on your rental suite; you will be wasting his time and your money.

---

### 🄢 SOPHISTICATED INVESTOR ACTION STEP

Aim to build relationships you can count on with quality contractors and tradespeople. If the relationship is not working, do your best to fix it or move on. Learn to recognize the contractors who understand what you need and are capable of doing the work to your satisfaction. They become a "partner" in your business. Treat these relationships with the respect they deserve. Many novice investors launch their portfolios buying under-valued property they renovate with the help of family and friends. That can work; and it can also prove disastrous. To avoid costly errors, including cost overruns related to time, make sure your "partners" share your commitment to the business plan.

## TIP #65: D.I.Y.? IN MOST CASES THAT WASTES A VALUABLE COMMODITY.

*Time is a non-renewable resource that you should not waste. Make sure you spend your time where it matters most.*

Many people have difficulty understanding the concept of valuing their time. In fact, we as a society are so focused on price we often forget about the time it takes us to make savings.

For real estate investors this is particularly true. Investors create wealth when they identify and buy properties that are undervalued and have positive cash-flow potential. Sadly, so many investors get caught up in the "I can do it myself and save myself some money" syndrome, they miss the point of real estate investing.

Sure it is true that many of us could paint the property, or fix the drywall. But while we are busy doing that, a good investment deal will pass us by. In fact, we'll be so busy we won't even know it passed us by. Investors make their most money when they buy properties and rely on other trusted team members to do the other work, like management or renovations.

If you ever think that all the good deals are going to other people and there are none left for you, recognize that thought as a real indication that you are not spending your time on the things you need to focus on. Protect your time even more closely than you do your money. Money can be re-gained—time cannot.

### 🕑 KEY INSIGHT

For every job you do, someone else could do it in your place for much less than your time is worth. Even if you were ridiculous and started to pay a painter $50 an hour to paint your suite, it would still be cheap in the long run. Why? Because during the time that you are *not* painting, you could uncover a deal that nets you $15,000 or more. So even though you dramatically overpaid your painter, you still came out substantially ahead of where you would have been if you'd painted it yourself and "saved yourself some money."

Arlen Dahlin, a good friend and very successful investor, made this observation to me: "Most people are programmed to step over dollars to pick up dimes." Don't let yourself be one of those types of investors! Stay focused on the most profitable use of your time in the business.

**RED FLAG**

D.I.Y. is also a life killer. Think: No time, no fun, and no family or friends left to enjoy your long-term investment dream!

You are obliged to bring your talents to your business and to help it to become its most profitable at the net bottom-line. If you still choose to go the Do-It-Yourself route, that's perfectly okay. Just know that as you are scraping off the old wallpaper, other investors are out there grabbing up the great deals.

## What do you need to do?

**PAY YOURSELF**

Factor in a management fee even if you plan to manage the property yourself. This upholds the most basic of investment advice: Make sure you get paid first.

Put a clear and accurate cost to your time. Ask the question, "What am I worth to my investment business on an hourly basis?" Once you have this number, try to only do tasks that meet or surpass this number. Will you be perfect at this task? Probably not. However, the more time you focus on these higher-paying tasks, the more profitable your investment business will be.

**BE REAL**

Property management is a 24-hour-a-day, 7-day-a-week job. If you have the time and the inclination to add an additional full-time job to your life, feel free to do so. Just know the time spent managing investment properties limits the time you can spend finding and buying good properties. Keep a perspective on real costs. You can expect to pay 4% to 10% of your monthly rent to a management company. At $850 per month, an 8% fee only adds up to $68. That's an amazingly cheap way to buy back your time and still get 24-hour coverage, seven days a week.

**KEY INSIGHT**

Savvy real estate investors do two things right:

1) They guard their time like it's a product of the Canadian Mint.
2) They know investors make most of their money buying properties, not managing them.

# Tip #66: Calculate the "Sweat Equity" Equation.

*Your sweat equity has a price tag. Learn it.*

Still not convinced you should put an actual price tag on your own sweat equity? Consider this: The renovation-and-resell market is one component of the real estate investment market where you can always find people making money. But take a closer look. *It's also the one area where you're going to find more than a few people losing their financial shirts!*

That's what makes this tip so sweet. Believe it or not, you can put a price tag on your sweat equity. And you can use that price tag to determine whether a particular reno-and-flip project is worth your time.

## What do you need to do?

### PRACTISE THE SWEAT EQUITY EQUATION

The Sweat Equity Equation says the first 100 hours you put into a moderately neglected property will increase its value by 10%, as long as you follow a proven system for renovations and you know what you are doing. Just putting in time will not increase the value, but putting in time in the right areas can make a *huge* difference.

> **Example**:
> You buy a house for $100,000.
> 100 hours of "sweat" will typically increase its value by $10,000, perhaps more.
> That equals $100 per hour.
>
> You can make this $10,000 in two hours by finding a property that is below market value and buying it. Which would you prefer to do? Two hours for $10,000 or 100 hours for $10,000? Keep this in mind when you put pencil to paper to figure out the investment value of the specific reno-upgrades outlined in the next tip!

**RED FLAG**

I have met investors who like to "hide" in their renovation projects so they don't have to face other things that are occurring in their lives or their investments. If this is true for you, just acknowledge it for what it is. And be honest with yourself. Is this the best use of your time?

## Tip #67: Figure Out the Best Bang for Your Reno Buck.

*Learn to identify what needs doing—and what makes you money.*

There are a lot of fixer-uppers on the real estate market and investors with a good eye for the renovate-and-resell market are always looking for ways to increase property values without compromising their investment system's cash flow.

Wise investors typically follow a quick checklist. It helps them zero in on the specific upgrades that need to be done, after which they can assess costs and calculate returns. Make sure you check out the complete *Renovation Secrets* program at www.realestateinvestingincanada.com.

If you are considering renovations, learn from others' mistakes. Spend the dollars where they will have the biggest impact on either rental or re-sale and always put yourself in the shoes of the prospective buyer or renter. Try to think like they do and walk into your property with a fresh pair of eyes, looking for things that would turn you off the property.

## What do you need to do?

**CONSIDER A FACELIFT**

Some of the least expensive upgrades include cosmetic features like paint and carpet and floor cleaning. These simple upgrades are not structural and usually require more time than money, but they dramatically increase the perceived value of the property, thus allowing you to charge higher rent or a higher selling price.

Specific additions include new lighting, which has an immediate impact on perceived value and is very cheap to upgrade. If you paint, go with warm, neutral colours—not typical "renter beige." You want shades that are likely to match almost any furniture the new buyer owns, yet not be boring.

Fix anything that is obviously broken. Windows, doors, locks, countertops and chipped bathtubs and sinks headline the list. If not fixed, these become instant turnoffs and show the prospect that you just don't care.

### BOOST CURB APPEAL

Mow the lawns, weed the gardens, trim the shrubs and repair and paint the fence. Replace the house numbers with large numbers (*not* the stick-on kind!). Install a new mailbox or slot.

Take another look at that front door: It is the first item that most prospects touch on the property. Make sure it feels "safe and secure" and is in good shape. You may want to replace it with a new bevelled metal door with a small decorative window. New doors provide tremendous return on investment.

Check all the locks and door handles both in and outside the property. This is how your prospect interfaces with the property and if these are cracked, broken or loose, the prospect gets a poor perception of your property, no matter what else you've done to increase its curb appeal.

### UPGRADE THE APPLIANCES

This is where an investment in renovation starts to get costly. Upgrading the appliances, however, is often worth the money because it boosts your monthly rental charge, can attract a better class of tenant (investor code for tenants with fewer property management issues!) and can dramatically reduce the chance of appliance repair bills.

There is no need to go to the top of the line. But do make sure that they match (white preferred) and that they are in great working order.

## Ⓢ SOPHISTICATED INVESTOR ACTION STEP

If you own a property with three or more suites, find out how much it will cost you to install a coin-operated washer and dryer. If you share the revenue with the coin-op company, you remove the hassle of broken-down washers and dryers from your life, since the laundry company is responsible for maintaining and cleaning the machines.

### ADD A SUITE

This is one of the best ways to increase cash flow on a rental property. *A suite in the basement of a single-family home can increase your monthly cash flow by 30% to 60%.*

Suites can also add significant value to the property. When you're looking at a single-family home, look at the basement. A partially finished basement could significantly drop your reno costs, especially if you plan to develop lower-level space for an additional tenant.

Make sure that the space you're considering fits the local zoning laws and that you provide the tenant with easy, private access and egress to their suite. Review Tip #60.

### GO FOR THE MAJOR OVERHAUL

This category is for the handyman's special and fixer-upper. Like development, this arena is fraught with traps for the rookie investor. It sounds very alluring to buy a junker and turn it into a quality rental or re-sale property. But knowledge is critical. If you plan to use the major overhaul strategy, make sure you have a talented team around you. This is not recommended for the faint of heart.

 **RED FLAG**

> This is a good place to lose a small fortune! The biggest mistakes beginners make when analyzing a junker deal is to overestimate what the property will be worth after a major renovation is done and to drastically underestimate what it will cost to renovate the property. They may also forget to value their own time into the deal.

### CHANGE THE PROPERTY'S USE

Change of use is a wonderful way to add value to a property. There are many strategies that you can follow, for example:

- Change the property's zoning to allow subdivision of a larger piece of land.
- Buy an apartment building and convert it to individual condominiums for sale on the open market.
- Convert old derelict warehouses into funky lofts.
- Add a suite or two to a property that is under-utilized within the current zoning.

The strategies are truly endless. Complications aside, this kind of deal could push up your property value by 100%, 200% or even more.

**RED FLAG**

These investments carry significant risks. Deep pockets are often required for a change-of-use strategy. Are you prepared to hold the property for 10 or more years if the zoning application is turned down?

### INCREASE THE INCOME

Increase the Net Operating Income (NOI: gross income less expenses) of a revenue property, and you increase the property's value. Here, the investor identifies multi-family properties with below-average rents, then undertakes a cosmetic-level facelift and raises the rents.

Calculate your Net Operating Income (NOI) as follows: (Gross Rental Revenue + Laundry Income) – Vacancy Allowance – Operating Expenses = Net Operating Income.

**Revenue Increase Example**: You buy a 10-unit apartment building where units rent for $400 a month, but market rent for those units is $450. Increase that rent by the $50, producing an extra $500 a month or $6,000 a year.

To estimate how this affects value, multiply the NOI by 10.
NOI = $6,000/year x 10 = $60,000.

Each region will have its own prevailing rate of return on a rental income increase. Speak with a quality investment real estate appraiser to discover your local multiplier. However, for rough estimates 10 is an easy number to use.

**KEY INSIGHT**

There are other key formulas you can use to quickly get value estimates. They are:

**Approximate Market Price**. This calculation will give you an approximate price for the property based on prevailing market conditions and the Net Operating Income. Although this value is not the "true and final" market value, it does provide you with a number from which to work.
**Approximate Value = Net Operating Income / Prevailing Capitalization Rate**.

Key Insight continues

> **Capitalization Rate**. This calculation tells you if the vendor is in line with the prevailing marketplace. You will need to know the asking price and the Net Operating Income.
>
> **Cap Rate = (Net Operating Income/Asking Price) x 100**

## DECREASE EXPENSES

Most investors are focused on driving income upwards and pay only a small portion of their effort toward reducing expenses. That's short-sighted, since cutting monthly expenses by $1,000 achieves the same NOI as increasing rents by $50.

Remember, it is what comes out at the bottom line that counts, so make sure you are continually looking at ways in which to reduce your expenses without being detrimental to the property.

 **RED FLAG**

> Don't fall into the trap of deferring needed repairs and maintenance. This will (absolutely) cost you money in the long run. A savvy investor can, however, often find simple and easy ways to decrease the property's operating expenses. These include installing low-flow taps and toilets, increasing the efficiency of the furnace, adding insulation, re-caulking windows, and installing long-lasting light bulbs.

## IDENTIFY OTHER INCOME SOURCES

Garages and storage buildings can be mini-gold mines when rented separately from residential buildings. You can also buy land with harvestable timber. If you recoup your investment by selling off a portion of the timber, it's like getting the land free!

# PART 6

## NEGOTIATE THE DEAL YOU WANT (PRACTICE MAKES PERFECT)

# TIP #68: IDENTIFY MOTIVATED VENDORS. AVOID "FISHERS."

*Your investment success depends on closing real estate deals. Save yourself a ton of time by learning to avoid unmotivated vendors.*

Regardless of how you meet a potential vendor, through a realtor, a friend or an ad in the newspaper, it is critical that you quickly discern two things. First, you have to find out if the property has a remote chance of working as a real estate investment. Second, you have to assess how motivated the seller is.

The higher the vendor's level of true motivation, the better chance you can make a deal that is fair for all parties involved. No matter what you are purchasing in your life, be it a new car, refrigerator or an investment property, the quality of the deal is determined by one thing: the vendor's willingness and eagerness to sell.

You always need to take a step back from the emotion of a possible deal and remember that an unmotivated vendor can waste a lot of your very valuable time and leave you with nothing in the end. We call these vendors "fishers." They are the people who drop their bait into the water just to see who bites. They have zero attachment to whether they sell and they're often just looking to see what their property is worth. In other words, they are not going anywhere and have all the time in the world to hold out for their price and their terms—no compromise.

All markets, hot and cold, also have vendors who want (or even need!) to sell their properties. As an investor, it's your job to help them do that. Motivated vendors will be much more flexible on price, closing dates and other terms. Remember, you are not taking advantage of their situation. You are helping them move on to the next stage of their lives, whatever that may be. A motivated vendor will be predisposed to making a deal—and you can help them do that.

But how do you know one from the other? Sophisticated investors will tell you time is money and they don't like to waste it. They'll ask a potential vendor a few simple (and very direct!) questions, then use his answers to guide their next steps.

## Ⓢ SOPHISTICATED INVESTOR ACTION STEP

Never give up outright on a property you would like to add to your portfolio. Time and circumstances change a vendor's motivation level. If a vendor is currently unwilling to work with you on a deal, leave them a short note that states that you would like to discuss purchasing their property when the time and circumstances are right. Give them your contact information and then just forget about it. I have heard of deals coming back to investors up to six months later. When that kind of call comes out of the blue, it signals the vendor is now motivated and much more open to making a deal.

## ⓥ RED FLAG

Never second-guess whether a vendor will eventually become motivated. There is an old theory that says vendors become motivated after their property has been on the market for a "long period of time." This is utterly false. Even if a great deal of time has passed, a vendor may not be in a rush to sell. Unless their circumstances change, you'll find the same old unmotivated vendor no matter how many times you go back! The willingness to make a fair deal arises only when there is a corresponding willingness to sell.

## What do you need to do?

### ASSESS THE VENDOR'S MOTIVES

Think of questions you can ask to determine the seller's motive. You want to know why they're selling the property, when they have to move and whether the move is motivated by a lifestyle decision or the need for money.

Be serious about getting answers to your questions. If you can't talk to the vendor personally, write your questions down and ask your real estate agent to get you the answers. Also, look at the property records to find out how long the vendor has lived in the property. If it has been many years, your plans to ensure the property is well maintained may help negotiations.

### STUDY THE MOTIVE AND FIGURE OUT HOW YOU CAN HELP

Once you understand the vendor's motivation, start thinking about that motivation as a problem you can help solve. Does the vendor need money fast? Have they already bought another home? Do they want to stay in the home until their kids have finished the school year?

## LEARN HOW MOTIVATED VENDORS HELP YOUR BUSINESS

Motivated vendors have a problem to solve and they will welcome virtually any opportunity to help them sell their property. Remember not to take advantage of a desperate seller. By helping them solve their problem, you will be rewarded with some or all of the following:

- A below-market price. This is not your biggest concern but it's a definite bonus if the deal works out this way.
- Terms and conditions that suit you. You may get a closing date that is months into the future, but includes a locked-in price that protects you from market increases. You may also get a lot more fixtures or chattels than you would with an unmotivated vendor.
- Access to the property before closing so you can do minor renovations and conduct showings to potential renters/buyers. This condition gives you a wonderful opportunity to get the property ready for your renter. As long as you are not doing major renovations, you will find that most vendors will allow this. Even if you don't plan to fix up the property, the ability to show it to potential renters is a great advantage.

### 🛈 KEY INSIGHT

Sophisticated investors know purchase price is one of their least concerns. While the masses may zero in on price, investors choose to focus on terms. That's why most high-quality investors advise others to "buy at market value today and sell at market value in the future." They know you will lose many great deals if you argue over the last one or two thousand dollars, since that kind of cash means very little in the end. A more successful strategy demands you keep moving forward. If you lose a property with a $50,000 profit potential because you argued over the last $1,500, you prove you are a master at "stepping over dollars to get to dimes!"

*Always* ask the following critical question of *every* vendor you speak with, whether you are buying from them or not: "Do you or anyone you know have any other properties you are thinking of selling?" You will be surprised at how many people say yes to this question. It's a low-effort way to learn about more properties you might want in your portfolio.

## Tip #69: Negotiations Make the World Go 'Round: Learn the Secrets.

*Negotiation does not mean you argue over a price. Negotiation means coming to terms. Follow these rules for best results.*

Many people are intimidated by the word "negotiation." That's because their only experience with what they think of as "negotiation" occurred when they bought a car. Let me be brutally honest. That is not a negotiation. That is a discussion about price between two people with opposing agendas.

Real negotiations have something to do with price, but that's only a small part of the equation. Even if the other party believes that price is your primary motivation, you can use your knowledge about the real purpose of the negotiation process to get to a deal that works best for you. To see this in action, learn as much as you can about negotiation, then put that information to work. And don't wait until you are a master before you buy your next piece of property. Since the vendor will have little or no negotiation skills in 95% of property purchase situations, investors who know the following rules will be far and away ahead of the game!

There are many wonderful books on negotiation strategies. For real estate investors, we have boiled it down to very clear and concise strategies (all of which are described in detail in Chapter 16 of *Real Estate Investing in Canada*).

### 🅚 Key Insight

Use these negotiation strategies in all aspects of your life, not just real estate.

## What do you need to do?

**STUDY THE RULES OF NEGOTIATION (ALL 15 OF THEM!)**

There are 15 rules of negotiation you can master. The first three are about preparation and they lay the foundation for negotiation confidence. Never skip these first three!

## The Rules of Negotiation

1. Set goals and write them down—every time. Know your limits, including the most you can pay for the property and the earliest you can take possession. These are your outer limits: Stick with them and you will never get stuck with a bad deal.

2. Have an agenda and a plan. Negotiating by the seat of your pants is the biggest—and most common—mistake people make. (Re-read Rule 1!) With a clear agenda and an action plan firmly in your hands, you will know exactly where you are going and the path to get there. This prevents distractions and lets you keep emotions completely out of the equation.

3. Create a relationship, not an armed camp. Pay attention to the person on the other side of the table. Find out their likes and dislikes and if you have anything in common. Use this information to create a relationship rather than a confrontation. This will help both of you negotiate terms with a clearer head.

 **RED FLAG**

Adversarial or confrontational negotiations get you a quick, stress-ridden trip to nowhere. This approach also wastes time because people dig their heels in—for no real reason. Always try to get to the point of the discussion. If negotiations become unmanageable or overly confrontational, walk away. There are many more great deals out there, and since your time is money, you'll want to spend it wisely.

4. Seek the win-win deal. Of course you want to get the best deal for yourself, but don't try to squeeze the last dollar off the table in every situation. Veteran real estate investor Tim Johnson taught me to "always leave something on the table for someone else." It's a credo the authors of this book live by.

5. Separate the people from the problem. Unsophisticated investors make negotiations personal. Your key is to completely separate the personalities

from any real problem that arises. If the discussion gets personal, bring it back to the facts.

6. Focus on motivations, not positions. As we discussed in the previous tip, you need to learn the vendor's real motivation and work with that information. You accomplish this by being a good listener. It is a powerful negotiation strategy to find out where the vendor's motivations lie and help fulfil them, without jeopardizing your own. You'll find this much easier than you think.

7. Search for agreement. Throughout the negotiation, use the magic words, "Do you agree?" This strategy helps set the stage for a positive final agreement. The more small items you agree to, the easier it is to remove emotion and personality from the process.

8. Listen only to reason, not pressure. If someone gives you a deadline or tries to pressure you to make a decision, avoid getting pulled into their trap. The seller's agent may tell you, "another offer is just about to come in, so you better deal now so you don't miss out." This may be the case, but we stress "may." Explain that you can only deal with your own offer and you can't control whether another offer comes in. That approach turns the tables.

9. Be willing to walk away. This is the most powerful tool sophisticated investors use. The masses believe they'll miss out if they let a single deal go. Sophisticated investors know another deal will come along—and may even be more profitable. Say, "It looks like we can't come to a fair agreement for both of us. Call me if things change in the future as I would like to buy this property." Those words work like magic and flush out any bluffs they may have been playing on you.

10. Remember: Silence is golden. When in doubt, keep your mouth shut and let the other party do the talking. The other party will invariably want to fill the silence, and often will fill it with a concession to you.

11. He who mentions a number loses first. Let the other party state the price they want. Ask them to state their bottom line and work the price down.

12. Negotiate only with the decision-maker. Never get caught negotiating with someone who doesn't have the authority to make the agreement. If a property is jointly owned, both spouses must be in attendance to approve the deal. Some nefarious vendors will negotiate a deal with you, then come back two days later saying their "partner" doesn't agree to the terms and the discussions have to start all over again. This is the real estate version of the old "good cop/bad cop" routine we've seen in movies for years.

13. Be patient. Allow the deal to take what time it needs—but don't get caught up if it becomes an obvious waste of time.

14. Be confident. You may need to fake this rule until you can make it ring true. But be honest with yourself: If you have followed the first three negotiations strategies, you already have a huge advantage over the other party and you deserve to go in with confidence. If you can't muster the conviction, be clear and calm in all your discussions as this will give you the air of confidence.

15. Follow through. Once the deal is done, fulfil the terms you agreed to.

 **KEY INSIGHT**

This list reiterates some points covered in other tips! But that's the wisdom of system duplication. When rules are proven, practise them to build success.

## TIP #70: THE PROBLEM WITH TELEPHONES.

*Telephones are great for setting up meetings; not so great for negotiation.*

Every real estate investor will eventually find herself having to handle some negotiations over the phone. *Rookie investors should avoid this like the proverbial plague!*

When you can't avoid the situation, be aware of the potential for problems. Veteran negotiations trainer Randy Shuttleworth of The Training Company put together a tremendous supplement for real estate investors who are forced to negotiate by telephone. Follow these guidelines for the best results.

## ⓢ SOPHISTICATED INVESTOR STRATEGIES

### Extra Tips for Negotiating on the Phone

Due to the busy schedules we all have, there comes a time when negotiating over the telephone is unavoidable. Here are some common pitfalls that you must keep in mind:

- The caller always has the advantage of surprise and is the best prepared.
- Important points are easily omitted or assumed.
- It is impossible to read the other person's body language.
- It is much easier for the other party to say *no* when they don't have to look you in the eye.

Avoid negotiating over the phone whenever possible. But when using the phone is unavoidable, take it seriously! Here are some quick Do's and Don'ts:

### Do's

1. Talk less! The less you talk, the more your opponent will feel the need to fill the space.
2. If your opponent calls you, just listen and take notes. Then call him or her back with your side of the story. This will allow you time to prepare a proper response.
3. If you have to initiate the call, develop a checklist to avoid omissions and assumptions.
4. Re-state agreements in your own words and confirm the terms upon which you both have agreed.
5. Have an excuse ready to break off the discussion. This will allow you to bow out gracefully if needed.
6. *Be prepared!* Don't ignore rules just because this is a phone call instead of an eye-to-eye meeting. Telephone negotiating can work, but only if you are prepared!

### Don'ts

1. Don't push yourself into a quick decision. Telephone negotiating can create a false sense of urgency where parties feel pressured to close the deal.

*Sophisticated Investor Strategies continues*

2. Don't negotiate an issue to conclusion until both parties understand the process for solidifying the deal. For example, how will things be put into writing? By a lawyer, a letter of confirmation, notations on a faxed order form, etc.?

3. Don't negotiate when you are involved in another activity, e.g., during a meeting or staff review, as you will not be completely focused on the negotiating process.

(Source: The Training Company, www.training-company.com)

PART 7

# PURCHASING AND CLOSING:
# THE ART OF THE DEAL

## TIP #71: A DUE DILIGENCE PRIMER ON PURCHASING AND CLOSING.

*Your investment system's success depends on closing deals. Do it often. But do it right.*

Closing on profitable properties that fit your system is something you really can't do often enough. Once you complete your due diligence to the point of purchasing a property that fits your system and remove emotions from the decision-making process, it is time to get that deal done and add that property to your portfolio. The next step is to carry out due diligence on the closing. We will offer specific advice on what you can do to make sure you get the deal you *think* you've agreed to. Sometimes, it differs from what all the other parties believe.

To ensure you are fully informed, we'll look at closing from the buying and selling sides.

### 🅚 KEY INSIGHT

A lawyer who specializes in real estate from an investment perspective is a critical person to have on your team. Make sure these types of transactions are the lawyer's number-one focus; that way you won't end up paying for their mistakes or oversights long into the future. Never use one lawyer over another based solely on price—go discount somewhere else, but not with your legal or accounting advice. Make your choice based on experience. Once the lawyer is a member of your team, make sure he or she reviews all documents and agreements.

Our goal is not to produce fear, but to get you to acknowledge facts. *Due diligence is the foundation of a successful real estate investment system. When you follow it, you plan for success. When you ignore it, you invite trouble.*

Even if you're working with trusted business partners, or face a great deal that demands a quick decision, never skip a step. Here are five tips in one, each of which could save you literally thousands of dollars and hours of wasted time in your upcoming transactions.

## What do you need to do?

**READ YOUR MORTGAGE APPROVALS FROM START TO FINISH**

Your lending institution will send you a written mortgage approval document, whether you are buying a small property or a multi-unit building. No matter what the lender tells you verbally, this document specifies exactly how the mortgage is going to be structured. It will include details such as the amount, the interest rate, the payment schedule and the list of fees.

To this point you have relied on certain unwritten statements to bring the deal close to completion. These may or may not be reflected in the mortgage approval document you have in your hand. So, check for specific conditions that you believe were agreed upon. Match up the numbers, interest rates and other figures and dates with your notes. If you find something in the document you do not understand, ask to have it clearly defined.

If all the terms fit, and your lawyer concurs, sign it. If there are changes to be made, no matter what your timeline looks like, never agree to the terms just to get the deal done.

###  Key Insight

*Never ever* remove the financing conditions on your offer to purchase based solely on a verbal agreement. More often than not a verbal approval can turn into an outright rejection or saddle you with mortgage terms and conditions that are not what you required. Wait until you see it in writing before you call the vendor to remove your conditions.

###  Red Flag

Mortgage and legal documents bind you to action. Never sign anything you are not in full agreement to or don't understand completely! There are no stupid questions—ask until everything is clear.

**WHEN SELLING, KEEP THE KEYS**

Simply put, never give the keys to a buyer until the deal is done. Once a buyer, even a trusted friend, has the keys, they lack motivation to finish the deal. Getting the purchaser to the table, with their money, their lawyer and their motivation is much easier when you still hold the ultimate prize—the keys to the property.

Once everything is in place for a timely closing, you can work with them on providing early access to show the property to prospective tenants.

## LET YOUR LAWYER BE YOUR LAWYER

Never let the vendor's lawyer become *your* lawyer at closing. Although this sounds like a way to save a few dollars, it can be a recipe for disaster. In these transactions, you need a lawyer who represents your interests and requirements alone. With one clear focus, he or she can protect you where needed and point out opportunities or problems. Expecting a lawyer to act for both sides of a deal puts her in the position of advising one party who might not realize he's not getting the best deal possible.

## GET THE FACTS ON ARREARS

Assumable mortgages can make a sweet real estate investment deal. The buyer gets a good price on the property. The seller gets to move on.

When you get a number from the lender, have it broken down into:

- the principal being assumed
- the arrears total
- legal fees.

Without this information, you could find yourself planning for an assumed mortgage based on the principal, then find out you're responsible for the other costs as well.

## STICK BY YOUR OWN RULES

Every investor develops his or her own approach to due diligence. The rules are based on what works, or what hasn't worked in the past. Every time you break a rule, you compromise your system.

Never let anyone force you to deviate from your proven system. Often these deviations have an underlying reason that is not explained to you. It may be to make someone else's life easier, or so they can get their commissions faster, or to save the lawyer time in their busy schedule. The bottom line? They work for you, not the other way around. Take control of your system, run it the way you need it to go and stick with it.

Never, ever skip a step in your due diligence just to make it easier on someone else. That skipped step will eventually come back and bite you financially, be it tomorrow or five years from now.

# TIP #72: FIX YOUR CASH PAYMENT.

*Make sure your cash payments stay fixed.*

In some cases, a vendor's current mortgages can be assumed at the time of purchase. Almost everywhere in the country you will still have to qualify with the bank to take over the mortgage. The exception is Alberta, where you can still find mortgages that are fully assumable with no qualifications. These are becoming increasingly rare, but they still exist.

When assuming a mortgage, with or without qualifications, you will come to an agreement with the vendor on the specific amount of cash you will be putting into the deal. If you are not careful, this number can fluctuate at closing due to mortgage and tax adjustments, etc.

As a sophisticated investor, it's your job to ensure the cash amount stays fixed. You can do this by attaching a Fixed Cash Schedule. (See the sample form that follows.) On an assumable mortgage, if the mortgage goes down, the cash goes up, so make sure you have the right figures when you first negotiate the deal.

## What do you need to do?

**GET THE RIGHT NUMBERS**

When it comes to having the "right figures," don't take someone's word for it; get it in writing from the lender.

**KNOW YOUR OPTIONS**

If the figures change and you don't want to put in more cash, add something like a second mortgage. It can fix the total purchase price and cash at the rate to which you and your partner first agreed.

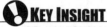 **KEY INSIGHT**

Use a formal written document, like the one printed on the next page, to fix your cash amount.

## FIXED CASH SCHEDULE FORM

The following form was developed and implemented by veteran real estate investors Arlen Dahlin and Valden Palm. Use it to fix your cash amount!

Addendum to Agreement of Purchase and Sale

RE:    PROPERTY: _____
SELLER: _____
BUYER: _____

1.1 If, on the date of closing, the actual, verified balance of the existing mortgage is less than the figure stated on the "Assumption of Mortgage" line, the difference shall not be added to the total of all deposits, but shall instead be deducted from the Total Purchase Price, and the Total Purchase Price shall be amended accordingly and so indicated on the Statement of Adjustments.

1.2 If, on the date of closing, the actual, verified balance of the existing mortgage is more than the figure stated on the "Assumption of Mortgage" line, the difference shall be deducted from the total of all deposits, and shall not be added to the Total Purchase Price, it being understood and agreed that the total of all monies paid to the seller, either by deposit or balance payable at closing, shall reduce by the amount of the said difference, with the Purchase Price remaining the same.

1.3 If the seller places a new mortgage and the buyer will assume, the Statement of Adjustments will be prepared crediting the buyer for the original principal balance of the new mortgage. The mortgage will be assumed without adjustment credit to the seller for any pay down of mortgage principal.

    The purpose of the above clauses is to confirm that the total buyer's cash, as stated in the "Initial Deposit", "Additional Deposit" lines and "Balance Payable at Closing" are indeed maximums, and shall not be adjusted upwards for any reason. The minimum total buyer's cash shall always be at least $1.00 so that there is never a negative cash to close for the seller to pay. In addition, the following clauses also apply.

2.1 The buyer shall get the benefit of any property taxes already paid or to be paid by the seller to the tax collection authority or to a mortgage tax account with a lender and shall not be reimbursed or adjusted for by the buyer.

2.2 The seller is responsible for the current year's taxes, without adjustment, as well as any property taxes in arrears by the seller at the closing date or adjustment date shall remain the responsibility of the seller to pay.

| _____ | _____ |
| Witness | Seller |
| _____ | _____ |
| Witness | Seller |
| _____ | _____ |
| Witness | Buyer |
| _____ | _____ |
| Witness | Buyer |

# TIP #73: CALCULATE THE *TOTAL* CASH REQUIRED TO CLOSE.

*Savvy investors base their bottom-line calculations on solid data and informed estimates.*

Ask a group of real estate-wise investors about the "hidden costs" of a real estate deal and you'll see knowing smiles cross their faces. That's because, at one time or another, they have been caught with a "hidden cost" at closing. They forgot to factor something in, or some cost came as a total surprise. Sophisticated investors only get caught once! Then they take that experience and add the item to their due diligence checklists.

The reality is it takes money to close a real estate deal—much more money than you need to cover the down payment and legal costs. Novice investors may try to tell you the up-front costs of a real estate purchase are pretty easy to calculate. If you buy a $100,000 property, a conventional first mortgage would be about $75,000. That means you need $25,000 for a down payment and $1,200 for legal costs and you're in. Right? Wrong!

Sophisticated real estate investors use the Property Analyzer Form developed by the Real Estate Investment Network (REIN™) to walk them through the total costs associated with buying a particular property. This form covers the obvious and not-so-obvious costs and it ensures you do not get caught short of cash at the day of closing. To help you prepare for the real costs, here is a list and brief description of the closing cost items most commonly forgotten.

## Taxes
GST: This applies to new housing—and to some homes with substantial renovations. There may be a rebate available to investors (see GST tips, Part 9).

Property taxes: It's surprising how often these are forgotten at closing. The cost depends on how much of the tax has been prepaid by the vendor and how many months are left in the local tax year. Your lawyer and the lawyer for the vendor should make an accurate adjustment for this, but in some cases the information you get may not be 100% accurate. Do a little homework yourself.

Land transfer tax: In some provinces across Canada, the provincial government demands a "piece of the pie" every time a property passes from one party to another. Each of these provinces has its own guidelines and formulas for calculating this tax. Make sure you are prepared for this cost by knowing in advance your local land transfer tax formula.

 **KEY INSIGHT**

In some provinces there are situations that do not warrant the land transfer tax, such as when one family member sells to another, or when the family farm is sold or transferred to a child. Have your lawyer look to see if your situation fits any of the exemptions.

### Insurance

Mortgage insurance premium and application fee: Mortgage insurance is one of the most expensive life insurance options out there. It is designed to ensure that if the party responsible for the mortgage dies, the mortgage gets paid off. It's a good idea, especially for a homeowner, but most sophisticated investors and homeowners decline the bank's expensive coverage and arrange for a third-party life insurance with the beneficiary. It's set up to pay off the mortgage, with any remainder going to pay a relative or charity of their choice.

Property insurance: It has become increasingly difficult to get great insurance coverage for rental properties, but this coverage is an absolute essential to have in place before you take possession (and will be one of the conditions of a mortgage). Because there are a limited number of quality insurance companies willing to work with the average investor, you will find the costs quite high. Check with an investment real estate insurance broker well in advance of closing on a property.

 **KEY INSIGHT**

Because it is getting more difficult to insure certain rental properties, it is highly recommended that you include a clause in your purchase offer that allows you to check if the property is insurable or not. Include this statement: "Subject to property being insurable satisfactorily to the buyer."

## Other Fees/Expenses

Lawyer (notary) fee: Find out in advance what your closing lawyer will charge. The lawyer will take these funds out of the monies you provide for closing.

Disbursements: These are unavoidable government and registration fees for the transfer of the property and are often worked into the bill from your lawyer for legal fees.

Appraisal fee: In most cases, a bank will require an independent valuation or appraisal of the property. Appraisal costs vary wildly, depending on the region and size of property. If you have a good, long-standing working relationship with your banker or mortgage broker, you can often work with them to pay some or all of the appraisal fee.

Survey and compliance fee (Real Property Report): This is the cost of having a survey done on the property and having the local government stamp that it still fits the guidelines.

Title insurance: This has become increasingly popular over the last few years as a replacement for the above-mentioned survey. Although the costs are very similar to a formal survey, the added benefits are well worth pursuing. Do note that different title insurance companies offer different coverage. You need to research the options and make sure you get the coverage you need to fulfil your requirements at the bank.

Prepaid utility bills: In rare cases, a vendor may have prepaid their utilities in order to get a discount. If this has occurred, the vendor will want compensation for any remaining credit.

Service charges for utility hookups: There is a fee to transfer utilities from the vendor's account to yours. New investors are sometime caught off-guard by recent utility company demands for a large deposit prior to opening up an account. We've heard of demands as high as $2,000-plus-deposit for small, multi-family properties.

Moving costs: If you are moving to the property, make sure your contingency plan includes the money to cover the move and the cost of cleaning the new property.

Condominium fees: If your vendor is not current with their condo fees, you could be responsible for these missed payments, depending on the jurisdiction. This can quickly add up to thousands of dollars. Have your lawyer check on this figure early in the process.

Home inspection fees: For each property a sophisticated investor purchases, a detailed inspection should be done. Make sure it is completed by a licensed expert with liability insurance. There are many people out there who call themselves home inspectors. Make sure you're dealing with a legitimate one.

Renovation and repairs: In about 75% of the properties you buy, some renovations or fix-ups will be required to make the property liveable or to bring it up to your rental standards. Factor these in from the beginning of your analysis. This figure can be as low as $1,000, or cost tens of thousands of dollars.

Water quantity and quality certificate (for homes with well service): If the property is on a well and septic system, you will want an expert to test the quality of both.

Staying Power Fund: Every rental property you have should have its own reserve fund to cover at least one month of mortgage and taxes. (More is better!) Do not think of this as money you might not need. Think of it as money you will need to cover a vacancy or repair.

## What do you need to do?

 COMPLETE THE PROPERTY ANALYZER FORM

You can review the form in *Real Estate Investing in Canada* by Don R. Campbell and commit to making *real* costs part of your business plan. Understand this form is a critical part of a non-emotional investment system.

### ⌖ RED FLAG

> Never ever skip the Property Analyzer step. It is specifically designed to make sure you remember *all* the costs of operating and purchasing a property. It eliminates surprises.

## TIP #74: INCLUDE A COVER LETTER WITH THE OFFER TO PURCHASE.

*Cover letters boost the chance of offer acceptance.*

Do you want to give your offer a significantly greater chance of acceptance? Then add a cover letter to every offer to purchase you submit. This letter will clearly define what you are offering the vendor and why. It clarifies communications and allows the vendor to make a better-informed decision on your offer.

## What do you need to do?

### MAKE IT DEAL-SPECIFIC

Write a letter addressed specifically to the vendor that clearly communicates why she should accept your offer. Highlight any aspects of the offer she will find most attractive based on your assessment of her motivation for selling.

If the closing date helps the vendor's need to vacate one home for another, draw attention to that point. If the purchase price is only slightly lower than the asking price, explain why it's fair given the current market or the results of your home inspection. If you are asking for any special compensation based on obviously required renovations, clearly state to the vendor why this work must be done.

Add a line or two about your experience and perhaps a couple of testimonials from previous vendors from whom you've bought property.

Treat the vendor with respect. If the vendor is a homeowner who has taken obvious pride in the property, comment on the property's condition. If the vendor is an investor, focus on the deal's numbers.

Always sign and date this letter and include your contact information as well as that of your real estate agent.

### WRITE ONE LETTER FOR EVERY OFFER

Sophisticated investors may make more than one offer on a property. This allows the vendor to choose which ever offer best suits their needs. Use separate cover letters to draw attention to the details of each offer.

### AVOID MISREPRESENTATION OR MISCOMMUNICATION

A formal offer to purchase (using a form you developed for your region) helps you make exactly the offer you want to make. A cover letter helps you convey your message to the vendor. It ensures a vendor gets the message you want, versus someone else's biased interpretation of what you want from the deal. Your letter may, for example, draw attention to how your offer facilitates the resolution of a specific vendor motivation, be it a price or possession date.

**KEY INSIGHT**

Make sure this cover letter forms a part of the offer to purchase and is delivered directly with and attached to the formal offer.

**OPTIMIZE YOUR LETTER'S IMPACT**

The letter should be brief and to the point. Always sign in blue ink, so the vendor knows it's not a photocopy. Staple the letter to the offer so they can be presented together.

If it is addressed to a homeowner, and you have very clear handwriting, feel free to hand-write the letter. Sometimes this can be less intimidating.

 **KEY INSIGHT**

Not everyone uses cover letters, or is familiar with the strategy. Ignore those who tell you "we don't do that here," or "it's not necessary." This is your strategy. Successful investors know it works and that's why you've adopted it.

## TIP #75: THE LAWYER GETS THE CHEQUE.

*This is not a tip.* **It's a rule.**

You've done your due diligence, the deal still looks good and you're ready to write a deposit cheque to hold the property while the last of your conditions are being met. This is often called the initial deposit and it is sent along to the vendor with the initial offer.

A lot of trouble can arise from these deposits and there are a lot of misconceptions about their purpose. With more than 20 years of real estate investment experience behind each of this book's authors, we are confident in telling you your offer will be taken seriously as long as the deposit cheque is at least $1,000. *There is no reason to attach an initial deposit cheque for more than this amount as that will have little or no effect on the vendor's acceptance.*

What you can do is provide the vendor with an initial deposit of $1,000, then increase that to a higher amount upon removal of all your conditions. Write this into the offer to purchase and explain it in your cover letter.

After you've decided how to structure your deposit, the question always arises: To whom should the deposit cheque be made out?

The answer is very, very simple. It is *never, ever* given directly to the vendor. The legal recourse to get it back if the deal doesn't go through is long and painful and puts you in a vulnerable position. The initial deposit *must* go into a trust account that is held on your behalf. In most cases, this will be your lawyer's trust account. It is increasingly rare for this cheque to go to *your* real estate agent's trust account (not the vendor's agent).

## What do you need to do?

• Write the cheque to your lawyer, in trust (i.e., Ritchie Mill Law Office in Trust).
• Never write the cheque to the vendor, no matter how tempting it is.
• Don't write the cheque to the vendor's lawyer in trust.

Always keep the cheque in your control. You don't have a relationship with the vendor's lawyer or his real estate agent. This fact never changes—even if the deal is with your own mother. Your lawyer is the only human being on earth who should get that cheque.

 **KEY INSIGHT**

> In most cases, the deposit will not be a problem. It becomes a part of the monies used to close on the property and the vendor gets it at closing. However, the one time you break this "lawyer's trust" rule will be the time the deposit goes into dispute. You do not want that to happen because it will take months before you get even a whiff of your money again.

## TIP #76: HOW TO AVOID THE HASSLE OF "HURRY UP AND WAIT."

*"The cheque is in the mail" just doesn't cut it!*

When dealing with funds for closing, you should always deal strictly in funds that are immediately cashable. This goes from the money you provide your lawyer for closing, to the funds your lawyer uses to buy the property, to the funds sent to you by the lenders as proceeds of a mortgage.

Most law firms that focus on investment real estate know that only certified or electronically transferred funds should be used. However, there are still horror stories out there from rookie investors using unsophisticated lawyers or notaries who don't understand that it takes about 10 days for an uncertified cheque to clear and another couple of days to process. If the bank or lender is not given clear instructions about how to handle this, they will post the required funds, using regular mail. This holds up closing by weeks and will cost the investor countless dollars in additional interest and possible penalties.

Make sure your lawyer has a system that eliminates the old "hurry up and wait" routine.

##  RED FLAG

Veteran and rookie investors play the waiting game far too often. It is even more disconcerting when the funds don't show up on time and no one in the loop (the banks or lawyers) can advise where they may be. The whole process equals a financial headache for investors. In addition, if the funds are coming to you because you sold or refinanced a property, it's *your* money—but it's not in your account.

## What do you need to do?

**USE A BANK DRAFT OR CERTIFIED FUNDS**

Avoid the "hurry up and wait" hassle completely by asking your lawyer to use a bank draft or a certified cheque to send funds to the lender.

## SOPHISTICATED INVESTOR TIP

Some experienced real estate investors take the whole issue of fund transfers to another level and refuse to use even a certified cheque. As far as the bank is concerned, the money leaves your account as soon as a cheque is certified. If that cheque goes missing, you lose that money and it's very, very hard to get it back. With a bank draft, however, you keep one copy of the draft and, if the other goes missing, you get a form from the bank, fill it out with a lawyer, then get another bank draft. Too many investors also don't realize that certified cheques can actually have stop payments placed on them with many financial institutions. Don't always count on a certified cheque being as good as cash!

## USE A PROFESSIONAL COURIER SERVICE

Many lenders have a policy of mailing cheques to personal addresses, but courier them to businesses. Make sure you request that any substantial funds being sent to you be couriered, not mailed. This gives you the opportunity to trace the process and avoid the "cheque's in the mail" syndrome.

Remember, no matter how large the cheque they are sending you, it is small potatoes to the bank and it won't be as important to them as it is to you. Avoid problems by being clear in your instructions.

## DRAW ATTENTION TO THE RIGHT ADDRESS

A surprising number of cheques go astray because they are sent to the wrong address! In real estate transactions, there is a tendency to send the cheque to the mortgage address, which in the investor's case is often an investment property with a tenant in it. Prevent that from happening by emphasizing the correct address in your letter.

When you or your lawyer advises the banker as to the address, shine a big spotlight on the address you wish the cheque to go to. If it is different from the property you are purchasing, make that abundantly clear! Make the correct address physically noticeable with capital letters in bold print, for example:

**John Q. Investor**
**123 Investment Street**
**Any Town, Any Province**
**Postal Code**

As with anything involved with investment real estate, the small details are often the most critical. Make sure you design a checklist that reminds you of all the little details along the way. In addition, ask to see your lawyers' closing checklist to see if there is anything you wish to add to it. If they don't have a checklist, be concerned, as checklists are really the only way to ensure that nothing is missed along the way.

# Tip #77: Know the Assets You're Buying.

*Clear communications will help you get the assets you expect—the good, the bad and the ugly.*

Surprises are the investor's worst nightmare. Pressure and excitement to close a deal often lead to major mistakes because of a perceived lack of time for proper due diligence. These mistakes or surprises will cost you money, either immediately or very soon in the future.

The bottom line? When it comes to knowing what you're about to buy, you need to follow your due diligence system to the letter, including visiting every single unit you're about to buy and uncovering the real facts about the tenants.

Make sure that you never, ever get pressured into skipping any of your vital due-diligence steps. Whether buying a large multi-family property or a single-family condo, the rules are always the same and they are designed to eliminate costly surprises.

## What do you need to do?

**INSPECT EVERY UNIT, NO QUESTION!**

There is no compromise on this point. You either know *exactly* what you are buying, or admit you're jumping in blindly. Imagine your shock when you take possession and the photos don't really match the condition of the property on possession day! It wouldn't be the first time that happened with real estate.

For instance, at the early stage of a purchase of a large multi-family property, you may be able to inspect a few sample units before you submit your offer to purchase. You should ask to see one of the best condition units, one of the worst and one in between. This gives you a quick overview and lets you get a feel for the property and how it's being managed. Since many vendors don't want you disturbing their tenants unless you have a serious offer on the table, be prepared to get access to only a minimal number of suites before you give them an offer.

However, do *not* remove your final offer conditions until you have seen each and every room in each and every suite. This can take a lot of time, but it is critical that you know the full condition of what you are buying. Even a detailed engineering report won't cover the condition of all the suites. It is up to you to physically walk through every one. Take your prospective property manager along with you for insights into the property's potential, both good and bad.

Many sophisticated investors bring along their building inspector or handyman as a second pair of eyes on these inspection tours. Having a professional at your side is way better than trusting your instincts.

## Ⓢ SOPHISTICATED INVESTOR ACTION STEP

Take photos of every room in every suite and keep track of which photos go with which suite. To make this easier, take a photo of the door number before entering the suite. You'll know that all the photos after it, up to the next door photo, are of that suite. Make sure you take additional photos of damage or any other condition of interest for future negotiations. These photos serve two purposes: 1) They are a visual record of the condition and the assets that form a part of your offer to purchase, and 2) You can use them to schedule and plan future renovations.

## ⓥ RED FLAG

Haste makes waste. If you rush through the inspection or due-diligence process, surprises you would have caught if you had been more careful will raise their ugly heads only *after* you own the property. A thorough inspection saves you money.

### GET THE LEASES AND RENT ROLLS

Look at the leases and rent rolls from the month previous to your purchase. Look for anomalies (lots of move-outs, lots of unpaid rent, etc.). These may be a sign the vendor is moving the tenants to their other buildings, or that they weren't great tenants to start with. Never rely on an old rent roll and leases list.

Examine every lease and compare it to the formal rent roll. Make sure the rent amounts noted in the leases are the same as those listed on the rent roll. If you can't get a copy of the written lease agreement, use a rental confirmation form, sometimes called a tenant estoppel certificate. It's a form an existing tenant signs stating his rent, security deposit, expected discounts and move-in date.

For more on how to avoid problems with existing tenants, see Part 8 on tenancy issues.

## Tip #78: *Caveat Emptor*: Never Remove Conditions Until the Report Is In!

*If the property is worth buying, it's worth getting the full report!*

Most vendors are honest citizens, with no malicious intent. Now that we have that out of the way, you need to know you should never trust a vendor.

It is your job as a sophisticated investor to ensure you live by the *caveat emptor* credo. Loosely translated, it means "let the buyer beware" and, since you are the buyer, you must be aware.

Investing in real estate is a serious business and must be treated as such. That means every time there is to be an agreement between the vendor and purchaser, it must be detailed in writing and be signed by both parties. Verbal agreements may well be comfortable for everyone, but they are very difficult to uphold when "selective" memory kicks in down the road.

The second part of the *caveat emptor* warning involves the condition of the property and disclosure by the vendor of any "issues of concern." One legal view holds that if a seller knows something that would affect any reasonable purchaser's buying decision, then the seller has to disclose that information. This would be wonderful if it worked in the real world, but sadly it doesn't.

In real life, it is *caveat emptor*, or buyer beware. Investors should understand that *caveat emptor* is a large part of real estate law. Proof of a seller's misrepresentation is difficult to establish and there is absolutely no guarantee of what will happen if you go to court. That's why it's best to make purchasing decisions using *caveat emptor* as your guide.

For new homes, old homes and in-between homes, the sophisticated real estate investor's rule of thumb is always the same: Hire a professional home inspector and make sure his inspection report is acceptable before final conditions are removed from the deal.

# What do you need to do?

### MAKE INSPECTIONS A PRIORITY
Every purchase should be contingent on the results of an independent, licensed, professional home inspection. Think of a professional home inspection as inexpensive insurance on your investment. If the report indicates the property has problems that will be expensive to fix, then the cost of the report is a cheap way to insure you aren't stuck with a money pit. If the report comes back relatively clean, then the money was well spent for peace of mind.

A home inspection includes:

• A room-by-room walk-through of the home
• A detailed report with items ranging from a broken cabinet door to a leaking roof

- A detailed review of all the infrastructure of the property, mechanical, structural and aesthetic.

Include the following sentence in your offer: "Subject to the buyer obtaining a building inspection satisfactory to the buyer within 14 days of acceptance."

###  RED FLAG

Your inspector may have a software package that prints out a good-looking report, but that doesn't mean he's done a detailed inspection. A sophisticated investor doesn't care about the look of the report; we care about the quality of the building. Don't get fooled by flash and colour photos.

### 🛈 KEY INSIGHT

The details of a professional home inspection will help you calculate additional expenses that might be incurred with a property purchase. Some reports may lead you to walk away from a deal. Others may lead to more extensive negotiations where you ask the seller to do the necessary repairs, or to compensate you for them. Either way, a quality inspection means you're the big winner.

### GET THE DETAILS IN WRITING — PART 1

With *caveat emptor* as your guiding principle, get everything in the deal in writing and have it signed by the vendor. This is the rule of thumb for changes too. If the vendor agrees to leave the lawnmower and it was not a part of the original offer, then simply write that up and have it signed and dated by both parties. Similarly, if the vendor agrees to clean up the property, be very clear, in writing, what that means to you and what it will cost him if it isn't done. The written agreement for that condition could say, "Vendor agrees to remove derelict car from backyard on or before closing or will pay the purchaser $1,000 toward removal."

### GET THE DETAILS IN WRITING — PART 2

In some cases, a real estate agent will agree to take care of an issue as a way to get the deal done. This could take the form of monetary compensation, or stipulate specific work to be done. If this occurs, make sure you have the agreement in writing. Selective memory will cost you money!

**KEY INSIGHT**

This tip makes it sound like you shouldn't trust anyone when buying real estate—and that is not true. In almost all cases, the deal flows perfectly well and all agreements are fulfilled. Due diligence is about the exceptions to the rule. By making sure you do your own research and require all agreements to be signed and dated, you have a strong argument toward a settlement that works in your favour. *An additional note*: If someone agrees to something but is unwilling to put it in writing, take it as a signal that you've called their bluff and now know they probably weren't sincere about meeting that promise in the first place. That's good information to have up-front. Remember, great investments mean there are no surprises!

## TIP #79: AVOID PLACING FIXED DATES IN ANY PURCHASE CONTRACT.

*All parties to a real estate deal should be looking for a deal they can successfully close. Learn to focus on that successful close, but avoid setting dates that box you in.*

After you have been investing in real estate for a while, you come to know how long it takes to get things done. For instance, in some jurisdictions it takes at least 14 days to get a land transfer registered, while in others it takes substantially less time. In busy areas, getting a lender's approved appraiser out to the property can take weeks, while in other areas they can come the next day.

It is your job, as an investor, to know how long each step of the purchase takes and to use that information to be realistic in the condition dates you put into your offer to purchase. Conditions are clauses within an offer that stipulate items of business that must be met before a contract is unconditionally valid. The majority of conditions are set by the purchaser, but both parties can set conditions.

For example, these can include a condition for the vendor to arrange appropriate financing or a professional inspection by a certain date.

Another key date to be realistic on is the date of closing (or when you take possession of the property). If you know that it usually takes 21 days for the banks, lawyers and land titles office to complete a transfer, don't set unrealistic expectations with the vendor by telling them you'll close in 14 days.

## 🚩 RED FLAG

If you put an unrealistic closing date in your offer—just to get the deal done—you will box yourself in. That leaves you with only two options as the deadline approaches. 1) You will have to pay a large premium to all of the parties involved (banks, lawyers, inspectors, appraisers, etc.) to get them to move you up to the front of the line. This will cost you both money and reputation. 2) You will have to go back to the expectant vendor and ask for an extension on the closing date, thus opening you up for paying additional compensation or being in a situation where the vendor refuses, leaving you with a completely unrealistic deadline. In the worst-case scenario, you don't close on time and have to forfeit your full deposit to the vendor.

# What do you need to do?

### ALWAYS INCLUDE YOUR LAWYER IN THE DEAL

Every offer should include the subject line: "Subject to the buyer's lawyer's approval within 14 days of acceptance." This clause gives you a chance to have your lawyer review the purchase contract to ensure that everything is clear and acceptable and the timelines are realistic.

If you're working with a real estate lawyer, he will want to check out your offers to ensure there are no landmines hidden in the contract. If they do find any issues, this clause allows you to address them before the contract becomes unconditional.

Be prepared for some vendors to request less than 14 days. This can work—as long as your lawyer is available in that shorter period. Check your lawyer's availability in advance.

### AVOID SPECIFIC DATES

Sophisticated investors avoid specific dates on their contract conditions. Instead, use a specific number of days *after acceptance*. For example, rather than a statement that says, "Subject to buyer's lawyer's approval by May 11, 2006," use a statement such as the following: "Subject to buyer's lawyer's approval within 14 days of acceptance."

This protects you from being under any additional time constraints if negotiations go back and forth before the vendor agrees to the contract a couple of weeks after you start the process. Make sure you have designed the deal so the clock starts ticking after all the parties agree to the terms of the offer.

## MAKE THE POSSESSION DATE/CLOSING DATE CONDITIONAL

In most jurisdictions, the possession date and closing date are the same thing: the date the property becomes yours. Choose a realistic date that gives you time to get your financing in place and time for your lawyer to complete the transaction. This should be no fewer than 30 days from the date the vendor accepts your offer, and preferably longer. You will only know what is realistic in your jurisdiction by asking a veteran real estate investor or real estate lawyer.

## GIVE YOURSELF TIME TO ARRANGE FINANCING

If you need to arrange financing to buy a property, include a conditional clause such as: "Subject to buyer obtaining financing satisfactory to the buyer within _____ (insert number) days from acceptance of offer."

Always be realistic. You need to give your banker (with whom you are trying to build a long-term and mutually beneficial relationship!) time to arrange the financing deal you want. Sophisticated investors don't rush!

Speak with your banker or mortgage broker in advance to understand what timelines they see for mortgage approvals. Keep up to date on this timeline. It is a constantly shifting number based on how busy the bank's underwriters are and the region in which you are buying.

 **KEY INSIGHT**

Note the above clause clearly states the financing must be acceptable to you, the buyer. This clause helps you maintain the option of not accepting "any financing" you can get.

## FACTOR IN PROPERTY INSPECTION TIME

We've said it before and we'll say it again. A professional and well-respected home inspector should go through each and every property you buy. Make this a routine cost of doing business by including a condition such as the following in every offer you make: "Subject to the buyer obtaining a building inspection satisfactory to the buyer within 14 days of acceptance."

A quality home inspector should provide you with a complete report on everything, the good and the bad, around the property. Your goal is to gain useable information to guide the purchase offer. This condition lets you walk away from a deal and get your deposit back if your inspector finds a major problem.

As noted in Tip #78, a property inspection report may lead you to re-open negotiations with the vendor. You may ask him to do the necessary repairs, or request compensation for having to do them after the deal closes.

## Tip #80: Your Offer Must *Not* Be an Open Offer!

*Every deal should include one irrevocable date. That's the date a deal works, or both parties move on.*

The previous tip shows how conditional dates give you time to complete your due diligence and arrange appropriate financing. Conditional dates also make sure your lawyer has time to review a deal and enable you to make your deal contingent on the results of a quality property inspection.

The one key date that many rookie purchasers ignore is the "irrevocable date." This is the length of time your offer is valid for acceptance by the vendor—and it should never be open-ended. Your offer is a legal document that binds you to fulfil many different agreements. It is a huge mistake to allow this to be floating around in perpetuity!

### ⚑ RED FLAG

If you set a date that's too far in the future, you give your vendor or your vendor's real estate agent time to "shop your deal." This means he or she can talk to other purchasers and use your deal as a negotiating tool. You might not end up with the property. Worse yet, your hard work will be used as a catalyst to get the price higher! This is not a fair business practice. But it happens—and you can keep it from happening to you.

## What do you need to do?

### SET A SHORT FUSE

Set a date that tells the vendor how long you will keep your offer open for consideration. You want this date to be not very far in the future, but still give the vendor enough time to consider the offer. Many sophisticated investors use a time frame of "no longer than three days."

### STICK WITH YOUR PLAN

Be clear in the cover letter about how long the offer is open for acceptance. Tell them you are currently looking at a number of properties and have chosen theirs as the one you want. Let them know you can't wait forever for their decision as you will buy a property very soon and need to know whether theirs is it. I like to use the sentence, "Our lives are both busy, so there is no need to waste any of your or my valuable time ..."

## TIP #81: MAKE POSSESSION DATES PART OF THE NEGOTIATION.

*Know the implications of a changed possession date.*

Changing the possession date of an original deal can be a way to help out a buyer or seller. It may improve the buyer's ability to have repairs or renovations done before the property is placed on the rental or sale market. It may even help a motivated seller move on with his or her life. Beware: *It can also cost you money.*

Possession dates should be negotiated with instruction from your lawyer. That way, your lawyer can re-do the calculations. A new assumption date, for example, may mean you are now responsible for an additional mortgage payment. The interest portion of that payment will increase your costs and that impacts your business plan.

## What do you need to do?

### CHECK THE DATES

Check your contract and mortgage payment date before agreeing to any changes in possession. Have your lawyer rework the mortgage payment, tax and any other applicable adjustments.

# TIP #82: USE CLOSING DATES STRATEGICALLY TO MAXIMIZE YOUR CASH FLOW.

*Maximize your cash flow and minimize your vacancies when you strategically choose the appropriate closing dates.*

This tip builds on the previous two tips. It also demonstrates how sophisticated investors put in an extra 10% of effort to maximize their profit potential. Here, the investor must acknowledge how closing dates impact their cash flow—and then use that information to give their own portfolio a welcome cash infusion!

## What do you need to do?

UNDERSTAND THAT THE STRATEGY DIFFERS IF THE PROPERTY IS CURRENTLY TENANTED OR IS/WILL BE VACANT WHEN YOU TAKE POSSESSION

### Currently Tenanted Properties

Pick the fifth day of the month for your closing date. This gives current owners time to collect the entire rent for the month. It also means you receive the pro-rated rent for that month as a discount on your final cash-to-close statement from your closing agent (typically your real estate lawyer).

The timeline for a currently tenanted property, using November (30 days in the month) as an example, looks like this:

- Offer accepted Friday, September 23.
- Conditions removed Friday, October 7 (14 days after accepted offer).
- Closing date Saturday, November 5 (29 days for closing).
- Monthly rent $800, collected on the first of November by current owner.
- You receive a credit on your cash-to-close statement for 25 of the 30 days of rent ($666.67).

If you want to boost your cash flow:

- Choose November 5 as the closing date.
- The first full mortgage payment will be due one month after closing (December 5).

- Phone the bank that holds your mortgage and ask to move your payments to the first of the next month (January 1).
- The bank will either add the interest portion for the month to the principal balance, or require you to make an interest-only payment for the first 26 days (Dec. 5-Dec. 31).
- The net effect is that you collect almost three months' rent before you have to make your first full mortgage payment.

| | |
|---|---|
| November: receive a rent credit for 25 days | $666.67 |
| December: collect full rent | $800.00 |
| January: collect full rent | $800.00 |
| Total | $2,267.67 |

Pay your first full mortgage payment on January 1, and collect almost three months' rent before you make your first full mortgage payment.

 **KEY INSIGHT**

This approach equals a reduction in the cash to close funds that come out of your pocket. The approach also standardizes all mortgage payments to the same day (1st of the month) and lets you collect almost three months' rent before paying your first full mortgage payment.

### Vacant Properties

Here, you want to choose the last Thursday of the month, four to six weeks after your condition removal date. The key with this strategy is to negotiate right-of-access prior to closing, after all conditions are removed. This can be as simple as including the following condition on your offer: "The seller to allow access to buyer upon condition removal and 24 hours' notice to show prospective tenants and/or contractors."

Once you get acceptance of this condition on your offer and after you have removed all conditions, you or your property manager can start marketing this property to your potential tenants. You will have four to six weeks to find an equity-building tenant or tenants!

Renters typically move in the last weekend of the month. If you take possession on the last Thursday of the month, your new tenants will move in almost as soon as you take possession. This eliminates any vacancy issues!

Here's how the strategy looks:

• Offer accepted Friday, October 7
• Conditions removed Friday, October 21 (14 days after accepted offer)
• Closing date Thursday, November 24 (last Thursday of month, almost five weeks after condition removal).

Now factor in the advantage of moving your mortgage payment date:

• If your closing date is November 24, your first full mortgage payment would be December 24.
• Ask the bank that holds the mortgage to move your first full mortgage payment till January 1.

| Summary: | |
| --- | --- |
| December rent | $800 |
| January rent | $800 |
| Total | $1,600 |

Pay your first full mortgage payment on January 1. Collect two months' rent before making your first full mortgage payment.

### 🄌 KEY INSIGHT

Sophisticated investors use information to make money. This strategy gives you five weeks to market vacant (or soon-to-be-vacant) property to find equity-building tenants. These tenants move in almost as soon as you take possession—and a change in mortgage dates means you put two months' rent into the bank before you make your first full mortgage payment.

## TIP #83: GUARD AGAINST FRAUD AND IDENTITY THEFT.

*Title insurance helps deals close—and close faster.*

When a lawyer acts for you on a purchase transaction, he searches title, checks the government records at the registry office and does

off-title-type searches to make sure you have a marketable title to the property at every level.

But you know what they say: Mistakes happen.

Title insurance is a tool your lawyer can use to make sure you have a
marketable title after a deal closes on a property with fewer than three units.
It should never replace the basic due diligence of title searches. Once it's
on your title, however, you won't have to worry about details your lawyer
may have missed, or fret about errors made by the municipality. Because it's
faster to get than title search data, title insurance also speeds up the process
of closing a deal.

## What do you need to do?

**ASK YOUR LAWYER FOR TITLE INSURANCE**

Title insurance is becoming more prevalent in today's real estate markets—
and it's cheap insurance for investors. Investors and their lawyers like it
because it's faster than municipal searches and comes with the added pro-
tections against mistakes or zoning issues. Even though it's pretty standard
practice, depending on your jurisdiction you may have to ask for it.

**CONSIDER THE REAL COSTS**

Title insurance has largely replaced surveys in most regions of the country.
Surveys have their place, but a land survey on a single-family home will cost
about $1,000. Title insurance will cost you roughly the same as a survey but
comes with many added benefits.

Sophisticated investors know most insurers pay out. That means you
won't have to hire a lawyer to sue your lawyer for negligence if it turns out your
title has a problem. If you have to sue, you will have to *demonstrate* the services
you're claiming weren't done and were part of your lawyer's retainer.

Title insurance also covers errors made by the municipality.

**GUARD AGAINST FRAUD — THE NEW HIDDEN DANGER IN CANADA**

Title insurance provides some protection from title fraud, whereby people
impersonate the title owners and register or transfer a mortgage by using
fake identification.

**GO RETRO!**

You can keep your bellbottoms and disco records in the closet for now. When we talk about going retro, we mean you should buy retroactive title insurance on properties you already own.

Ask your lawyer about the benefits of buying retroactive title insurance for properties already in your portfolio. In some cases it might be a waste of time and money. In others, where there are potential issues with the title, zoning or other compliance issues, retroactive title insurance can save the day.

# PART 8

## Tenancy Issues:
## Make Defence
## Your Best Offence

# TIP #84: GO FOR THE (PROPERTY MANAGEMENT) GOLD.

*Quality property management makes—not costs—you money.*

What do vacancies, unnecessary repairs, tenants who don't pay the rent and tenants who won't leave all have in common? Inadequate property management. And it only gets worse! Problems with deferred maintenance, calls in the middle of the night, ruined vacations and costly legal bills related to tenancy are all solidly linked to poor property management.

## What do you need to do?

**PAY ATTENTION**

Quality property management is a cornerstone of successful real estate investment. It's also the one item market newcomers are quickest to write off, since they don't get the salient investment point: Efficient property management makes you money!

**BUYING IS EASY. MANAGING IS HARD WORK**

Think about how long it takes you to buy a property. Even with strict attention to the due diligence of your system, we're talking hours, maybe days. Property management lasts the lifetime of your investment.

 **KEY INSIGHT**

Poor property management is one of the biggest single causes of real estate investment failure. Quality property management makes life easy, keeps the income rolling in and helps keep you confidently investing in more properties.

**KNOW THE FINANCIAL COSTS**

Poor property management equals decreased revenue, negative cash flow, substandard maintenance, high tenant turnover and increased advertising costs. Often times, hiring a high-quality property management company is well worth the cost (usually running from 4% to 11% of gross rental income).

Your job doesn't end when you hire a quality manager. It's now your responsibility to ensure you manage the managers and make sure they are truly doing an amazing job for you. Remember, the bottom-line results are your responsibility, even if you are not actively managing.

### RECOGNIZE THE EMOTIONAL COST

Properties have two costs. The first is the obvious financial one. The second and much more important cost is emotional. Sometimes a property looks like a good investment. But after you own it for a period of time, you realize it keeps you up worrying at night. This is a sign the emotional cost is not worth the financial reward. Sell the property and move on to a property that has a lower emotional cost.

Poor property management equals higher stress levels, sleepless nights and lost relationships. Visit www.realestateinvestingincanada.com to discover the latest property management and real estate investing systems for Canada.

### HIRE A FIRST-RATE MANAGER FIRST

There is a vast difference in quality among property management companies, and it is not reflected in the prices they charge.

You can contract full-service property management companies that do everything for you, then send you the cheque at the end of the month. This will cost you a monthly percentage of the collected rent. If you wish to do more of the management yourself, you can contract a rent-up service. They find you a quality tenant and usually charge a one-time fee.

No matter what level of management you choose, make sure you complete your due diligence on the company. Ask for references, drive by properties they manage and see for yourself what they offer in terms of quality and attention to detail.

Talk to the tenants in properties they are managing so you can gauge the relationship and their responsiveness to the tenants. Recognize the vast difference between managing a property through times of peak versus low demand. Make sure the company you hire has experience in the good times—and knows what to do when the rental scene gets tougher.

Fellow investors are a good place to get the names of quality management companies. The investing world is not very large and a property management company's poor reputation will spread like wildfire. Even when a company is referred to you, make sure you do your due diligence.

**KEY INSIGHT**

Problems with property management will interfere with your system. Contact your local landlord association or a local chapter of the Real Estate Investment Network to ask about courses on pro-active landlording. Being a proactive landlord will quickly free up your time, reduce your hassles and prove you are an investment realist. You need to think about what to do *when* a problem arises, not *if* a problem arises. Prepare yourself in advance.

## TIP #85: MATTERS SURROUNDING TENANCY RULES.

*Keep your regulatory knowledge current.*

Every province has its own tenancy regulatory board, which is aligned with the federal Department of Consumer and Corporate Affairs. Their regulations guide landlord and tenant issues. (A list of government web sites outlining landlord and tenant laws in each provincial and territorial jurisdiction is provided in the Appendix.)

These rules and regulations are continually changing and it is the landlord's responsibility to work under the most current legislation. In some provinces, the regulations favour the tenant, while in others the legislation is much fairer. Sadly, the rules are typically designed to control bad tenants and landlords. As a sophisticated investor, you want to do whatever you can to ensure you never have to use the majority of the confrontational rules.

Throughout this part, we will discuss how the tenant and landlord relationship can be mutually supportive instead of confrontational.

The names of the various boards vary. In British Columbia, it is the Residential Tenancy Branch. In Alberta it is the Landlord and Tenant Advisory Board and in Ontario it is the Ontario Rental Housing Tribunal (even the name sounds confrontational, doesn't it!).

### What do you need to do?

**CONTACT YOUR LOCAL BOARD**

Use the government web site to find the name of the regulatory body in your province or territory. Download the complete regulations to keep as a reference. Most provinces also have tip sheets or regulation summaries to help you with the most common issues.

Many of the boards also give you a package containing all the pertinent forms for administering your properties and your tenant relationships.

 **RED FLAG**

Not knowing the law is never an excuse for breaking it.

### BE ACTIVE: JOIN A LOCAL OR NATIONAL ASSOCIATION

In real estate investment, as in life, it is best to surround yourself with people who are doing the same thing as you. This helps you avoid making the same mistakes as others and it give you great access to key suppliers and potential mentors.

Attend your landlord association's meetings and be an active member, not a passive one. Use its information packages and take its educational programs. It's apt to cost you more time than money, and the information you glean will be worth every second and every penny.

### CHANGE YOUR MINDSET

If you are convinced tenants are bad and will phone you in the middle of the night to clean out their toilets, get rid of this old myth! It is just not true. A roomful of 600 active real estate investors were recently asked, "How many of you have ever had a middle-of-the-night call from a tenant?" Only two put up their hands and, once we heard their stories, we told them exactly how they could have prevented that call by solving the problem in advance.

A second myth you need to toss aside says the relationship between a tenant and landlord needs to be confrontational. This is absolutely false. The relationship is only confrontational when the landlord hasn't chosen his tenants well, or hasn't worked to build a more supportive relationship. There are literally millions of wonderful, long-term, hassle-free tenants in every community across the country. These tenants will gladly pay all the expenses of operating your property, including the mortgages and taxes. All you have to do is provide them with appropriate housing!

**KEY INSIGHT**

Veteran real estate investor and author Tim Johnson created a definition of a tenant from a landlord's point of view. That definition is something *all* real estate investors need to keep in mind when choosing their tenants. According to Johnson, your tenant is: "A partner in business who will open up the shop each morning and lock it up at night. They will look after security, inform you of problems or potential problems in the business. They will cut the grass, rake the leaves, shovel the snow, pay all the utilities. They will even pay all of your mortgage payments and property taxes. Then, in the end, they will relinquish all monetary interest in the business and walk away, leaving you with the profits."

## TREAT REAL ESTATE LIKE A BUSINESS

Many beginning landlords seem to believe the real estate business is different from other businesses. As you will quickly learn, this is a huge mistake that could cost you thousands of dollars in poor decisions.

For example, stop thinking of your tenants as tenants and begin thinking of them as paying clients. Your job is then focused on attracting good, long-term, paying clients—not tenants. Why is this important? Simply, it gets you out of the "old-world" of real estate advertising (classified ads in the back of a newspaper) and into a whole new world of marketing. You can now look at the marketing strategies used in other industries and transfer them into your business. Always be on the lookout for ways other businesses effectively attract their clients. Then ask yourself, "Can I adopt this strategy in my real estate business?"

Remember, the clients you are trying to attract will be paying you thousands of dollars per year (in rent). An $800 per month renter is not an $800 client—they are a $9,600 client.

Once you understand the importance of this change of mindset, you will start to look at the market from a competitive point of view. Rather than blindly purchasing an investment property because it fits your system, make sure you are doing an analysis of competing properties in the region. What do they have that you don't, and vice versa. Highlight these differences.

## 🕐 Key Insight

Picture your rental property as if it were a video rental store. There are two other competing rental stores in the area and you need to find out how to attract clients to your store versus the competition. You also want to find ways to keep these clients for the long term. Now apply this analogy to rental real estate. You are surrounded by competitive rental units and you must attract the renters, then keep them for a long term. The best way to do that is to provide potential tenants with a clear reason why they should choose your "store" (rental unit) over the competition. If you can't think of a reason right now, you had better start!

## 🚩 Red Flag

Being a lazy investor is a great way to bankruptcy. Step out of the box with your thinking and you'll leave the problems behind in the dust!

## Tip #86: Be Creative in Your Advertising Strategies.

*Learn the key to maximizing your cash flow.*

As in every business, advertising plays a critical part in building cash flow. Advertising is especially critical in the real estate business, because your whole goal is to attract quality tenants who pay top market rents.

With this in mind, we will discuss strategies to make you stand out in both a hot market and a cold market. The key is *not* to follow old beliefs or old strategies. The following details are from a comprehensive 10-year study of sophisticated investors.

## What do you need to do?

DETERMINE WHAT SOURCE OF ADVERTISING IS MOST COST EFFECTIVE IN YOUR MARKET

There are many creative ways to attract tenants in any market. Here are some, both creative and mainstream. Tap into as many as you can to attract the perfect tenant in the least amount of time.

## 🛈 KEY INSIGHT

Classified ads in newspapers will provide you with the least cost-effective way to attract tenants. In some cases, it is still worth the effort and expense. However, you may wish to note that most sophisticated investors attract the best long-term tenants by being pro-active with their marketing. They don't just rely on classified ads.

Here are some proven cost-effective strategies to attracting quality tenants:

1. "For Rent" signs in the window and on the lawn. Most of your tenants will come from this marketing if you do it right.
2. Referrals from current tenants. Ask your good tenants for referrals, and give them incentives for doing so.
3. Share names with your fellow real estate investors. This is another critical reason for surrounding yourself with like-minded real estate investors. Once their suite is filled, they'll often have a few quality prospects left over from their advertising. Tap into that resource.
4. On-line ads.
5. Local military bases.
6. Large construction sites.
7. Human resource departments of major employers.
8. Local police authority, especially one that transfers its members from town to town.
9. University or college newspapers or on-line ads.
10. Flyers on vehicles in nearby office buildings.

### BE CREATIVE

It is important to be creative as you work through this list. Consider where your "target market" would see your advertising. Be different; don't be afraid to stand out. Your job is to attract the type of prospect you want. Remember, the volume of calls is nowhere near as important as the quality of calls.

### HAVE A MARKETING STRATEGY

Having a marketing strategy is critical to your business, whether you are in real estate or auto repair. Without an effective marketing plan you will continually feel as if you are behind the 8-ball. Marketing includes writing ads that will attract positive attention to your suites, from how they look to how they smell.

**🚫 KEY INSIGHT**

As a landlord, attracting and keeping the right tenants—cost-effectively—will be the single most important action you take. Advertising represents a small portion of your overall marketing plan. But once you master advertising, it will lead to higher rents, fewer vacancies, longer tenancies and higher sales prices.

# TIP #87: MAKE THE MOST OF ON-LINE ADVERTISING.

*Guest tip: Jason Leonard, editor-in-chief of Gottarent.com, offers sage advice on how to make the most of your virtual ad campaign.*

Rising vacancy rates, high costs for print advertising and an extremely large user base are the driving forces behind landlords turning to the Internet to source prospective residents.

Early adopting landlords of on-line advertising have been rewarded with lower vacancy rates and higher quality prospects, and are realizing significant savings over those who rely exclusively on print advertising.

Advantages of on-line ads versus print ads:

- There are no restrictions on how much you can say about the property. On-line ads are typically not sold by the word or character.
- You can show photos or give virtual tours of the property. This is especially good for those moving to your city from a distance.
- You can show floor plans.
- An interactive map to the property can give driving directions.
- You can track how many people viewed your ad. You'll know your exact cost per prospect.
- On-line advertising has extremely wide reach. You gain a competitive advantage by finding renters who are moving to your city *before* they move there.
- You can discontinue your advertising as soon as you've found a tenant, and eliminate further calls.

### Reduce Advertising Costs and Manpower Requirements

In most cases, Internet marketing is relatively inexpensive to implement. In fact, if you create a well-written ad on a rental site with good traffic, it will significantly reduce advertising costs while adding efficiency to your operations.

Consider how many calls it would take to deem a $25 Internet advertisement good use of your advertising budget. Twenty, forty, fifty...? Now compare that with what you normally spend in print and the results you get. The truth is the best Internet listing web sites in Canada outperform their print competitors on a cost-per-call basis by a wide margin.

| Medium | Cost per month | # of calls | Cost per call |
|---|---|---|---|
| Internet Ad | $25 | 50 | $0.50 |
| Classified Ad | $200 | 100 | $2.00 |
| Magazine Ad | $500 | 150 | $3.33 |

There are two things to note about the above chart. First, the Internet will almost always produce fewer calls than other mediums, and secondly, your cost per call is always lower than with the other mediums. How is this possible? Internet advertising is inexpensive because it doesn't have the high costs associated with print. These savings are passed on to you.

The Internet draws fewer calls not because fewer renters use the Internet but because on-line ads act as a filter. With the sheer amount of information presented to prospects, only those truly interested in your property will call you. In fact, while a good closing ratio for calls coming in from, say, the newspaper would be 20%, it is not unheard of for more than 50% of prospects from on-line sources to sign a lease. As a result, you also see a savings in the manpower requirements to screen prospects, often an overlooked expense.

### So, who uses the Internet?

I often hear landlords say, "Our clientele doesn't use the Internet." The fact is, almost everyone from every walk of life is now making his or her way on-line. They are accessing the Internet at home, work or school, in libraries, cafes, seniors' centres and community centres. The Internet does not care about one's economic status, age or ethnicity. It would be a huge mistake to assume your target market is not using the Internet, since very few people in society now lack access.

# TIP #88: PROPERLY SCREEN PROSPECTIVE TENANTS.

*Real estate investment is a business. Make sure your due diligence extends to tenant selection.*

Did you think your due diligence was complete after you bought the property? For some unfortunate or unthinking investors, this is true. However, as a sophisticated investor you will quickly learn that doing the extra 10% of due diligence on a potential tenant makes all the difference in the world.

A robust residential real estate market typically spells some trouble for the rental industry. When more people are buying homes, fewer are renting. As a matter of fact, many unsophisticated investors use a region's higher vacancy rate as an excuse *not* to have full properties. Once again, they allow outside influences to affect how they run their businesses!

## 🔵 KEY INSIGHT

In every real estate market, hot, cold and in between, there are renters—lots of them. It does not matter what the vacancy rate is. Your job as a "business owner" is to ensure you attract as many "clients" for your business as you can, with no excuses. Some investors slow down their marketing efforts when they hear vacancy rates are going up. This is the *exact opposite* of what you should do. When others slow down, you ramp up. This is how you make sure the smaller number of renters available keep coming to *you* instead of to the competition.

Another terrible mistake unsophisticated investors make is to become impatient because their suite has been vacant for two months. In frustration, they rent to anyone who responds to their ad. This is a *huge* mistake and it will ultimately cost the landlord substantially more in time and money. Never (never!) think you have to rent your property to the first person who looks like he has the cash to move in.

Sophisticated investors use due diligence to support a tenant-search mantra that goes something like this: Quality property. Quality tenant. Quality property. Quality tenant.

# What do you need to do?

## PRE-SCREEN TENANTS

Before you show a property, conduct a telephone screening to make sure the next step in the screening process is worth your time. There is no need to show the property to everyone who calls and is interested. Remember, you're looking for a long-term "client" for this property.

## USE A FORMAL QUESTION CHECKLIST TO GUIDE THE CONVERSATION

You are choosing the tenant, not the other way around. Make sure you take control of the conversation early. During the initial telephone call, ask key questions such as:

- "When are you looking to move to the new place?" You'd be surprised at how many calls are just "thinking about moving." Just take their name and number and move on. Don't waste your time if they want a suite far in the future and you need to rent now.
- "How long do you plan to rent this place?" This question is critical. They may only need your place for three months while their new house is under construction. If you want a long-term tenant and you don't ask this question, you may be sorely disappointed when they move out after a few months.
- "How many people will be living there?" You want to know if this is a good match or not. If you are renting a one-bedroom suite and your prospect is a family of four, this is probably not a good match for the long term.
- "Do you have any pets or plan on getting any?" Keep this question open-ended. By stating "pets" instead of naming specific animals (dogs or cats) you will get a much clearer answer.
- "How long have you rented the place where you currently reside?" You are trying to filter out short-term "hoppers." If they say less than a year, ask them about the length of time at the previous place to see if there is a trend.
- "Where did you hear about this place?" As a business owner, you will want to know what marketing is working and what is not.
- "What kind of work do you do?" Many beginning landlords ask, "Do you have a job?" That isn't the right question, since most people will say yes even if they work only six hours per week at the local coffee shop. You want someone who can afford to pay your rent over a long period of time.

- "How long have you been at this job?" Look for stability.
- "Have you given your current landlord proper notice?" This helps identify the potential for future problems. Some tenants don't follow rules well, and if they say no to this one, then you might want to continue your search—no matter what their back story is.

*Spend your time showing the property only to prospective tenants who make it through this telephone interview.*

### KEY INSIGHT

Many tenants believe only one security deposit exists and you will hear about current landlords who won't release security deposits until the middle of the month. Never agree to wait. *Never* let a tenant change your rules. And never give possession of a property until you have cash (not a cheque) for the full first month's rent and the security deposit (or last month's rent, depending on your local laws).

### CONDUCT A BACKGROUND CHECK

Once you complete the telephone interview and show your property, you may think you know whether you want to rent to this tenant. This is wrong. You have just begun your due diligence!

Ask prospective tenants to complete a formal application to lease. This covers the information you already collected over the phone, but includes contact names and numbers for follow-up checks.

Make sure you have a line on the application that allows you to do a complete credit and criminal background check. When you become a member of your local landlord association or the Real Estate Investment Network, you can get template application forms that work for your jurisdiction. In order to do a complete check, the prospective tenant needs to provide you with complete and accurate information. Tell them clearly that you won't be processing their application until you have all the information.

### RED FLAG

Don't waste your time with prospective tenants who do not complete the form (no matter what their excuse). If they don't have the time or inclination to fill out a form regarding something as important as a place to live, you can imagine what other excuses may arise once they become tenants.

Always phone current and previous employers and build some rapport. Tell them you are a business owner (manager) and so are they. Mention that you realize they are sick and tired of employees who don't live up to their resumes, just like you are tired of prospective tenants who aren't totally honest on their rental application. Ask them how the prospective tenant treats company assets and other employees. Ask if they would rent a property to this individual. Ask about their prospects of long-term employment.

## 🔵 KEY INSIGHT

When talking with an employer, ask them if they are confident that the prospect will be responsible. If they say yes, ask them if they are confident enough to co-sign the rental agreement, thus guaranteeing the rent will be paid. You are not asking them to do this. You are looking to see how confident they are in this prospect.

Always call the prospect's most recent landlord, but take a sophisticated investor approach to the call. You want to find out the prospect's real rental history and if they are telling the truth on the application. As you get your answers, remember that a current landlord may not tell the whole truth if she is looking to rid herself of a problem tenant.

Build confidence in your information by talking to at least two previous landlords.

## 🟢 SOPHISTICATED INVESTOR ACTION STEP

Some prospective tenants who lack a sound rental history will often ask their friends or relatives to "play the part" of the previous landlord. They prepare this relative with what to say when you call. The one thing they don't know is that you are a sophisticated landlord and you understand that this might go on. You can circumvent this by calling the "landlord" and saying, "I understand that you have a suite for rent." There are two possible answers to this question. First, they say they're full, or second, they ask what you're talking about and say you've got the wrong number! This is a quick way to discover the difference between a real landlord and a set-up.

### CONDUCT A COMPLETE BACKGROUND CHECK

There are a few services that provide landlords with the ability to do complete background checks on potential renters. This complete background check includes:

- *Credit history*. Look for solid credit, but don't expect it to be perfect. You're simply looking for potential financial reasons why they won't make your rent payment.
- *Criminal background*. You want to know whom you are renting to. Many landlords have absolutely no issues with renting to people with a criminal history. Still, it's in your best interests to know the facts.
- *Rental history*. There are some services that keep a database of tenants, using information provided by your fellow landlords. The database will tell you about the tenant's rental behaviour and allow you insights into issues that could arise with this tenant. You must have written permission from the tenant to access any of this information, and the wording must be very specific on your rental application form.

### 🕐 KEY INSIGHT

It is critical that you do complete due diligence on your prospective tenant. A gut-feeling decision can lead to a real pain in the gut over the long term. If this due diligence sounds too daunting, there are companies that will do the majority of the screening and due diligence for you. However, as the owner of the property, you may still wish to do the final approval. Remember, you are ultimately responsible for who they put in there. It affects your bottom line, not theirs! Sophisticated investors won't risk their investment on a "gut feeling" that everything is going to be all right.

## TIP #89: DO A MOVE-IN INSPECTION AND KEEP MAINTENANCE CAUGHT UP.

*Your due diligence continues before, during and after your tenants move in.*

A full pre-move-in, walk-through inspection with the tenant is an absolute must for any landlord. You can use this walk-through for three important points:

1. The most obvious—to inspect the condition of the property before any of the tenant's property is moved in.
2. Just as important—to help you set the stage for your expectations of the tenant. This can cover what day their rent is due (and the penalties for

not hitting that day), as well as what they are responsible for as far as maintenance and yard work.

3. To solidify the relationship between you and the tenant. Use the time to build some rapport, discuss their likes and dislikes and show them this is not going to be a confrontational relationship. Since most tenants are used to confrontation with their landlord, it's your job in this walk-through to be very clear that you will always be fair, if they are always fair.

## What do you need to do?

### CONDUCT A MOVE-IN INSPECTION

Never ever let a tenant move anything into a property unless you and the tenant have done a complete room-by-room inspection and have both agreed to the conditions. Use a "Move-in Inspection Form" that addresses each and every room. Keep detailed notes on the current condition and have the tenant agree to and sign this form as confirmation of their agreement. Each province has different laws outlining what must be stated on the inspection report; check with your local authority.

Make sure that *all* tenants sign this inspection. Make this a specific policy and you will avoid being forced to take responsibility for problems related to the property's condition when your tenants move on.

### 🕐 KEY INSIGHT

As you do the walk-through with the tenant, take many digital pictures. Make sure your camera has the date function turned on so you can verify the date. As an added protection, have the tenants in a few of the pictures. Burn these photos onto a disc and then save this in your property file. This serves two purposes. First, the act of taking the pictures in front of the tenant tells them you are serious about the condition of the property. Second, if there is ever a dispute about condition, you will have verifiable proof.

### KEEP PROPERTY MAINTENANCE UP-TO-DATE

Respect your tenants and build mutual loyalty by keeping the "quality property" component of your real estate investment. Your goal is simple: Make your property the kind of place people will want to rent.

Annual inspections are critical for all sophisticated investors. Do a complete walk-through at least once a year to confirm there aren't any maintenance issues you haven't been aware of. While you're there, change the furnace filter and check that the smoke detectors are working. This shows your commitment to maintaining a quality property.

## Tip #90: Be Proactive When the Rent Isn't Paid.

*Don't let the hassle of dealing with a tenant in rental arrears become an eviction horror story.*

"Take immediate action" is the underlying mantra of the sophisticated investor. Waiting or hoping that a problem will go away will only bring pain and heartache. As a business owner, you need to make sure you are being paid a fair market price for your "product" (rental property) and not allowing people to "shoplift" from your store.

That's how sophisticated investors think of the process. Living in your property is the product and rent is the payment for it. If rent is not paid, it is just the same as if they walk into your video store and take $800 of videos without paying. If this happened in your video store, you would take immediate action. The same principle needs to apply here.

All landlords should have an arrears policy in place before the first tenant moves in. This system must work within the local landlord and tenant laws. If you consistently have people who don't pay their rent on time, it is a direct reflection upon you, your business systems and those you choose to put in your suites. In other words, it is your responsibility.

That being said, there are many proactive ways to eliminate or dramatically reduce rental arrears. For instance:

• Design up-front penalties renters must incur if they miss submitting their rent on time. These penalties should be written into their lease document—which, of course, they must sign.
• Clearly define these penalties in a follow-up letter sent a couple of months after they move in (not immediately as it will get lost in the move). Use a pleasant tone in the letter. Use words such as, "I know you aren't the type of person who would not live up to their legal obligations by missing a rent payment; that's why I chose you for this property. However, it is part of my system of clear communications to make you aware of what was in your lease:

1. Rent is due on or before noon on the 1<sup>st</sup> of the month.
2. If rent is late, there is an immediate penalty of $xx.
3. For each day the rent is late, a penalty of $xx is added.

"Once again, I know you're not the type of person who wants to waste your money on penalties, so I'm sure these don't pertain to you. This is a place you will be proud to call home for years to come. If you ever have any maintenance issues, please don't hesitate to call me at (555) 555-1212."

- If a renter is late in paying rent, you live by your rules. Of course, you have complete discretion as to which of your rules you want to enforce. Take the emotions out of it; this is a legal business transaction. *Your goal is to make rent matter. You want your tenants to know you are serious about collecting rent—and that there are penalties for those who do not pay.*

## What do you need to do?

**GET FIRST MONTH'S AND A SECURITY DEPOSIT (OR LAST MONTH'S RENT) UP FRONT**

It sounds a little harsh, but you are a landlord, not a bank. Make sure you get the security deposit (or last month's rent) up front with the first month's rent. (Make sure you know your local tenancy laws and use the details to protect your investment.)

Get the deposit and first month's rent in cash, certified cheque or money order. Never, ever accept an exception to this rule. This sets the tone that you are serious about the payments you are expecting. As any good landlord will tell you, it is much easier to get nicer than it is to get harsher as the relationship progresses.

 **RED FLAG**

> If the cash, certified cheque or money order is not in your hand, your tenants don't move in. Period.

**INCLUDE PENALTIES FOR LATE PAYMENT**

Wherever legally possible, build penalties for late fees and NSF cheques into your lease. To make tenants understand that you are serious about arrears, make these fees substantial. Sophisticated investors make the choice easy for the tenants who think they can choose between paying or not. They make it financially painful if they choose not to pay rent.

### GET POST-DATED CHEQUES

In most provinces, you can ask for post-dated cheques for rent payments. Your time is money and you do not want to make rent collection part of your monthly agenda. If you do, you will pay for missed appointments, return trips and a wagonload of excuses!

Do not take cash unless it is the last-ditch effort. It's a security risk and there is no paper trail. *Always* provide a signed receipt for the rent paid.

Always think ahead: If you accept cash as a partial payment, how will you prove rent arrears? The practice opens up a lot of grey areas.

 ### KEY INSIGHT

Some sophisticated investors have arranged to have both credit card and debit card payment options for their renters as a convenience. Renters have really gravitated towards this approach. It is easier for them and there is a paper trail.

### ALWAYS FOLLOW YOUR OWN ARREARS POLICY

When you meet a tenant to sign a lease, go over your rental arrears policy. Make sure it says exactly what will happen if a cheque fails to clear. For example: *If the cheque does not clear, I will issue 14 days' notice to vacate.*

If the tenant pays in full, including applicable penalties, the vacate notice may be dropped. If it is not paid, the notice to vacate remains in force, the landlord retains the security deposit for unpaid rent and gets the property back.

### LEARN THE LAW

Rest assured the law is on your side, as long you make sure your actions are in step with the law.

All landlords should join a local landlord association. It will provide educational opportunities regarding the local residential tenancies act. It is also good to get a quality advocate or bailiff on your side as it's their job to deal with any uncomfortable tenant situations. In almost all cases, you will never need them. Still, it is good to know who to call.

**KEY INSIGHT**

The landlord/tenant relationship is governed by law. Write a tenant lease based on that law and be prepared to take immediate action if a cheque fails to clear. Be strong, yet fair and always keep the relationship as open as possible. Because you don't own thousand of suites, your close relationship with your tenant is one advantage you have over the big guys!

## Tip #91: Confirm the Existing Tenant Details.

*The place you want to buy is being marketed with "existing tenants." Make sure those two words aren't investment-speak for "assumable headaches."*

Revenue property may be sold with tenants' agreements in place. Some vendors may even promote those tenants as an added asset to the deal. After all, beginning investors often believe the advertising and due diligence involved with acquiring tenants costs real time and money. Who wouldn't see existing tenants as money in the bank?

That's not how the sophisticated investor thinks. *Experience shows existing tenants demand the same due diligence as new ones. Since you didn't negotiate any of the terms of their tenancy, you must assume you know nothing about those terms.*

Sophisticated investors want to have as much information as possible on the current tenants and their terms of tenancy. This way they can make a very clear decision as to whether they wish to take the property as tenanted or vacant.

To get these details you should use a Tenant Confirmation form (an example is provided at the end of this tip). This form, which confirms all of the terms of their tenancy, is to be completed and signed by each tenant. Since a landlord and tenant's recollection of the tenancy terms often differ, it is best to get these straightened out long in advance. It helps you determine whether the rental income statements given to you by the vendor are accurate. If you are in a jurisdiction where security or last month's rent is in the landlord's hands, this form will clearly outline what amounts are to be credited to you at closing. Being clear keeps everyone honest.

 **RED FLAG**

Make sure this written form is signed and dated by all tenants.

# What do you need to do?

**REVIEW THE STATUS QUO AND MAKE SURE YOU HAVE ALL THE DETAILS**

Do not accept anyone's "word" on tenancy terms. Meet your new tenants face-to-face. Ask how they feel about the property and their plans to stay or go. Only good can come from being completely honest with your questions. This should be a part of your due diligence.

Review their lease agreement and make sure you can live with its terms. Poor leases are not uncommon, but you don't have to get stuck with one!

If a tenant doesn't have a formal lease, clearly explain to the tenant that a lease will be put in place that outlines your rules. If the tenant will not accept this, you may wish to move on to another property.

## 💲 SOPHISTICATED INVESTOR TIP

If you don't want to rent to any of the current tenants or plan to undertake extensive renovations, you can always request vacant possession as part of your offer to purchase.

## 🚩 RED FLAG

Read a copy of each lease that is in place. Look for situations that may not be appropriate for you. The need for caution is especially strong if the existing tenancy isn't based on a formal lease agreement! When the current tenants' leases expire, make sure you get them to agree to your new lease, with all of your rules and regulations.

## ❶ KEY INSIGHT

Bad surprises are a natural consequence of due diligence that falls short of its mark. That's why you are studying a real estate investment system that stresses property score cards, analyzer forms and checklists for everything from vendor motivation to prospective tenants! Apply your due diligence strategy to *every* tenant relationship and every property you own and you'll start to see why sophisticated investors can talk about "quality tenants and quality property" as an investment strategy.

## TENANT CONFIRMATION

Date _____
     (Day)   (Month)   (Year)

My name is _____
     (First)     (Middle)     (Last)

I Currently Rent Suite # _____ at _____

_____   _____
     (Address)     (City)

**DETAILS** of my tenancy are as follows:

1. Current Rent: $ _____ /month

2. Security Deposit: $ _____

3. Date I Moved In: _____
     (Day)   (Month)   (Year)

4. I have a written lease with my landlord:   YES   NO

4a. If NO, please describe tenancy arrangement: _____

5. Date my current lease expires: _____
     (Day)   (Month)   (Year)

6. I am currently up to date with my rent payment:   YES   NO

6a. If NO, I currently owe: $ _____

7. There are no side deals, pre-paid rent or rent-discount (i.e., free-rent) arrangements between my landlord and me, other than that I am a tenant as set out above.

Dated this _____ day of _____ , 20_____ .

Tenant Name _____   Witness Name _____

Signature _____   Witness Signature _____

Tenant Name _____   Witness Name _____

Signature _____   Witness Signature _____

Other Comments: _____

PART 9

LEGAL INSIGHTS AND
TAX TIPS: WHAT YOU'VE
GOT TO KNOW
(SO IT WON'T HURT YOU)

# TIP #92: HONESTY IS THE ONLY POLICY.

*Swim in the grey waters and you will eventually be bitten by the sharks.*

The great thing about the Canadian real estate market is that it gives people a chance to create long-term wealth if they follow a system and have patience. The bad thing about the Canadian real estate market is that many people believe they must make money quickly or they're not being successful. Late-night TV and huge "get rich" ads have programmed Canadians to have very little patience in any wealth-creation strategy. In reality, "get rich quick" is a marketing hook, not real life. The saddest part of this equation is that those who chase the fast dollar often have to wade into what is politely called "grey water." This is where all of the real estate sharks hang out—and wait for their next prey.

How do you avoid the grey water? It's easy. All you have to do is be completely honest and above board with all your transactions.

Novice real estate investors get to meet a lot of people while assembling the team they'll work with en route to achieving their personal goals. You need real estate agents, bankers, mortgage brokers, lawyers, accountants and other investors. However, novice investors are also often prey to the grey-water sharks who teach or advocate strategies that, when looked at in the bright light of day, are either outright fraud or will quickly lead them to bankruptcy.

You need to quickly spot the difference between the ones who are "selling you" and the ones who are supporting you. This can be complicated, because the "grey-area sharks" are amazing sales people and have mastered the "I'm here to help you" speech. This makes them difficult to pick out. The bottom line is you need to steer clear of anyone who even hints of the illegal or grey-water deal.

This warning is not made lightly, nor should it be ignored. The rules are pretty simple.

## Warning: Grey water ahead

1. Be wary of those who try to teach *and* sell you real estate. The potential for a conflict of interest is just too high.
2. If you are told to sign a document that is not true because you need to get a mortgage or close a deal, recognize that advice as a sign that

you're already swimming with the sharks and it is time to get out of the water.

3. If you are not able to get a second legal opinion on a deal, no matter how small, see this as a *huge* red flag.

4. If you are being told not to declare every aspect of your real estate transaction to every party involved (i.e., withholding information from a banker, lawyer or purchaser), then you have just jumped into grey waters. Be prepared to be bitten.

5. If someone recommends a particular course of action (e.g., structuring your corporations, buying in a certain town, arranging for a bunch of new credit cards), make sure you check to see if they have a personal interest (usually financial) for that advice. For instance, arranging to set up three corporations before you buy your first property may not be a great strategy for the novice investor. It is, however, a great strategy for lawyers and accountants who make fees every year from these corporations—whether you own property or not.

6. If your "gut" tells you something isn't right, dig deeper before you are pushed into grey waters. In other words, always "look behind the curtain!"

First, always remember the difference between a below-average investor and an over-achieving investor amounts to a mere 10% increase in effort. In other words: You don't need to cheat to win.

Second, as you get your system in place, keep these two general business rules front and centre:

> *I will only make commitments I have every intention of fulfilling.*
> *I will never sign a document that isn't really true.*

## What do you need to do?

**LEARN TO RECOGNIZE FRAUD**

You may, for example, encounter a mortgage broker who says you have to sign a document stating that you're going to move into the property you're purchasing as a primary residence, even though you plan to use it as investment property. They'll tell you that "other people are doing it," or "it's not illegal unless you get caught."

They'll tell you this is necessary to:

a) secure a good interest rate or,
b) secure good mortgage terms.

*They are wrong. This is fraud and it's illegal.*

An expert mortgage broker has the ear of the top players in the lending world and they can get you amazing terms and amazing interest rates without your ever having to sign a false document. If your mortgage broker or banker tells you differently, get a new mortgage broker who actually understands how it all works.

### TAKE A STEP BACK

The arrangement described above, because it's not based on fact, borders on bank fraud. If the lender decides you have committed a fraud, the bank goes after you—not the broker. If the deal is worth enough, the police will also get involved. Good-bye free world after that!

It's wrong to think mortgage fraud only hurts the bank. Fraud can be used to manipulate housing prices in particular neighbourhoods. It can also give organized crime access to property that can be used to grow or manufacture street drugs.

### FRAUD CAN COST YOU YOUR BUSINESS

Major mortgage insurers such as Canada Mortgage and Housing Corporation (CMHC) and GMAC have substantially increased their investigations into homeowner loans. They're looking for people who say they're moving into a property as a primary residence and who obtained a loan on that basis, even though these borrowers really purchased the property as an investment.

The cost of getting caught runs high. In Edmonton in 2004, 55 people were caught in just one small investigation. They're losing their properties and their credit rating, and they're being sued for damages. In November 2005, four more were jailed for transactions like this.

### BE HONEST

Ask yourself, "Is this something I can tell my mortgage company?" If the answer is no, don't do it.

## AVOID DISHONEST PEOPLE

Stay away from mortgage brokers who suggest dishonesty as a good policy. You don't need fraudsters on your team.

Avoid lawyers or accountants who seem to be creating overly complex structures and transactions if you are just starting out. Get a second legal or accounting opinion *before* you sign on.

There are wonderful brokers, lawyers and accountants out there who will work hard and find you the right deal—without ever thinking about putting you in harm's way.

## 🚩 RED FLAG

Once exposed, a fraudulent deal can trash the only reputation you have. If it's the same reputation you plan to use to access financing, build a team of professionals and attract joint venture partners, then you don't want to take the risk!

## 🛈 KEY INSIGHT

Honesty is always the best policy. In fact, sophisticated investors will tell you it's the *only* policy. New investors, especially if they have a little nest egg ready to go, may attract the interest of some less-than-scrupulously honest business people. Here, as in life in general, if a deal sounds too good to be true, it probably is.

## 🚩 RED FLAG

Never become a "straw buyer." One of the ways people are attracted to "fast money" in real estate is through the opportunity to be a "straw buyer." A straw buyer is someone who puts up their name, credit history and signature to arrange for a mortgage on a property. The fraud artist then puts up the down payment, assumes payments on the mortgage and pays the straw buyer $5,000 for their services. It sounds like a no-risk deal to the straw buyer, but it's fraud, pure and simple. Many of these cases end with the fraud artist not making payments on the property. The straw buyer then assumes the debt—and has to explain why he signed a false document. *Never ever* give up your name or credit for quick cash (unless you only want to see your friends during visiting hours!).

**RED FLAG**

Steer clear of anyone who tells you a "negative cash flow" property will save you money on taxes! Nicknamed "alligators" because they eat you alive, negative cash flow properties take money from you each and every month. They also take you farther and farther away from financial freedom. Still not convinced? Ask yourself this question: How many negative cash flow properties can you afford to own before you end up broke?

## TIP #93: DISCHARGE THAT CAVEAT.

*Keep your titles clean.*

The legal implications of having a caveat registered against a property you own underscores the importance for real estate investors to make sure they understand basic real estate legal terms.

First things first. While a *mortgage* gets registered on its own as a mortgage, a *caveat* is the device by which the land titles office registers certain documents alongside a mortgage.

An *assignment of rents* is a legal document that is sometimes registered alongside a mortgage. It assigns all rents and income from a property to the mortgagee. If the buyer stops making payments, the mortgagee may have the right to assume management of the property and collect rents to get their money.

An assignment of rents and an *option or a right of first refusal* are examples of how others with an interest in property held by someone else can register a caveat against a land title as a way to protect their interest in the property.

A caveat against a title matters because a caveat is a charge against a property. Let's say you are an investor who sells a property by way of an *agreement for sale*. That means the title stays in the name of the person selling, but the buyer registers a caveat against the title. That caveat essentially says, "I'm buying this property by way of an agreement for sale and I have a buyer's interest in the property."

This kind of caveat protects the buyer from the seller being able to sell the property out from under them.

Now, that's the easy part. The critical piece comes if a caveat is not acted upon. In this case, the "agreement for sale" buyer doesn't end up closing on the property. If that is the case, the vendor takes back the property and looks to sell it to someone else. And here's where the situation gets interesting: *Unless the vendor remembers to get the old "agreement for sale" caveat discharged, it will be still be listed on the title and become a major legal problem in the future!*

## 🚩 RED FLAG

A caveat may be registered against your property by a prospective buyer. If that deal falls through, you must have the caveat discharged. Until that happens, no one will buy your property. As long as that caveat is there, it says you're not the only person with an interest in that property. Every time a caveat or even a lien is placed on your property's title, the lien or caveat will continue to stay on the title until you request it to be physically removed by a discharge document signed by the caveator (the person who placed the caveat). Keep your titles clean.

## What do you need to do?

### ALWAYS ASSUME A CAVEAT HAS BEEN REGISTERED

If you are selling a property by way of an agreement for sale and your buyer files a caveat, you have to understand that is what buyers do. It protects them from your changing your mind. It also protects them from your using their offer as a way to sweeten the price pot and sell the property to someone else!

### CLEAN UP THE TITLE

If that buyer backs out of the deal or fails to close, you need to let him or her move on—as soon as they formally sign a "discharge of the caveat." Make sure the discharge papers are handy. Make sure you register the discharge so you are ready to sell to someone else.

## 🛈 KEY INSIGHT

No one wants to see a sale go bad because the buyer can't get his financing together or backs out of a deal. But it does happen and you need to be ready when it does. Discharging a prospective buyer's caveat is not a sign of defeat. It's a sophisticated investment move that ensures the property is caveat-free before the next buyer comes along.

## TIP #94: FORECLOSURES EQUAL INVESTMENT OPPORTUNITY.

*These deals can be a win-win for both sides.*

The best thing about foreclosures and pre-foreclosures is that buyers can sometimes get properties at a good price and motivated sellers can get out from under their debt before it is too late. Investors will often find that pre-foreclosure situations provide some pretty unique opportunities to present creative offers, a fact of life which makes these deals a kind of Holy Grail for some investors. However, the information on foreclosures is much more difficult to find in Canada than in the United States.

A pre-foreclosure property has not yet gone through all the legal steps of a full foreclosure. This means vendors are extra motivated to get out from under a debt they can't afford and you can solve their problem and get yourself a good deal at the same time.

The good deals aside, investors interested in the foreclosure and pre-foreclosure market should educate themselves about how these deals work in the real world, since it's not like it's taught on late-night TV! There are many legal implications that surround these deals in Canada, and they get even more complex if they are a part of a bankruptcy.

 **RED FLAG**

Much of the hype and misconception around the "great deals" that can be had on foreclosures comes over the border from the United States, where rules and laws are substantially different from our Canadian laws. Be aware that most foreclosures in this country get sold at market price or only slightly below. It is not like you hit the lottery jackpot when you buy a Canadian foreclosure.

## What do you need to do?

**UNDERSTAND THE BASICS**

Often in foreclosures you find vendors who are close to bankruptcy or in bankruptcy. If they are in bankruptcy, there will be a *bankruptcy trustee*. The trustee is in control of the bankrupt person's affairs. The bankruptcy trustee must be involved in any negotiations regarding the bankrupt's property. Their job is to protect creditors by getting as close to market value as possible.

### FOLLOW THE PROCESS

In many provinces across the country, you are allowed to be in the court and to stand up and speak to the issue regarding your intent to buy a foreclosed property. Be clear and to the point when your time comes. Make sure you take good notes regarding the judge's instructions. These will be re-written by the bank's foreclosure lawyer and be sent to your lawyer. Good notes regarding the judge's specific instructions will be a major help if there's a discrepancy.

### 🚩 RED FLAG

If you don't believe the order accurately reflects what the judge said, you can order a court transcript and use it to argue for a new order. This is an expensive document and good notes can help avoid this step.

### 🕐 KEY INSIGHT

The bankruptcy trustee is there to represent creditors of the seller, usually parties other than the lender. They're not there to protect the bankrupt seller. If you want to buy foreclosed properties, you will need to work with bankruptcy trustees. They want the deal to be done quickly and fairly. Prove to them that you're not there to steal the property; you're there to get a fair deal. This approach may lead them to call you first regarding future properties.

## TIP #95: ALL CONDOMINIUMS ARE NOT THE SAME (OR: MY BIKE CAN'T GO THERE—AND MY PARKING SPACE HAS A TITLE?!)

*Condominium plans are complicated. So go slow—and get help.*

The word "condominium" refers to a type of real estate ownership. Regardless of whether the property is an apartment-style building, a town-house development, a side-by-side duplex or a single-family home, owners will have title to a specific unit, and shared interest in common areas.

You can even have condominiums that comprise a number of single-family homes all sharing title to the common-area lands that surround it. Never assume when you hear the word condominium that it refers to an apartment in a big building.

Because each condo is run by a different condominium association, the rules change from condo corporation to condo corporation and province to province. All owners will pay maintenance fees (assessments) to the condominium association, with those fees paying to maintain, repair or improve the common areas.

Before you buy a condo to place on the rental market, there are a lot of things you need to know. The most important is whether the condominium bylaws allow rentals in the building. If so, how many are allowed and how many are currently in the building? Many novice investors have been caught buying properties in buildings where the rental allotment was already filled, so they had to keep their property vacant or re-sell it.

You also need to know about special assessments required, contemplated or unpaid. These are upcoming major payments, over and above the monthly condo fees, that each owner must pay to the condominium corporation for maintenance of the common areas.

Other details of condo bylaws are just plain quirky. Tenants may not be able to park their bicycles on the balcony, a fact that could negatively impact a prospective tenant if the target demographic for a funky high-rise includes tenants who want to bike a few blocks to work or school.

Others may restrict all home-based businesses. That could be a problem for a target tenant that includes families who may want to rent your townhouse and set up a home-based service like a daycare or hair salon.

Some condo bylaws even assign titles to parking spaces, a potential landmine when there may be twice as many parking spaces as unit titles! Others may require condo directors (instead of the management company) to sign legal documents on behalf of the condo corporation. Imagine how that complicates a closing date if even one director isn't available when the buyer or seller needs him to be!

 **RED FLAG**

You'll only know all these critical things if you have read the condominium bylaws and condominium board minutes. Successful condo investments depend on knowing exactly what the condo bylaws say you are responsible for and what you can and can't do as an owner.

## What do you need to do?

**CALL IN THE EXPERTS**

Sophisticated investors ask, "What's behind the curtain?" When it comes to condo purchases, that can mean looking behind several curtains (or the same curtain, several times!). Review financial statements, the condo reserve fund study, the condo reserve fund plan and the minutes of the most recent AGM, plus one year of board meeting minutes. Have your lawyer review legal documents, including the condo plan, to ascertain if there are any legal actions against the condominium corporation generally, or against the unit you are buying.

Ask specifically about titled parking spaces. The only way to know for sure is to review a copy of the condominium plan. That plan will also detail what else owners have agreed to.

**GET SPECIFIC INFORMATION**

If someone acting for the corporation tells you there are no special assessments required, contemplated or unpaid and there is no deferred maintenance, get it in writing. (See the following tip.)

**KNOCK ON DOORS**

Knock on the doors of other owners and talk to them about the condominium. Get their perspective on how it works and whether residents are happy.

**ALWAYS COMPLETE THE *FULL* CONDO DUE DILIGENCE CHECKLIST**

See the Appendix for a detailed condo due diligence checklist that every investor should complete before removing final offer conditions on a condominium purchase.

## TIP #96: STUDY THE CONDO'S DEFERRED RESERVE PLAN.

*You need to find out how the condominium association manages its owners' money.*

Condominium owners hold title to their units and share ownership on some property in common. This has the potential to be good or bad, depending on how the condominium board is being run. When everything's working right, it's a pretty "worry free" approach to owning your own home. But condo owners, including investors who manage the units as rental properties or buy individual units for short- or long-term investment, need to ask some tough questions about what happens when things aren't working so well.

Condominium associations set up a **reserve fund** as part of their initial organization. Individual owners pay into the reserve, creating a pool of funds to be used for basic maintenance, repairs and upgrades. Later, after the initial set-up (two years), the condo board (using an Alberta example) must carry out a "deferred reserve study" (DRS) by a qualified person. The board must next prepare a "deferred reserve plan" (DRP), which is used to implement the findings of the study.

There can be a big difference between the DRS carried out by a "qualified" person (i.e., an engineer) and the DRP, which is implemented by the condo board. A DRS is often an extremely conservative bum-covering document which, if implemented, would raise fees excessively. Boards often cut back on the DRS in the DRP.

If maintenance gets behind, the condo association may levy a **special assessment** to deal with problems. If these assessments aren't paid, the work may still not get done! In the end, that's **deferred maintenance**—and deferred maintenance costs money.

## What do you need to do?

### ASK FOR THE DRS AND DRP

In most provinces, condominium corporations are required to have an outside company produce a financial study (often called the Condo Reserve Fund Study) that clearly outlines the current condition of the common areas, the predicted future replacement timeline of major common components and the costs for doing so over the coming years. This is in addition to the annual budget plan the condominium board sets out.

### MATCH THE DOCUMENTS

Now review the plan and study together. Is the condominium board doing what the study says it should be for maintenance and building a reserve fund? The condo board does not have to do everything the study suggests. But if they are not building an adequate reserve fund to cover obvious major future expenses as set out in the Condo Reserve Fund Study, then you can expect to receive a hefty bill in the future.

### COVER THYSELF

If the deferred reserve study isn't complete (perhaps it's in the process), you need to talk to your lawyer about an addition to your contract. Include something like this: "Seller warrants there are no special assessments required, contemplated or unpaid." If you want to have the vendor clearly state their knowledge on the condominium's financial and structural situation, you can get them to sign a Statutory Declaration. See the Appendix for a sample you and your lawyer can use as a template.

## TIP #97: TAKE ANOTHER LOOK AT THAT CONDO DEAL.

*Make sure your "great investment" doesn't lead to your great downfall.*

Condominiums that haven't yet been built can look like pretty good investments. Before you sign the developer's contract, however, you better be darn sure you can assign your interest in the unit, or sell it to another investor, without the developer's permission.

You also want to be very clear that the builder has the money and talents to actually bring the building to completion. Too often, you will see investors' money disappear because the builder disappears. Make sure you do your due diligence on the builder.

 **RED FLAG**

*Never ever* pay future value for a property. In other words, in the case of a property not yet built, make sure you are paying what it would be worth on today's market, not what it is projected to be worth when it is completed. Be smart and don't let greed grab hold of you.

## What do you need to do?

### READ THE CONTRACT

You have to go over the contract in detail. Remember, it was written by the builder's lawyers so you know whom it is written to protect. Have *your* lawyer read through it carefully and explain any potential land-mines she may uncover.

You must be sure of the price. You have to know if you can expect a GST rebate (and you can, as long as you are the owner/occupier). The GST rebate rule is not the same for investors as for owner-occupiers. (If you're buying more than one condo, it's going to be tough to convince the Canada Revenue Agency you're an owner-occupier!)

You have to know whether you can assign your interest in the unit or sell to someone else without permission. Never assume this is possible.

### INVOLVE YOUR LAWYER

Condominiums purchased as investment properties demand additional due diligence. Basic contract forms may be a good start, but you don't want to sign them until you've had legal advice, since you're apt to need changes. At the very least, you need to be sure you understand what you've agreed to do.

### ASSEMBLE YOUR BUYERS

If one condo looks good, 10 must be better. Right? Wrong. If you don't have your buyers lined up for re-sale when the deal's about to close, your financing could be at risk. And don't expect the developer to give you any extensions on the deal. He's busy building and selling. Besides that, he's got your deposit cheques, which he keeps if the deals don't close.

 **KEY INSIGHT**

Fast money is a great motivator. It also tends to mask the real truth about fast-money deals. Namely, they are speculative and financially risky. Keep perspective at all times when investing. For instance, if you are buying a pre-built condominium hoping to sell it for a quick profit or rent it when the property is finished, make sure you remember you are not the only one with this plan. As the building gets close to completion, the dozens and dozens of investors who bought alongside you will also be planning to cash in. This means you will have a ton of competition to sell your property, or a ton of competition to rent it out. The basic rules of economics state that if there is a fixed demand and a high supply, prices must come down. Sophisticated real estate investors go into investments that are *not* speculative. They look for opportunities where others aren't lining up right beside them. A good deal is only good if it fits your long-term wealth system. Make sure you are being honest with yourself. Always ask, "Is the property I am looking at a speculation or a real-life investment?"

# BONUS TIP! TIP #98: UNDERSTAND GST ON COMMERCIAL REAL ESTATE.

*GST is like tax law generally: complicated.*

Canada's Goods and Services Tax (GST) is not generally payable on the purchase of real estate where the property is a residential complex. Commercial real estate is a different matter.

Commercial real estate is GST payable and any rent collected in a commercial building also has a GST component. You also need to know the following.

**1. The purchaser pays.**
Where GST is payable, it is the purchaser who must pay the GST directly to the Receiver General. If GST is not remitted to the Canada Revenue Agency (CRA), the CRA will pursue the buyer, even if you have receipts that show you paid the GST to the vendor. You would be surprised at how often this situation occurs and the purchaser ends up paying the GST amount twice.

 **RED FLAG**

*Never* pay the GST to the vendor and rely on the vendor to pay it to the Canada Revenue Agency (CRA).

**2. You need to check that GST number.**
If GST is payable but the purchaser is registered for GST, the vendor can rely on what is now Section 221(2) of the Excise Tax Act and not collect GST from the purchaser.

 **RED FLAG**

Check the GST number to make sure it's valid. Section 221(2) of the Excise Tax Act says the vendor does not have to charge and collect GST if the purchaser is registered for GST. If, however, the vendor relies on a *misrepresentation* of information regarding proper registration, the vendor is responsible for its collection and payment!

## What do you need to do?

**REMIT THE GST ON YOUR PURCHASE DIRECTLY TO THE CRA**

**IF YOU'RE SELLING, CONFIRM THE BUYER'S GST STATUS**

Call the CRA Business Window (1-800-959-5525) and provide the purchaser's name and GST Registration Number to ensure that it is valid. The CRA official will confirm registration status over the phone. You can also ask for official, written confirmation of that status.

# BONUS TIP! TIP #99: FIND OUT ABOUT THE GST REBATE FOR INVESTORS.

*Guest tip: Real estate lawyer Alan Silverstein highlights the good news for new home and condominium investors who are now eligible for GST rebates upon meeting certain requirements.*

Here's really great news for anyone investing in a new home or condominium.

You can now qualify for a GST rebate, just like an owner-occupant. And that can save investors a surcharge of up to 2.52% of the purchase price.

### "Revenue Neutral"

Why does the GST rebate even exist for new homes and condos? Before the GST was introduced, the rate of federal sales tax on new construction was just over 4%. To keep the net tax burden "revenue neutral" (remember that infamous expression?), the GST New Housing Rebate was launched.

It cuts the 7% GST on new homes/condos (plus substantially renovated properties) by 2.52% to 4.48% when the purchase price excluding GST is below $350,000. Between $350,000 and $450,000, "tax-excluded," the rebate falls by $8.75 per $100 of purchase price. Over $450,000, excluding GST, there's no rebate.

Up go the numbers when new homes/condos are sold for one "all-inclusive" price. In these purchase agreements, the builder pays the GST from the sale proceeds, while the buyer transfers the GST rebate to the builder.

Now the top-qualifying price for the full rebate is $365,750. A smaller rebate is available for "tax-included" prices between $365,750 and $481,500. Over $481,500, the rebate is gone.

Almost all builders today market new homes/condos for one all-inclusive price. (Still, buyers should always ask whether the price is "GST included," or "plus GST.")

After all, it's easier for buyers to stomach a $300,000 price that buries the GST than to shell out $287,136.29 for the home (what the builder earns after GST) plus $12,863.71 for GST. And that's why new home/condo buyers who pay a "tax-included" price won't collect the rebate. The house is priced with the rebate earmarked for the builder.

Unlike other incentive programs, the GST rebate isn't limited to first-time buyers. But not everyone qualifies for it, either—only individuals who bought a new home/condo for use as their primary place of residence, or that of a relation, right after closing.

This owner-occupant condition effectively jacked up the price paid by investors for a new home/condo by the amount of the rebate. How? Investors ineligible for the GST rebate had already transferred it to the builder in the purchase agreement. That forced investors to cough up the "lost" rebate as a closing adjustment with their builder.

Years of lobbying to equalize the rules paid off in the February 2000 federal budget, when the GST New Residential Rental Property Rebate was introduced. The numbers for this investor rebate mirror those of the owner-occupant rebate. So the full rebate of 2.52% is available if the sale price doesn't exceed $350,000 (excluding GST). For prices from $350,000 to $450,000, excluding GST, the rebate is phased out. Over $450,000, it's totally eliminated.

But there are a number of key differences between the two rebates:

• As before, investors must pay their builder the amount of the "lost" rebate as a closing adjustment. But investors now can recoup the GST investor rebate from the Canada Revenue Agency after closing, if all other conditions are met.
• The investor rebate is not limited to individuals; it can be paid to corporations.
• Both Canadian residents and non-residents are eligible.
• The unit bought by the investor must be a "self-contained residence" with private kitchen facilities, private bath and private living area. Alternatively, it can be a suite or room in a hotel, motel, inn, boarding house, or in a residence for students, seniors, or the disabled.

- The first tenant is "reasonably expected" to occupy the unit as their primary place of residence for at least a year. Smart investors will insist on a written lease with a minimum one-year term, instead of any month-to-month arrangement.
- Construction, substantial renovation or conversion of the building must have begun after February 27, 2000.
- Investors in new homes/condos must repay the rebate if they sell the property during the first full calendar year after closing, unless the purchaser acquires it for use as their primary place of residence, or that of a relation. Effectively this means there are two separate one-year qualification rules for the GST investor rebate: Own the property for a year, and rent it for a year.

To claim the GST Investor Rebate, investors must file a prescribed form, GST 524, along with the purchase agreement, statement of adjustments, lease with the first tenant, and insurance policy on the property. Investors have two years after closing to apply for the rebate.

More information is available from the CRA web site: www.cra-arc.gc.ca.

*Alan Silverstein is a Toronto real estate lawyer, commentator and author. (Originally published in the* Toronto Sun *on April 24, 2004. Reprinted with permission.)*

## BONUS TIP! TIP #100: RRSP MORTGAGES DEMAND EXTRA ATTENTION TO DETAIL.

*Another look at secondary financing, with an RRSP twist.*

There are two things you need to know about registered retirement savings plan (RRSP) mortgages. First, if you lend money from an RRSP, the Canada Revenue Agency (CRA) says it can only be to an *arm's length party. Lending to direct relatives is not possible*. The mortgage must also be administered the way a third-party mortgage would be administered, including market interest rates and collection procedures.

Second, it has to be **commercially reasonable** to make it a qualified investment in your RRSP. Commercially reasonable means that if the RRSP mortgage loan is audited by the CRA, they are going to look at all aspects of the mortgage loan to see that it fits within the market guidelines.

In other words, you haven't given a sweetheart deal to someone as a favour and you are keeping the collections up on the monthly payments.

## What do you need to do?

**SET IT UP RIGHT**

The first thing the CRA auditors will look at is a certified appraisal of the property. That's how they will establish the value of the property and assess whether it is commercially reasonable. Make sure you have one on file.

**FACTOR THE LOAN-TO-VALUE (LTV) RATIO**

Lending rules don't allow a bank to lend more than 75% of the value of the property because those loans are deemed too risky. If you get above the 75% mark, and it is not insured by CMHC or another mortgage insurance provider, you will need to go to a secondary lender where the interest rate will be higher. If your RRSP mortgage sits in the 75% to 95% area, CRA will be satisfied with a higher interest rate. If the loan doesn't meet the "commercially reasonable" criteria, it won't pass a CRA audit.

**KEEP A PAPER TRAIL**

You need paperwork that justifies the loan. The more paperwork in your file when you put the RRSP loan together, the better. Make sure you have done all background checks as if you were the bank. Conduct credit checks, employment checks, etc. The CRA will look for proof that you followed these commercially acceptable steps. They will also look for a certified appraisal, some comparisons of interest rates and some comment on why the LTV is higher or lower than what is normally commercially given.

### ⚑ RED FLAG

The higher the LTV, the more risk you have. Make sure you are very clear as to the risk level you are willing to take in your RRSP and that you are getting paid an appropriate amount of interest for the risk level. Before you lend out of your RRSP, make sure you know *all* the rules. This is a complex investment strategy and if done incorrectly it can lead to major tax implications. Some great information is available in the "RRSP in Real Estate" section at www.realestateinvestingincanada.com.

**BE FASTIDIOUS**

Conventional lenders approve loans after a detailed application process. Apply the same level of scrutiny to your RRSP loans. Most importantly, always remember you are the lender. You are making the lending decisions—and you are financially responsible. Do not let emotions get in the way of making the right decision. Play the role of the banker and protect yourself with quality due diligence on the borrower and the property.

## BONUS TIP! TIP #101: INVESTORS DRIVE RRSP MORTGAGES.

*If you want access to RRSP mortgage financing, it is YOU who MUST drive the details.*

With registered retirement savings plans (RRSPs) getting less-than-stellar returns, a growing number of investors are turning to investing in mortgages within their RRSP. This can give a sophisticated investor a consistent rate of return backed by a quality piece of real estate. In the right cases, the risks can be very low, the volatility next to zero and the return-on-investment substantial.

These RRSP mortgages don't just help the RRSP holder, they also help the real estate investor who can now access these mortgage funds to further their investments. These are serious and sophisticated investments, from both the RRSP holder and real estate investor's points of view.

The RRSP holder *must* complete at least as much due diligence as a bank would, making sure the lender and the property provide enough security for their RRSP. It is highly recommended the RRSP holder *never, ever* lend to over 90% loan to value, even if it is someone you know and trust. Even at 90%, make sure you get the full market interest rate or are legally participating in the equity appreciation. In fact, you should do as much due diligence on the property as you would if you were going to buy it yourself. You need to know what you are getting yourself into.

If you are a real estate investor who is borrowing these funds, always remember you are not dealing with a bank who can afford a loss or missed payment. You are dealing with a family's retirement money and you must never miss a payment or fail to fulfil any other obligations under the contract. Pay full market interest rate, make all the payments on time and help these RRSP holders achieve their retirement goal. That should be your only focus.

Real estate investors need to recognize two things.

1. RRSP mortgages are complicated and you must get a second mortgage lawyer's advice to complete the package of forms required by the borrower and lender. One slip of the pen and the deal can trigger substantial tax consequences. Never let this process be run by someone without extensive experience; it is too financially dangerous.
2. If you, as the sophisticated investor, wish to be a borrower from a self-directed RRSP, you must become the driver of the process. That means it will take quite a bit of your personal time to get the deal done. You will be walking the deal from start to finish and your lawyer will be by your side, but you must stickhandle through all the red tape and communicate with the various parties involved.

## What do you need to do?

**NEGOTIATE THE LOAN**

When an RRSP plan holder gets together with a borrower, they need to negotiate the formal terms of the loan. This agreement, which includes the dollar amount, interest rate, length of loan, payment structure, lawyer contact information and property address (legal and municipal), must also outline the current mortgaging in place. The agreement must be in writing and be signed by both parties.

The borrower (real estate investor) and lender (RRSP holder) then need to complete the package of forms required by the RRSP trustee. Make sure these are reviewed in detail by a legal expert familiar with the RRSP second mortgage process before they are submitted to the trustee.

### 🔘 KEY INSIGHT

RRSP mortgages are not to be considered real estate investments. These are financial transactions that have a real estate security behind them. If you are using your RRSPs to invest this way, make sure you know all your exit options. Get the key questions answered:
1. How do I collect my money if the borrower stops making payments?
2. Can I sell my mortgage to another party if I require the cash?
3. What occurs upon the expiry of the term on the mortgage? Is there instant renewal or am I paid off?

### SEE A LAWYER

Have your lawyer prepare the mortgage and other documentation so as to match the signed agreement. The lender and borrower should have separate legal representation. This ensures each party is clear on what they are signing and the commitments they are making, and avoids the potential for a conflict of interest.

### INSTRUCT YOUR LAWYER

A lot of investors forget the simple act of instructing their lawyers about what they want them to do with a file. This is important in a basic real estate transaction as well as more complex transactions such as an RRSP mortgage. The RRSP lender needs to check that his lawyer is adept at RRSP mortgage transactions. If not, find someone who is. The RRSP lender's lawyer will then be instructed to act for the lender and prepare the mortgage document and any transfer documents required by the trustee.

As the sophisticated investor looking to borrow from the RRSP lender, it is important for you to understand all the steps this process will take and to be prepared for it with proper documentation. A good start would be for the borrower to instruct her lawyer (who should also be familiar with sophisticated real estate investment, including RRSP mortgages) to develop a template letter the RRSP lender can use to instruct his own lawyer. The letter should include specific instructions for the RRSP lender's lawyer. The RRSP lender fills it out and gives it to his lawyer along with the trustee package of forms and the signed mortgage agreement from step #1 above.

### 🕐 KEY INSIGHT

RRSP financing is quite a different process from a regular mortgage. There are many additional steps and much more explanation required. It is the full responsibility of the borrower to make sure all steps are followed by all parties and all documentation is completed to get the deal done in a timely manner. This process can lead to the borrower speaking directly to the lender's lawyer or their RRSP trustee. The RRSP lender, on the other hand, often sits back, silently relying on the borrower to handle the deal. They are just looking for improved results in their RRSP.

> ## ◭ RED FLAG
>
> If you plan to borrow from an RRSP or lend money out of your RRSP, it is critically important that you understand all the intricate details and legal ramifications of the process. To learn more about how it works and the opportunities it holds for both parties, visit www.realestateinvestingincanada. com and click on the "RRSP Strategies" link. This is a complete program written by Canada's own "Mr. RRSP," Valden Palm.

## BONUS TIP! TIP #102: JOINT VENTURES: GET IT IN WRITING.

*Make sure your joint venture is worth more than the paper it's written on.*

Joint ventures (JV) are a great way to share the financial risk of an investment. These are formal relationships where two or more parties decide to work together on a specific real estate project pooling money and expertise. This can be a venture that combines companies, people or other joint ventures. These relationships must be taken seriously and the legal documentation must be in order. Although complex in nature, joint ventures can be the quickest and least risky way to enter into real estate deals.

But things can (and will!) go wrong if every aspect of the JV isn't treated as a formal business relationship. Indeed, the fastest way to derail a JV is to make the error of confusing friendship and business partnerships.

In brief: Friendship evolves with time. Joint venture relationships evolve according to the details of a written document. Joint ventures are serious business and emotions can't get in the way of solid business decisions. In fact, getting into a joint venture relationship with a close friend can prove disastrous to the friendship if the legal documentation is not clear on rules and responsibilities.

Partners can, for example, opt against the "hassle" of financial reports that are properly prepared and routinely filed, because they trust each other. However, what do you do when your lender wants documentation of your investment success? And what if there is a financial dispute on the operations of the property? Where will the hard and fast numbers be?

A second problem is often lethal if the relationship is not formalized in writing. This occurs when partners modify their business plan or agreement on a handshake, with the changes to the initial JV agreement never formally made in writing. That's great until someone "can't remember" the amendment—which will occur more often than not.

Still not convinced *your* JV needs to be this formal? Then ask yourself the tough questions.

What happens if your JV partner moves, needs cash, gets divorced, dies—or simply changes his mind? If you don't have these contingencies in writing, you can find yourself in a very difficult situation—emotionally and financially.

What will you do when the estate of a deceased JV partnership decides it doesn't like the way the business operates and is not prepared to support your management decisions? This could leave you in a joint venture with a hostile party that can bring your business creation crashing down around you—all because you didn't get these contingencies in writing at the beginning.

 **SOPHISTICATED INVESTOR TIP**

No matter how large or small the relationship, and no matter how well you know the person, it is paramount that you make your agreement in writing, signed by both parties. Always design the "divorce" in advance as it is much easier to agree to those critical steps early in the relationship—before there is conflict.

 **KEY INSIGHT**

A joint venture is only as good as the parties involved. The parties must bring different strengths to the relationship in order for it to be successful over the long term. A typical successful joint venture would include a real estate expert and a silent financial partner. A classic mistake of novice investors is to enter into a joint venture with someone who is in the same position (knowledge or financial) as they are. For instance: two beginning investors with no cash get together to try to buy a piece of property—a big mistake. This is a relationship that is doomed to struggle. Only enter relationships that become stronger when the parties are combined as a team.

# What do you need to do?

**KEEP YOUR JV FIRMLY ON TRACK**

Write a formal joint venture agreement and operate the JV according to that document. Make sure the contract stipulates proper financial reporting be made to each party. If the JV needs to be modified, negotiate any changes and amend the formal agreement in writing.

## 🕐 KEY INSIGHT

Joint-venture relationships are an amazing way to build your property portfolio by pooling money and expertise to buy more properties. Novice investors can use JVs to learn how the investment business works if they complete a joint venture with a veteran and trusted investor. Think of it as a win-win mentoring relationship, whereby you exchange investment cash for financial gain and knowledge.

## 🚩 RED FLAG

Novice investors should know there are veteran sharks in the waters and they're looking for rookies to take advantage of. Make sure you have done complete due diligence on the potential partner, including criminal background checks, securities violations and past projects. Don't just jump in because they have a high profile and you seem to like them. Dig deep and dig hard. Many of these sharks have mastered the "trust me" sales pitch. Be careful if they aren't being very open about past dealings or they don't want you to use your own lawyer for independent advice. There are even "seminar leaders" or "experts" who set up business to take advantage of the rookie investors. These people are motivated by self-interest and may direct vulnerable clients into dangerous deals that are slanted to favour the "seminar leader." The deals they offer may even sell property to seminar clients without disclosing key financial components of the deal. These relationships are especially dangerous and require an extra level of due diligence on the novice investor's part. Make sure the deal is fair for both parties, that the joint venture relationship is clearly laid out in writing and that you have an independent lawyer review the agreement. Don't let blind trust and enthusiasm replace the all-important due diligence.

# BONUS TIP! TIP #103: GET THE REAL GOODS ON CAPITAL GAINS.

*Property rollovers are more than a new trick for an old dog!*

Many real estate investors get into the business hoping that profits made on their investments will qualify as capital gains, meaning they will be taxed in a much more favourable manner. This is quite true in many cases, especially for those who are holding properties to build long-term wealth. However, there are many cases where capital gains tax deductions are not applicable. These cases can cost you thousands of dollars on each transaction.

## ⚑ RED FLAG

Not all real estate transactions are treated as capital gains. Many novice investors miss the key rules around capital gains tax and end up paying full business or personal income tax on their real estate transactions. It is *critical* that you have a quality real estate-specific tax accountant on your team. For instance, if you buy a property and do few or no renovations, hold it for a short period of time (less than two years) and sell it into the market at a higher price, Canada Revenue Agency (CRA) may deem those profits as business or personal income rather than a capital gain. Suddenly, your tax bill skyrockets and your profits disappear.

Get full accounting advice but remember a typical calculation for capital gains says you are taxed on only 50% of the gain. Business or personal income means you are taxed on the full amount! It's a huge difference, so know your rules.

Some people also blindly use the strategy of buying a property in their personal name and then transferring it to their corporate name a month later. It sounds like a simple strategy, yet this transaction can trigger personal income-tax issues if not done correctly.

Things get a little trickier when you try to use a capital gain tax-saving strategy that involves rolling a property over into a spouse's name. Similar complications can arise when you transfer a property title after a significant amount of time has passed since the initial purchase. (There may even be some issues about who owns the property to start with!)

Section 73.1 of the Income Tax Act is one of the sections most commonly applied to real estate investment. It allows the "rollover" of property to a spouse at no capital gain.

That's the good news. On the flip side of the ledger, capital property transferred between spouses, even if a rollover under Section 73.1 applies, could still be subject to the rules in *other* sections of the Income Tax Act.

Say we have a husband who wants to roll a property over to his wife. Sections 74.1 and 74.2, for example, require that both the capital gain and the rent earned after transfer be "attributed" to the transferor (in this case, the husband). Under these provisions, the transferor will have to calculate the capital gain and the rent earned after the transfer into his own income. (These "attribution rules" are discussed in more detail in Canada Revenue Agency's Interpretation Bulletin IPT-511.)

The attribution rules do not apply if fair market value is paid by our member's wife and the husband elects to not have Section 73.1 pertaining to the rollover apply. Other rules may apply if you're transferring property to a corporation, especially if the property's rolling over at a different value than when you bought it.

Clear as mud? That's why sophisticated investors make tax decisions on the advice of their tax professionals. Before you sell or transfer any properties whatsoever, make sure you have the opinion of tax professionals who completely understand real estate transactions. Many believe they do, but only a select few have the experience and knowledge of the intricate details.

## What do you need to do?

**GET PROFESSIONAL TAX-PLANNING ADVICE**

The Income Tax Act is a whopping 1,500 pages long and its application is complicated.

There are many ways to operate your real estate business in a tax-friendly rather than a tax-heavy environment. That's why there are large law firms and large chartered accountant firms where everybody is a tax expert. Find a tax expert who has extensive investment real estate experience.

### MEET REGULARLY WITH YOUR EXPERT TEAM

Work with your professional to deem what your best strategies are based on what you want to achieve. Each year, sit down and sign your annual returns—and plan the coming year as far as acquisitions and sales go.

### BE PROACTIVE

Look for tax-advantaged ways in which to operate. It is much easier to make the adjustments up front rather than after the transaction takes place. Sadly, many investors wait until they see their tax bill before they want to make changes. These retroactive changes, although possible in some cases, come with major costs that could have been avoided if a plan had been in place.

 ### RED FLAG

It's tough to un-do a business transaction that impacts your tax bill. Make tax planning part of your investment business—or pay the state piper!

### SOPHISTICATED INVESTOR ACTION STEP

Don't allow yourself to get caught up in the way the masses think about paying taxes! Paying a lot of tax is a good thing: It means you are making a lot of money. *The key is to have strategies in place where you are paying the least amount of tax legally allowed.* Remember, never swim in the grey waters and always have a good plan to deal with your purchases, your operations and your sales. If you do this, you can simply smile when you write your tax cheque—because you'll know without question that you have created additional long-term wealth for you and your family and haven't wasted money on needless expenses and taxes.

# APPENDIX

- PROPERTY GOLDMINE SCORE CARD
- ALL PROPERTIES
  DUE DILIGENCE CHECKLIST
- CONDOMINIUM PURCHASE
  DUE DILIGENCE CHECKLIST
- STATUTORY DECLARATION
- SUPPORT TOOLS AND
  KEY CONTACTS

REAL ESTATE
INVESTMENT
NETWORK™

#1018, 105 – 150 Crowfoot Cres. NW, Calgary, Alberta T3G 3T2
phone (403) 208-2722 fax (403) 241-6685 www.reincanada.com

# Property Goldmine Score Card

Property Address: _____

Town: _____ Prov: _____

Source: _____ Tel: _____

## Property Specific Questions

☐ Can you **change the use** of the property?
☐ Can you buy it <u>substantially</u> **below retail market value**?
☐ Can you <u>substantially</u> **increase the current rents**?
☐ Can you do small **renovations** to <u>substantially</u> increase the value?

## Area's Economic Influences

☐ Is there an **overall increase in demand** in the area?
☐ Are there currently **sales over list price** in the area?
☐ Is there a noted **increase in labour and materials cost** in the area?
☐ Is there a lot of **speculative investment** in the area?
☐ Is it **an area in transition** – moving upwards in quality?
☐ Is there a major **transportation improvement** occurring nearby?
☐ Is it in an area that is going to benefit from the **Ripple Effect**?
☐ Is the property's area in **"Real Estate Spring or Summer?"**
☐ Has the **political leadership** created a "growth atmosphere?"
☐ Is area's **average income increasing** faster than provincial average?
☐ Is it an area that is attractive to **"Baby Boomers?"**
☐ Is the area **growing faster** than the provincial average?
☐ Are **interest rates** at historic lows and/or moving downward?

_____ = Total ✓'s

Does This Property Fit Your System?  ☐ yes ☐ no
Does It Take You Closer to Your Goal?  ☐ yes ☐ no

© 2004 www.reincanada.com

# ALL PROPERTIES
## DUE DILIGENCE CHECKLIST

Due diligence is critical for ANY property you are considering investing in. Whether you are a silent partner or the actual person finding and investigating a property, you must do your own independent due diligence. This checklist will provide you a foundation from which to work, and will assist you in asking the critical questions. Remember, it does all come down to the accuracy of numbers. DO NOT SKIP ANY STEPS! (If you are purchasing a condo, use this form PLUS the Condo Due Diligence Checklist together.)

**Location:**

❑ How many checkmarks does the area get using the **Property Goldmine Score Card**? *(6 checks or more is best)*

❑ What is the nature of the local economy?

Diverse _____ or Single Industry _____

❑ In what area of town is the property located?

Older _____ Newer _____ Transitional _____

❑ What is the type and quality of the surrounding properties?

Type: _____

Quality vs. rest of neighbourhood: _____

❑ What amenities and services are nearby?

Transit _____ Shopping _____ Schools _____

University/College _____ Major Employer _____

**Building:**

❑ What is the overall Curb Appeal?  (scale 1 to 10)          _____

❑ What is the overall Interior Appeal?  (scale 1 to 10)          _____

❑ How well has the property been maintained? (scale 1 to 10)   _____

❑ Are there any deferred maintenance repairs required
in the next 12 months?                                       _____

  If YES, list them:  _____

  If YES, estimate cost of repairs:                     $ _____

❑ Are there any appliances you need to purchase?          YES / NO

❑ Has a complete professional inspection been completed?   YES / NO

  If NO, when are you scheduling it for?  _____

❏ Is a Real Estate Property Report (site survey certificate)
    available from vendor?                                    YES / NO
    If YES, is it acceptable to your lawyer for closing?      YES / NO

**Financial:**
❏ Have you completed a **Property Analysis Form**?           YES / NO
    *(You must complete the form for EVERY property*
    *before you make your offer.)*
❏ Do the results of the **Property Analysis Form**
    fit your investment system?                               YES / NO
    (if NO, look for a different property)
❏ If currently a rental—are financial statements
    available for the property?                               YES / NO
    What is the expense-to-income ratio?
    (35 – 45% is workable)                                    _____
    Are the numbers believable?                               YES / NO
    Do they fit market norms?                                 YES / NO
❏ What is the current rent on the property?
    *(If not currently rented, what should it*
    *rent for when analyzing the market?)*                  $ _____
❏ What are rents for similar properties in the area?       $ _____
❏ What is the vacancy rate history of the property?          _____ %
When vacant, does it seem difficult to re-rent?              YES / NO
What is the vacancy rate history for the area?               _____ %
How does that compare with the property's history?           _____ %

**Additional Critical Due Diligence:**
Check the following items to ensure you're not buying unknown trouble:
- ❑ Confirm taxes and other charges are current (city hall).
- ❑ Confirm no outstanding work orders or compliance orders (city hall—health department).
- ❑ Open or past complaints registered to the address. Known as a problem property (police).

❑ Who will be managing the property? _____
If YOU—is there a reliable company when you get
tired of managing?                                    YES / NO
❑ What banker/broker has a program to assist you with the financing on
this property? _____
❑ What is the vendor's REAL motivation level?
(0 = none, 10 = extremely) _____

❑ Do you plan on keeping the current tenant—
do they fit YOUR tenant profile?                      YES / NO

❑ Do you need vacant possession to
make it fit your system?                              YES / NO

# CONDOMINIUM PURCHASE
## DUE DILIGENCE CHECKLIST

In addition to completing your Property Analysis Form, when purchasing a condo or group of condos you need to take a very close look at the following:

### 1. Building:
❑ How many units in the building?    *(25+ is best)*     _____

❑ What is the ratio of owner occupied to rentals?     _____
   *(Looking for potential "anti-renter" situation)*

❑ What is the age of the building?     _____
   *(Age is important for financing; state of building's maintenance is important for costs)*

❑ Are there any Deferred Maintenance issues pending? _____
   *(See Condo Reserve Fund Study and minimum 12 months of condo board minutes)*

   If YES, review and estimate total cost of:
   *(Remember each unit will be responsible for their portion of these costs)*

   A.  Roof replacement or repair                    $ _____
   B.  Mechanical
       *(Does it need engineer inspection report?)*     $ _____
   C.  Interior or exterior refurbishment              $ _____
   D.  Post-tension deterioration                      $ _____
   E.  Parking lot resurfacing                         $ _____
   F.  Intercom system repair/replace                  $ _____
   G.  Other                                           $ _____
   ❑ Is the parking area of adequate size?
       (Important to your tenants and your exit strategy)    YES / NO
   A.  What is the ratio of stalls to suites?         _____ / _____
       *(A minimum 1 stall per unit advised)*
   B.  Can you rent additional stalls?                   YES / NO
   C.  Is there adequate on-site visitor parking?        YES / NO
❑ What is the typical rent for the property?     $ _____
❑ Does the opportunity to increase the rent exist?       YES / NO
   A.  If YES by how much?                           $ _____

❏ What is the building's previous year's vacancy rate? _____ %
   A. How does that compare to area average? _____ %
❏ What is the typical renter profile in building?
   (e.g., age 25-40, SM/F etc.) _____
❏ Does this fit your desired renter profile? YES / NO

## 2. Legal:
❏ Is there pending litigation against the condominium
  corporation? YES / NO
   *(The Condo Board must reveal this to you—also check board minutes)*
❏ Is there a recent Phase 1 Environmental Study available? YES / NO
❏ Is the property approved for CMHC financing? YES / NO

## 3. Condominium Corporation:
❏ Talk with representatives of the Condo Board to get a feel for
  the atmosphere.
❏ Review 2 years of Condo Board meeting minutes for potential prob-
  lems.
❏ Review the Annual Condo Budget.
   A. Compare last year's budget for accuracy with actual operating
     costs.
   B. Review the upcoming year's budget to see if appropriate
     adjustments have been made.
❏ Review the Condominium's Bylaws.
   A. Do they hold any penalties towards renter units?
     *(e.g., renter restrictions, large damage deposit to condo corp., etc.)*
   B. Define whether there is an easy grievance arbitration procedure.

❑ What are the monthly Condo Fees
and what do they include? $ _____
   A. If they seem high do they include heat and/or power? YES / NO
   B. If they seem low, is there an adequate amount allocated to the
      Reserve Fund for future repairs, or will a condo fee increase be
      needed? YES / NO

❑ Read the Rental Management Contract *(and rental pool agreement if in place)*.
   A. Are the contracts coming due for negotiations? YES / NO
   B. Are management costs slated to increase in
      near future? YES / NO
   C. Speak with management company
      representative AND on-site manager to get
      a feel for their thoughts on the building.

❑ Is there a Rental Pool in place?
   A. What is the unit factor for distribution
      of pooled rents? _____
   B. Who manages the pool? What is their fee? _____ %
   C. Read the guidelines—can you participate? YES / NO

❑ Is the Building Insurance Policy adequate? YES / NO
❑ Review the condominium's financial statements
   for an adequate reserve fund vs. upcoming
   required repairs.

❑ Are there any pending or current cash calls
   to be paid by the owners? YES / NO

❑ Ensure you complete a **Property Analyzer Form** with accurate market
   numbers.

# STATUTORY DECLARATION

**CANADA**                    **IN THE MATTER OF TITLE TO:**
                             Legal Description:        _____
**PROVINCE OF**_____          _____

                             _____


                             **AND THE SALE THEREOF FROM:**
                             Vendor:   _____
                             Vendor:   _____

**TO:**

                             Purchaser: _____
                             Purchaser: _____

**TO WIT:**
WE / I _____
of the City of _____ , in the Province of _____ ,
**SOLEMNLY DECLARE THAT:**

1. To the best of my / our knowledge, information and belief there are no special assessments contemplated by the Condominium Corporation, that voting rights have been assigned and that there are no legal actions pending or contemplated by or against the Condominium Corporation.

2. I / we have not received a notice convening a special or general meeting of the unit owners of the Condominium Corporation respecting any of the following matters:

(a) the termination of the government of the condominium property;

(b) any substantial alteration in or substantial addition to the common elements or the renovation thereof; OR

(c) any substantial change in the assets or liabilities of the Condominium Corporation.

3. I / we have not received any notice or communication whatsoever from the Condominium Corporation or its agents requiring me / us to carry out any repairs to or restoration of the subject unit and / or the common elements, including that portion of the common elements designated in the declaration as being for the exclusive use of the vendor of the subject unit.

4. I / we have not made application to the Condominium Corporation for its approval of any structural change, additions, improvement to or renovation of the unit in accordance with the registered declaration and bylaws of the Corporation; nor have I / we or any other owner or owners collectively, to the best of my / our knowledge, information and belief, made application to the Condominium Corporation for the approval of any alteration, addition, improvement to the common elements whether substantial or not, and in this regard I / we have not received a notice or other communication of any meeting of the membership held or to be held by the Condominium Corporation for the purpose of considering any alteration, addition, improvement to or renovation of the common elements. Similarly, I / we are not aware of any change or proposed change in the assets of the Condominium Corporation as reflected in its most recent and audited financial statements, save as follows:

_____
_____
_____
_____
_____
_____
_____
_____
_____
_____
_____
_____
_____
_____

5. Neither I / we, nor to the best of my / our knowledge, information and belief, my / our predecessors on title have made any unauthorized change, addition, improvement to or renovation of the unit or the common elements contrary to the registered declaration and bylaws of the Condominium Corporation.

6. There have been no claims or demands whatsoever during my / our period of ownership by the Condominium Corporation or in any way related to my / our ownership and occupation of the subject unit and the common elements.

AND I / WE MAKE THIS DECLARATION CONSCIENTIOUSLY BELIEVING IT TO BE TRUE, AND KNOWING THAT IT IS OF THE SAME FORCE AND EFFECT AS IF MADE UNDER OATH.

SEVERALLY SWORN before
me at the City of _____
in the Province of _____

this \_\_ day of _____ Vendor: _____
200 \_\_

Vendor: _____

A COMMISSIONER ETC.

## SUPPORT TOOLS AND KEY CONTACTS

Real estate is a team game and the strength of your team will help determine how quickly you achieve success. In addition, keeping on top of key economic trends as well as changes to laws that affect real estate investors is absolutely critical.

With this in mind, here are some additional support tools, web sites and education materials that can greatly assist you.

### Landlord and Tenant Government Web Sites

The following is a list of government web sites that outline landlord and tenant laws. Many of them provide shortened versions of their acts in plain English. It is important for you to review information for your areas.

**British Columbia** http://www.pssg.gov.bc.ca/rto/

**Alberta** http://www3.gov.ab.ca/gs/information/landlord/

**Saskatchewan** http://www.saskjustice.gov.sk.ca/legislation/summaries/landlordtenantact.shtml

**Manitoba** http://www.gov.mb.ca/finance/cca/rtb/resource.html

**Ontario** http://www.orht.gov.on.ca/scripts/index_.asp

**Quebec** http://www.educaloi.qc.ca/TLR_Law/F01_ResumeCapsules/index.php3?no=19&noCat=6

**New Brunswick** http://www.legal-info-legale.nb.ca/pub-landlord-tenant.asp

**Nova Scotia** http://www.gov.ns.ca/snsmr/consumer/resten/

**Prince Edward Island** http://www.irac.pe.ca/rental/

**Newfoundland and Labrador** http://www.gov.nf.ca/gs/cca/rt/

**Northwest Territories** http://www.justice.gov.nt.ca/RentalOffice/rentalofficer.htm

**Yukon** http://www.gov.yk.ca/depts/community/consumer/landtact.html

**Nunavut** http://www.gov.nu.ca/Nunavut/index.shtml

# REAL ESTATE INVESTMENT NETWORK—REIN™

The Real Estate Investment Network™ (REIN™) is a group, led by bestselling author Don R. Campbell, dedicated to providing real estate investors with unbiased research and strategies for the Canadian marketplace. Members of REIN meet monthly in select cities across the country. Some of its members live outside Canada. It is now entering its 14th year of operation and has assisted members in riding the upward swings in the market while avoiding the downturns. Members have safely and securely purchased over $1.25 billion of residential real estate. REIN's members focus on long-term wealth as opposed to get-rich-quick schemes. This success comes from focusing on real life economic fundamentals and putting the ACRE system into action. This system takes the hype out of the marketplace so you can focus on what works right in your backyard.

REIN is an exclusive paid-membership program of more then 1,400 members across the country, which is dedicated to educating its members about how, where and when to buy Canadian real estate. From networking with other active investors to providing direct access to leading-edge experts, it is the most complete program of its kind anywhere in North America. You will never have to buy from, invest with or put money into any real estate deal with anyone in, or associated with, REIN.

REIN's single objective is to help *you* become an experienced, confident and wealthy real estate investor. There are no huge upfront fees; REIN believes that money is best spent investing in real estate—not on seminars.

To receive a FREE 12-page package on the benefits of being a member of Canada's most successful real estate investment program, with over $1.25 billion dollars purchased and 14 years of market experience, call 1-888-824-7346 today or e-mail your mailing address and telephone number to Don R. Campbell's office at info@reincanada.com or visit www.realestateinvestingincanada.com and click on the REIN button. We look forward to helping you achieve your own "Personal Belize."

# ABOUT THE AUTHORS

**Don R. Campbell** is the author of the Canadian bestseller *Real Estate Investing in Canada*, a book that all real estate investors should have as an action tool and reference. Don is president of the Real Estate Investment Network (REIN™), whose membership exceeds 1,400 successful Canadian investors and whose investment in Canadian residential real estate tops $1.25 billion.

In his real estate seminars, Don shares his years of hands-on experience as he teaches strategies in live workshops across the country (www.reincanada.com) that he has personally tested in the real world. He has helped investors achieve their dreams and along the way charities such as Habitat for Humanity have benefited from his enterprise.

**Peter Kinch** is the Owner and Senior Mortgage Broker of The Mortgage Centre—Canadian Mortgage Team in Vancouver, BC. Over the past several years, he has been working extensively with real estate investors and has gained invaluable expertise and insight into their unique financing needs. As such, investors are seeking him out as he has developed the 5-Year Action Plan™, which helps to determine the best mortgage solution, whether it be a single purchase or the development of a real estate portfolio.

Peter Kinch is the author of *The Mortgage Minute*™, which can be heard daily on NEWS 1130 in Vancouver, and is a regular featured guest on City TV, CKNW News Radio, Realty TV and the *National Post Business Report*, also heard on NEWS 1130. Kinch is a contributing author to the *Western Investor*, *Home Makeover Magazine* and other publications.

**Barry McGuire,** while at law school, had his first opportunity to invest in real estate. He had a friend who seemed to be buying every house near the University of Alberta, renting it out and building a real estate empire. McGuire was a student and needed a place to stay while going to law school, so he used his student loan for the down payment and quickly found five other students who also needed a place to stay. The positive cash flow was tremendous and replaced the missing student loan. Better yet, three years later, the property had tripled in value!

This early lesson was not forgotten, and Barry continues to enjoy a diversified real estate investment portfolio. Thirty years later, Barry's legal practice is focussed exclusively on real estate.

Over the years, Barry has had extensive involvement with the Alberta Real Estate Association in preparing and teaching credit courses for real estate agents. He has also taught these courses for the Real Estate Training Institute, an independent trainer of real estate professionals.

In his daily legal practice at Ritchie Mill Law Office in Edmonton, Alberta, Barry loves to assist clients with the planning and consulting issues that help ensure successful real estate purchases. He believes that a sound education in real estate fundamentals is one of the best tools in any real estate investor's toolbox.

**Russell Westcott** is a veteran real estate investor, researcher and educator. He is the General Manager of the Real Estate Investment Network™. Westcott is recognized for his creative buying strategies, which range from forming joint-venture partnerships to turning one property purchase into three or four through leverage financing. He has consistently purchased one property a month since he started to invest, and he shares his expertise with REIN members at REIN events.

Russell lives his life around four principles: 1) health, happiness and enjoyment of life; 2) family and relationships; 3) contribution and growth; and 4) abundance and gratitude. He lives by his credo: "You can have anything in your life if you provide massive value that significantly improves people's lives."

# INDEX OF TIPS